MULTICULTURAL EDUCATION SERIES

James A. Banks, *Series Editor*

(continued)

D1593867

Mathematics for Equity

A Framework for Successful Practice

Edited by

Na'ilah Suad Nasir,
Carlos Cabana, Barbara Shreve,
Estelle Woodbury, and Nicole Louie

Teachers College, Columbia University
New York and London

NATIONAL COUNCIL OF
TEACHERS OF MATHEMATICS

1906 Association Drive, Reston, VA 20191
www.nctm.org

KH

Published by Teachers College Press, 1234 Amsterdam Avenue, New York, NY 10027

Library of Congress Cataloging-in-Publication Data

Mathematics for equity : a framework for successful practice / edited by Na'ilah Suad Nasir [and four others].
pages cm. — (Multicultural education series)
Includes bibliographical references and index.
ISBN 978-0-8077-5541-9 (pbk. : alk. paper)
ISBN 978-0-8077-5562-4 (hardcover : alk. paper)
ISBN 978-0-8077-7306-2 (ebook)
1. Arithmetic—Study and teaching. 2. Arithmetic—Study and teaching (Secondary) 3. Mathematics—Study and teaching. 4. Educational equalization. I. Nasir, Na'ilah Suad, editor of compilation.
QA135.6.M378 2014
510.71'2—dc23   2014002131

ISBN 978-0-8077-5541-9 (paper)
ISBN 978-0-8077-5562-4 (hardcover)
eISBN 978-0-8077-7306-2

Printed on acid-free paper
Manufactured in the United States of America

21 20 19 18 17 16 15 14   8 7 6 5 4 3 2 1

12/17/15

Contents

PART III: TEACHER LEARNING AND PROFESSIONAL COMMUNITY

PART IV: MOVING ON AND LOOKING FORWARD

Series Foreword

"U.S. students lag around average on international science, math, and reading test" (Layton, 2013). This headline, published in the *Washington Post* after the 2012 Program for International Student Assessment (PISA) test results were released, epitomizes the response of many journalists, politicians, and policymakers to the performance of U.S. students on standardized tests. After describing the mediocre performance of U.S. students on the PISA, this news story praised the high achievement of students in "Shanghai, Singapore, and other provinces or countries."

The mean PISA scores of students in various nations do not reveal a number of interesting and significant educational trends and developments. Linda Darling-Hammond (2010) points out that the scores of Asian and White students in the U.S. are above the Organization for Economic Cooperation and Development (OECD) average in each subject area. However, when the scores of African American and Latino students are added, the U.S. national average drops to the bottom of the ranked scores. She makes this point to emphasize the important ways in which the fate of the U.S. is tied to the future success of ethnic minority students such as African Americans and Latinos. Students in South Korea are among the highest performing students on the PISA. However, when I visited South Korea in the spring of 2013, many of the educators with whom I interacted were bemoaning the extreme pressure that was being put on Korean students to perform well on achievement tests and were complaining that the emphasis in South Korean schools was on teaching students to memorize facts in textbooks rather than on teaching them to think critically. Ironically, as the U.S. is emphasizing the mastery of basic skills and student performance on standardized tests, many educators in South Korea and China believe that the schools in their nations should increase the focus on teaching students to think critically.

This revealing and engaging book is timely and important because it describes and illustrates ways in which students can both acquire the knowledge and skills they need to be mathematically adept as well as to think critically. This book describes how the students at Railside not only acquired sophisticated mathematical concepts and skills and learned to think mathematically, but also how they developed strong relationships with their teachers and with other students in robust learning communities. The teachers at Railside were able to create learning communities in their classrooms because they had created an effective learning community in their mathematics department.

In 1993, I stated, "equity pedagogy exists when teachers use techniques and methods that facilitate the academic achievement of students from diverse racial, ethnic, and social-class groups" (Banks, p. 6). The teachers at Railside used Complex Instruction—a concept created by Elizabeth Cohen and further developed by Rachel Lotan (Cohen & Lotan, 2004; Lotan, 2012)—to implement equity pedagogy. "Multidimensionality" is an important idea of Complex Instruction that was implemented at Railside. It conceptualizes academic tasks as involving multiple skills, and assumes that no student is equally competent in each of them, but that collectively the group is competent in all of them. By using groupwork to teach high-level mathematical skills and concepts, each student within a group was able to make a significant contribution to the solution of problems. The teachers at Railside valued many dimensions of mathematical work and encouraged students to solve problems in myriad ways.

When the teaching of mathematics is reformed in the creative, challenging, and affirming ways described by the authors of this helpful, needed, and affirming book, all students will benefit and flourish, including the large number of immigrant students who are now populating the nation's schools. Students whose first language is not English is the fastest-growing population in U.S. schools. The 2010 American Community Survey indicates that approximately 19.8% of the school-age population spoke a language at home other than English in 2010 (U.S. Census Bureau, 2010).

American classrooms are experiencing the largest influx of immigrant students since the beginning of the 20th century. Almost 14 million new immigrants—documented and undocumented—settled in the United States in the years from 2000 to 2010. Less than 10% came from nations in Europe. Most came from Mexico, nations in Asia, and nations in Latin America, the Caribbean, and Central America (Camarota, 2011). A large but undetermined number of undocumented immigrants enter the United States each year. The U.S. Department of Homeland Security (2010) estimated that in January 2010, 10.8 million undocumented immigrants were living in the United States, which was a decrease from the estimated 11.8 million that resided in the United States in January 2007. In 2007, approximately 3.2 million children and young adults were among the 11.8 million undocumented immigrants in the United States, most of whom grew up in this country (Perez, 2011). The influence of an increasingly ethnically diverse population on U.S. schools, colleges, and universities is and will continue to be enormous.

The major purpose of the Multicultural Education Series is to provide preservice educators, practicing educators, graduate students, scholars, and policymakers with an interrelated and comprehensive set of books that summarizes and analyzes important research, theory, and practice related to the education of ethnic, racial, cultural, and linguistic groups in the United States and the education of mainstream students about diversity. The dimensions of multicultural education, developed by Banks (1993) and described in *The Routledge International Companion to Multicultural Education* (Banks, 2009) and in the *Encyclopedia of*

Diversity in Education (Banks, 2012), provide the conceptual framework for the development of the publications in the Series. They are content integration, the knowledge construction process, prejudice reduction, an equity pedagogy, and an empowering institutional culture and social structure.

The books in the Series provide research, theoretical, and practical knowledge about the behaviors and learning characteristics of students of color, language minority students, low-income students, and other minoritized population groups, such as LGBTQ youth. They also provide knowledge about ways to improve academic achievement and race relations in educational settings. Multicultural education is consequently as important for middle-class White suburban students as it is for students of color who live in the inner city. Multicultural education fosters the public good and the overarching goals of the nation.

This book is encouraging because it describes and illustrates ways in which the teaching of mathematics can be reinvented so that students from diverse racial, ethnic, cultural, and linguistic groups can master complex mathematical knowledge and skills, which Robert P. Moses and Charles E. Cobb Jr. (2001) call a "civil right" because quantitative skills are essential to become an effective and successful citizen in our highly technological and global society. This book, however, is also a cautionary and discouraging saga because it describes how a series of bureaucratic and budgetary decisions by administrators derailed the innovative, creative, and empowering program that the teachers in the mathematics department at Raildside created and sustained for a number of years. A powerful and poignant lesson of this book is that an effective pedagogical program that takes years to create can be quickly destroyed by hasty and unimaginative administrative decisions.

—James A. Banks

REFERENCES

Banks, J. A. (1993). Multicultural education: Historical development, dimensions, and practice. In L. Darling-Hammond (Ed.), *Review of research in education*, 19, 3–39. Washington, DC: American Educational Research Association.

Banks, J. A. (Ed.). (2009). *The Routledge international companion to multicultural education.* New York and London: Routledge.

Banks, J. A. (2012). Multicultural education: Dimensions of. In J. A. Banks (Ed.), *Encyclopedia of diversity in education* (Vol. 3, pp. 1538–1547). Thousand Oaks, CA: Sage Publications.

Camarota, S. A. (2011, October). A *record-setting decade of immigration: 2000 to 2010.* Washington, DC: Center for Immigration Studies. Available at http://cis.org/2000-2010-record-setting-decade-of-immigration

Cohen, E. G., & Lotan, R. A. (2004). Equity in heterogeneous classrooms. In J. A. Banks & C. A.M. Banks (Eds.), *Handbook of research on multicultural education* (2nd ed., pp. 736–750). San Francisco, CA: Jossey-Bass.

Darling-Hammond, L. (2010). *The flat world and education: How America's commitment to equity will determine its future.* New York, NY: Teachers College Press.

Layton, L. (2013). U.S. students lag around average on international science, math and reading test. *The Washington Post.* Available at http://www.washingtonpost.com/local/education/us-students-lag-around-average-on-international-science-math-and-reading-test/2013/12/02/2e510f26-5b92-11e3-a49b-90a0e156254b_story.html

Lotan, R. (2012). Complex instruction. In J. A. Banks (Ed.), *Encyclopedia of diversity in education,* (Vol. 1, pp. 436-439). Thousand Oaks, CA: Sage Publications.

Moses, R. P., & Cobb, C. E., Jr. (2001). *Radical equations: Math literacy and civil rights.* Boston, MA: Beacon Press.

Perez, W. (2011). *Americans by heart: Undocumented Latino students and the promise of higher education.* New York, NY: Teachers College Press.

U.S. Census Bureau. (2010). *2010 American community survey.* Available at http://factfinder2.census.gov/faces/tableservices/jsf/pages/productview.xhtml?pid=ACS_10_1YR_S1603&prodType=table

U.S. Department of Homeland Security. (2010, February). *Estimates of the unauthorized immigrant population residing in the United States: January 2010.* Available at http://www.dhs.gov/files/statistics/immigration.shtm

Acknowledgments

Many mathematics teachers at Railside have said that, in retrospect, the work was the most invigorating of their careers, and also the most difficult. The challenge and passion in that work created an extraordinary learning opportunity for all of us. Our ongoing work as educators is continuously inspired by the courage and love of learning shown by the thousands of students we have been fortunate to meet and the many teachers who it has been our privilege to work alongside.

As editors planning this book, we could not help but tell one another stories of students and colleagues, and all they have taught us. We felt an enormous obligation to accurately capture the spirit of the stories—ours and theirs—as well as the details of the work and the many contributions from dozens of remarkable educators. If we have done justice to those students and teachers, then perhaps this book will inspire more stories from teachers who love their students as much as we have loved ours.

We are grateful for the love we have received from our families and friends, especially those who were wonderfully supportive in the creation of this book as well as when we immersed ourselves in our classrooms. We are deeply thankful to the many administrators, counselors, staff, and nonmathematics teachers at Railside, without whom the work described in this book could not have happened. We wish space and memory would allow us to name them all individually and to acknowledge what each has taught us.

We are honored to celebrate the extraordinary Railside mathematics teachers who participated in the work described in this book:

Esther (Mecking) Andrews	Dave Allen
Susan Baskin	Ashanti Branch
Erin Buzby	Carlos Cabana
Cliff Cheng	Suzanne Cristofani
Gary Cruz	Joanne Da Luz
Kristina Dance	David Danielson
Laura (Thomas) Evans	Alan Fishman
Walt Frey	Ilana Seidel Horn
Lisa M. Jilk	Geetha Laksminarayanan
Bill Lathlean	Mona Lee
Lucy Lowhurst	Ladan Malek
Breedeen Murray	Nisha Nagdev

Karen O'Connell   Eric Price
Emily (Cooper) Scheinman   Ana (Ruiz) Sheriff
Barbara Shreve   Linda Thomas
Philip Tucher   Ruth Tsu
Christina Werner   Pam Wilson
Hannah Witzemann   Estelle Woodbury
Dorothy Woods   Lisa Wright
Joe Yee   Gina Yu

Chapter 1

Introduction

*Na'ilah Suad Nasir, Carlos Cabana, Barbara Shreve,
Estelle Woodbury, and Nicole Louie*

The first decade and a half of the new millennium has held a myriad of challenges for teachers in urban public schools. Teachers face districts that are increasingly underfunded, students who have been underserved for their entire educational careers, and increasing pressure under federal education policies to raise test scores, even as resources to do so decrease (Darling-Hammond, 2010). In mathematics, these challenges are even more intense, as tensions between proponents of "reform" versus "traditional" approaches to the teaching of mathematics continue to plague both practitioners and scholars of mathematics education (Schoenfeld, 2008). These tensions are now playing out in the context of new national math standards that address both content and mathematical practices in which students build understanding. Against this backdrop, achievement gaps in mathematics remain significant, and equity-oriented approaches to the teaching of mathematics have rarely been described in detail, nor have they attended to addressing the deeply racialized inequities in access to good mathematics teaching or the ways that instruction for marginalized youth might need to specifically attend to the needs of such young people (Martin, 2009).

This edited volume provides a case study of the mathematics department at a school we call Railside High,[1] where teachers successfully developed and sustained an equity pedagogy in high school mathematics in an urban district. *Mathematics for Equity* includes contributions from several nationally renowned scholars of mathematics education, all of whom studied various aspects of the pedagogy, teacher community, or student experiences at Railside at different points in time. This volume also includes the unique perspectives of several teachers and students about the learning they did together. As a whole, it provides a rich discussion of the nature of teaching, learning, and teacher community at

Railside, and reflects on the complex nature of building and maintaining an equity pedagogy in mathematics through a period when the national educational policy climate focused on standardization and accountability. As the national education conversation shifts to address the Common Core State Standards, the experience of building a teacher professional community around equity and rich learning experiences for students and adults may offer valuable perspectives for practitioners in a time of change.

Mathematics for Equity is a celebration and tribute to all of the hard work of many people over many years at Railside. The approach to teaching mathematics that was developed at Railside has not only been studied and written about extensively by scholars and recognized by the national mathematics education community, it has also been a source of professional passion and fulfillment for Railside math teachers. This book is intended to describe the teaching practices, student experiences, and professional community at Railside.

It is critical to remember that the teaching practice at Railside was not the work of a small group of teacher leaders. Rather, it was a collective effort of many contributors to the department over the span of 2 decades. In these pages are the thoughts, ideas, and words of this larger group of teachers, and we hope we do their work justice in our descriptions. It is our intention that this book serve as an inspiration and a resource to teachers, math coaches, math department chairs, administrators, and district leaders seeking to improve the teaching of mathematics in their schools and districts.

The story of the Railside math department is also a cautionary tale. In recent years, local education politics—in the midst of an economic recession and a national emphasis on standardization and high-stakes accountability—have made it difficult for teachers to sustain the equity pedagogy they worked to develop at Railside. By the end of the 2009–2010 school year, the pressures became so great that several teacher leaders felt forced to leave the department, and the math teachers remaining reported being unable to continue teaching in ways they thought were best for students' learning.

HOW THIS BOOK CAME TO BE

This book project has been a collaboration in the truest sense of the word. The editorial team consists of two researchers, Na'ilah Suad Nasir and Nicole Louie, and three teachers, Carlos Cabana, Barbara Shreve, and Estelle Woodbury. Carlos, Barbara, and Estelle had all been department chairs in the math department at Railside and had taught there for many years. Na'ilah is a university researcher who studied the math department's practices from 2003–2007. In 2005, Nicole was a student of Carlos's in the Stanford Teacher Education Program (STEP), taking his course on teaching mathematics in heterogeneous classes; after teaching middle school mathematics for 4 years, she returned to graduate school as a doctoral student. We came together as a team in 2009, when we sat down together for coffee and the teachers shared their frustration and disappointment with district-level decisions that seemed to undermine and undo their work. Na'ilah and Nicole decided to conduct a study of these changes and began meeting regularly with Carlos, Barbara, and Estelle in an effort to understand what was happening to mathematics teaching and teachers at their school. Later that year, the teachers decided that they could no longer remain at Railside, and announced to their colleagues that they would be leaving. Soon after, Nicole and Na'ilah interviewed one of these colleagues, who suggested they document and publish the whole story of Railside mathematics—capturing what the department had learned, built, and achieved, as well as the extreme challenges the department later faced. This book comes out of that suggestion. We have worked as a collective to envision this book, to extend invitations to authors, to co-write chapters, and to edit and revise manuscripts. Our work together, however, has not simply been an act of writing—it has been an analytical endeavor. As we wrote the teacher chapters, we talked extensively about the teaching practices at Railside and reflected on both those practices and the philosophy underlying them. As we wrote, we came to better understand those practices, as well as the magic that had happened at Railside. As Estelle quipped in one of our brainstorming meetings, "This is what you are too tired to do at the end of June!" That is, this is the work of making sense of what worked, why it worked, and how it got accomplished, an endeavor teachers are often too tired to do by the time the school year ends.

CORE PRINCIPLES OF THE RAILSIDE APPROACH

As Barbara, Estelle, and Carlos reflected on what had been built at Railside, we were struck by how consistently several principles of teaching and learning seemed to emerge. We identified five recurring principles:

- All teachers and students are learners
- Working from strengths while making space for vulnerability
- Redefining "smart"
- Redefining what it means to do math in school
- The importance of relationships

Railside math teachers consciously worked toward many of these principles; others were less explicit but still very present in the work. The principles had never before been articulated as a list, much less officially posted somewhere. Some were adopted very early as guides for the math team's work, while others were recognized later on, through reflection, as central to the work that teachers did both with students and with each other as colleagues. In Carlos, Barbara, and Estelle's chapters in this volume (Chapters 3 and 11)—and implicit in others' chapters as well—these principles will come up again and again.

All Teachers and All Students Are Learners

In many American schools, teachers are expected to be authorities who pass down perfectly formed knowledge, while students are classified as those who are intellectually capable and those who are not (Darling-Hammond, 2010; Varenne & McDermott, 1998). This was not the case at Railside. Many of the reforms that we pursued were motivated by the conviction that all students can learn rigorous mathematics and a pressing need to make such mathematics more widely accessible. This belief is not simply an endorsement of a politically correct notion of equity, but rather requires an outright rejection of what Danny Martin has termed the racial hierarchy of mathematical ability. At the same time, as teachers we had a sense of exploring uncharted territory. When Railside teachers first undertook mathematics reform in the mid-1980s, department leaders clearly communicated that they were no experts and that everyone in the department—from the newest to the most veteran among us—had something important to contribute to the project. We worked hard to maintain that culture in the years that followed.

Working from Strengths While Making Space for Vulnerability

In viewing all teachers and all students as learners, we made space for each person to be intellectually and emotionally vulnerable, to make mistakes, to not know. We have viewed this vulnerability as essential for learning and growth. On the other hand, making space for students and teachers to work from their strengths and build on their successes has also been an organizing principle in our work. This has often meant conceptualizing what it means to do the work of teaching and learning mathematics in expansive ways, as the next two principles illustrate.

Redefining "Smart"

According to Western tradition, intelligence is linear and one-dimensional—that is, there is only one way of being smart, and people can be ranked based on how smart they are, for example, with IQ scores (Oakes, Wells, Jones, & Datnow, 1997). In mathematics, this view of ability has been closely associated with memorizing facts and producing correct answers quickly. At Railside, we decided that this way of defining intelligence was too limiting; not only does it imply that only a few people can be smart, but it also eliminates space for other valuable ways of thinking and understanding. Convincing ourselves and our students that there were better ways of conceptualizing intelligence, and finding those ways, was an ongoing task. Work on this has motivated our uptake of a particular pedagogical approach, Complex Instruction (which we describe in detail in Chapters 3, 8, and 11), and guided our day-to-day interactions with students.

Redefining What It Means to Do Math in School

In the United States, school mathematics commonly emphasizes the memorization and execution of disconnected procedures (Boaler & Greeno, 2000). This is alienating for many students; it also fails to accurately represent the discipline of mathematics. At Railside, we sought to redefine what it means to do mathematics in school, emphasizing disciplinary practices such as reasoning and justification, creativity and invention, and use of a variety of strategies and representations. This meant that students who were good at learning algorithms still had many ways to grow, while students who weren't had strengths that were relevant and important not only to their own learning, but to their classmates' as well. It also pushed us as teachers to learn mathematics more deeply ourselves, and to restructure our curriculum around big mathematical ideas instead of around small chunks of skills and procedures.

The Importance of Relationships

In our community of mathematics teachers at Railside, being a teacher meant much more than being a professional in the technical sense of the word. It meant building caring and trusting relationships not only with our students but also with our colleagues. We celebrated birthdays and milestones together, had regular working meetings over meals, observed one another's teaching, worked together to design courses, and celebrated our victories. These relationships connected us to our work in personal ways, and they made it possible for us to be vulnerable with one another and take the risks that we needed to take to pursue the ambitious goal of making rigorous mathematics accessible. Thus, our work building a professional community and enacting a new pedagogical vision of mathematics teaching was intertwined with and supported by the relationships we built with our professional colleagues.

Valuing personal relationships was also central to our work with students. We worked hard to build trusting and caring relationships with students, so that they were willing and able to take the significant emotional risks we were asking them to take with us in the classroom.

These principles will come up again and again across the chapters in this book. They are relevant both to thinking about how we engaged students, but also in considering how we came together to build a professional community that sustained our work together.

ROAD MAP OF THE BOOK

Mathematics for Equity is organized into four sections: The Railside Approach, Student Experiences at Railside, Teacher Learning and Professional Community, and Moving On and Looking Forward. Each of these sections includes research chapters as well as chapters written by former Railside teachers or students. We strove to strike a balance across the chapters between being descriptive (of our practices and pedagogy), being analytical (to understand and convey why and how things worked), and offering principles (to guide those who want to improve their own mathematics teaching or teaching in their schools and districts). In doing so, we were struck by how the development of teaching practices at Railside involved both intention and planning on the one hand and serendipity on the other; that is, some changes and innovations happened because we had a vision of moving instruction in particular ways, while other things occurred in response to pressures or happenstance events that turned out to be consequential. Below, we describe the chapters in each of the four major sections of the book.

The Railside Approach

This part focuses on detailing the pedagogical and curricular approach, and offers an overview of the effects of these approaches on student learning and engagement. It features two research chapters and one chapter by teachers. Chapter 2, the first research chapter, written by Jo Boaler and Megan E. Staples, describes the Railside approach to pedagogy and curriculum, and gives an overview of the student outcomes at Railside, as compared to those of students at two other schools without an explicit equity orientation. Chapter 3 is written by Carlos Cabana, Barbara Shreve, and Estelle Woodbury, and expands on the description in Jo Boaler and Megan E. Staples's chapter, highlighting two important aspects of the teaching practice at Railside: the use of groupworthy problems as the foundation of their curriculum, and their assessment practices. Chapter 4 is written by Megan E. Staples and presents a detailed portrayal of one Railside teacher's classroom, with a focus on understanding how collaboration can be fostered among students in detracked heterogeneous classrooms.

Student Experiences at Railside

This section includes three chapters that focus on the experiences of students in Railside mathematics classrooms. Chapter 5, written by former Railside student Maria D. Velazquez and Nicole Louie, highlights the perceptions of Railside alumni and analyzes how the organization of Railside math classrooms affected students' learning and trajectories in mathematics. Chapter 6 is written by Victoria Hand and draws on case study data of two students to highlight how students were framed as competent math learners in their interactions with teachers, in ways that fostered the creation of productive learning spaces. Chapter 7, written by Lisa M. Jilk, describes the experiences of one immigrant girl who is also an English language learner in mathematics at Railside; her story brings to life the ways that access to positive math identities were afforded to students at Railside, despite limited proficiency with English.

Teacher Learning and Professional Community

The third major section focuses on the dynamics and processes around the building and maintaining of teacher professional community at Railside and consists of four chapters—two research chapters, one teacher chapter, and one chapter co-authored by a former department chair who helped to launch the reform work in the department together with two university researchers and educators who provided the department with crucial support for reform. Chapter 8, written by Ruth Tsu, Rachel Lotan, and Ruth Cossey, offers some historical context for understanding the development of the teacher professional community and the practices at Railside. It details the history of the development of the community of teachers at Railside, and provides a recounting of how and why particular equity-oriented practices were taken up. Chapter 9 is written by Ilana Seidel Horn and describes the process and organization of teacher learning at Railside, comparing teacher peer interactions at Railside with those of another high school. Chapter 10 is written by Ilana Seidel Horn and Judith Warren Little and reports findings on the ways that the teacher community operated at Railside through an analysis of the routine problems of practice that arose in their work. The last chapter in this section, Chapter 11, is written by Carlos Cabana, Barbara Shreve, and Estelle Woodbury. It discusses how the professional community functioned and was sustained, as well as the processes by which new teachers were integrated into the department.

Moving On and Looking Forward

This final section consists of three chapters and is an epilogue of sorts. Chapter 12, by Nicole Louie and Na'ilah Suad Nasir, presents Railside teachers' perspectives on the erosion of their "signature pedagogy," their department community, and their ability to invest themselves emotionally in their work. On a more optimistic note, Chapter 13—written by two former Railside teachers, Lisa M. Jilk and Karen O'Connell—details efforts to bring lessons from Railside to inform work in another urban school district in a different state. Chapter 14 reflects on the prior chapters and considers the implications of the approach developed at Railside for teaching practice more broadly.

It is our hope that this book will reach those who are seeking a different vision for what secondary mathematics teaching can look like, and that it will serve as a reminder that equity, rigor, and high performance outcomes are not mutually exclusive. Indeed, they are fundamentally linked. We can meet the needs of all of our students by providing rich and rigorous instruction in mathematics, by having high expectations for both ourselves as teachers and for every student that walks into our classrooms, and by working together to enact a new vision of mathematics teaching and learning.

Part I

THE RAILSIDE APPROACH

At a time when schools and districts are wrestling with how to best support the learning of an increasingly diverse student population, models that illustrate the components and outcomes of an equity pedagogy in mathematics are much-needed and rare. Part 1 begins at the beginning. It considers, what is the evidence to support the notion that the pedagogy developed at Railside was effective? And what were the elements of this pedagogy, both with respect to the practices as well as the beliefs and assumptions that underlay those practices?

This section begins with a seminal analysis by Jo Boaler and Megan E. Staples in Chapter 2 that draws on multiple data sources, including mathematics assessments, standardized tests, and student surveys and interviews, to examine how the cognitive and motivational outcomes of Railside students compared to those of students in other schools. They argue that over time Railside students displayed deeper and more extensive understandings of mathematical concepts, had more positive feelings towards mathematics, and were more likely to plan to pursue mathematics in the future. Further, they explore the aspects of the Railside approach that contributed to these favorable outcomes, including the curriculum and structure of the department, the use of groupwork and Complex Instruction, and the creation of multidimensional classrooms in which students were viewed as competent and were encouraged to support one another's learning.

Chapter 3, written by Carlos Cabana, Barbara Shreve, and Estelle Woodbury, picks up on some of the themes identified in the Chapter 2 and offers examples from classroom practice and provides an analysis from the perspective of the teachers themselves of the components of math instruction at Railside. Specifically, the authors detail five aspects of the pedagogical practice at Railside, including (1) structuring lessons to support engagement in *groupworthy tasks*, (2) approaching math concepts through *multiple representations*, (3) organizing curriculum around *big ideas*, (4) using *justification* to push students to articulate their mathematical thinking, and (5) making students' thinking public and valued through *presentations at the overhead*. These elements were underscored by two big ideas about the teaching and learning of mathematics, including justification and student presentations at the overhead.

Finally, in Chapter 4, Megan E. Staples takes us into the classroom of one Railside teacher, Ms. McClure, to explore how she promoted collaboration among students working in heterogeneous groups. She describes the multiple ways in which Ms. McClure created a context within which productive student collaboration could flourish, providing descriptive detail and examples of what this looked like as it played out in the classroom. Critical to Staples's analysis is the idea that what Railside teachers did was to organize the conditions under which particular types of learning would emerge, and thus she uses ideas from complexity science to understand this process.

Taken together, the chapters in this section provide both breadth and depth in conveying the nature, components, and underlying assumptions of the equity pedagogy at Railside, and the learning outcomes—both longitudinally and in moments of learning in classrooms—that they supported.

Chapter 2

Creating Mathematical Futures Through an Equitable Teaching Approach

The Case of Railside School

Jo Boaler and Megan E. Staples

Soon after moving to California from England, I (Boaler, 2002a) was interested in conducting a study to follow through on the one I had conducted in England—looking at the impact of different teaching approaches upon student learning.[1] I had heard about an interesting school where the math teachers collaborated greatly and used an unusual pedagogical approach called "Complex Instruction." Complex Instruction is an approach to teaching developed by Elizabeth Cohen and Rachel Lotan that focuses on disrupting status differences in the classroom and utilizing groupwork for optimal engagement and learning. I visited the school and immediately saw a very unusual teaching approach, so we were thrilled when the department agreed to be part of a comparative study that would allow us to learn from their work.

The low and inequitable mathematics performance of students in urban American high schools has been identified as a critical issue contributing to societal inequities (Moses & Cobb, 2001) and poor economic performance (Madison & Hart, 1990). Thousands of students in the United States and elsewhere struggle through mathematics classes, experiencing repeated failure. Students often disengage from mathematics, finding little intellectual challenge, as they are asked only to memorize and execute routine procedures (Boaler, 2002a). But the question of how best to teach mathematics remains controversial, and debates are dominated by ideology and advocacy (Rosen, 2001).

In this chapter, we report upon a 5-year longitudinal study of approximately 700 students as they progressed through three high schools. One of the findings of the study was the important success of one of the schools. At Railside School students learned more, enjoyed mathematics more, and progressed to higher mathematics levels. What made this result more important was the fact that Railside is an urban school on what locals refer to as the "wrong" side of the tracks. Students come from homes with few financial resources, and the population is culturally and linguistically diverse, with many English language learners. At the beginning of high school, at the start of 9th grade, the Railside students were achieving at significantly lower levels than the students at the other two, suburban schools in our study. Within 2 years the Railside students were significantly outperforming students at the other schools. The students were also more positive about mathematics, they took more mathematics courses, and many more of them planned to pursue mathematics in college. In addition, achievement differences among students of different ethnic groups were reduced in all cases and were eliminated in most. By their senior year, 41% of Railside students were taking advanced classes of precalculus and calculus, compared to approximately 27% of students in the other two schools. Mathematics classes at Railside had a high work rate and few behavioral problems, and the ethnic cliques that form in many schools were not evident. In interviews, the students told us that they learned to respect students from other cultures and circumstances through the approach used in their mathematics classes.

The mathematics teachers at Railside achieved something important that many other teachers could learn from—they organized an effective instructional program for students from traditionally marginalized backgrounds and they taught students to enjoy mathematics and to include it as part of their futures. In this chapter, we present evidence of these important achievements and report upon the ways that the teachers brought them about.

We conducted our study of student learning in different schools with the knowledge that a multitude of schooling variables—ranging from district support and departmental organization (Talbert & McLaughlin, 1996) to curricular examples and classroom interactions—could impact the learning of students and the promotion of equity. Our study centered upon the affordances of different curricula and the ensuing teaching and learning interactions in classrooms. It also considered the role of broader school factors and the contexts in which the different approaches were enacted.

UNDERSTANDING MATH AT RAILSIDE

The Stanford Mathematics Teaching and Learning Study was a 5-year longitudinal study of three high schools with the following pseudonyms: Greendale, Hilltop, and Railside. These three schools are reasonably similar in terms of their size and share the characteristic of employing committed and knowledgeable mathematics teachers. They differ in terms of their location and student demographics (see Table 2.1).[2]

Railside High School, the focus of this analysis, is situated in an urban setting. Lessons are frequently interrupted by the noise of trains passing just feet away from the classrooms. Railside has a diverse student population, with students coming from a variety of ethnic and cultural backgrounds. Hilltop High School is situated in a more rural setting, and approximately half of the students are Latino and half White. Greendale High School is situated in a coastal community with very little ethnic or cultural diversity (almost all students are White).

Railside School used a reform-oriented approach and did not offer families a choice of math programs in which to enroll. The teachers worked collaboratively, and they had designed the curriculum themselves, drawing from different reform curricula such as the College Preparatory Mathematics Curriculum (Sallee, Kysh, Kasimatis, & Hoey, 2000) and Interactive Mathematics Program (Alper, Fendel, Fraser, & Resek, 2003). In addition to a common curriculum, the teachers also shared teaching methods and ways of enacting the curriculum. As they emphasized to us, their curriculum could not be reduced to the worksheets and activities they gave students. Mathematics was organized into the traditional sequence of classes—algebra followed by geometry, then advanced algebra and so on—but the students worked in groups on longer, more conceptual problems.

Another important difference to highlight was the heterogeneous nature of Railside classes. Whereas incoming 9th-grade students in Greendale and Hilltop could enter geometry or could be placed in a remedial class, such as "Math A" or "Business Math," all students at Railside entered the same algebra class. The department was deeply committed to the practice of mixed-ability teaching and to giving all students equal opportunities for advancement.

We monitored three approaches in the study—"traditional" and "IMP" (as labeled by Hilltop and Greendale) and the "Railside approach." As the numbers in the IMP approach were insufficient for statistical analyses, the main comparison groups of students in the study were approximately 300 students who followed the traditional curriculum and teaching approaches in Greendale and Hilltop schools and approximately 300 students at Railside who were taught using reform-oriented curriculum and teaching methods. These two groups of students provide an interesting contrast, as they experienced the same content, taught in very different ways. Class sizes were similar across the schools: approximately 20 students in each math class in Year 1, in line with the class-size reduction policy that was in place in California at that time, and 25–35 students in Years 2 and 3.

WHAT WE LEARNED AT RAILSIDE

Given our goal of understanding the highly complex phenomena of teaching and learning mathematics, we gathered a wide array of data, both qualitative and

Table 2.1. Schools, Students, and Mathematics Approaches

	Railside	Hilltop	Greendale
Enrollment (approx.)	1,500	1,900	1,200
Study demographics	40% Latino/a 20% African American 20% White 20% Asian/ Pacific Islanders	60% White 40% Latino/a	90% White 10% Latino/a
ELL[a] students	30%	20%	0%
Free/reduced lunch	30%	20%	10%
Parent education, % college grads	20%	30%	40%
Mathematics curriculum approaches	Teacher – designed, reform-oriented curriculum, conceptual problems, group work	Choice between "traditional" (demonstration and practice, short problems) and IMP (groupwork, long, applied problems)	Choice between "traditional" (demonstration and practice, short problems) and IMP (groupwork, long, applied problems)

[a] ELL is English language learners.

quantitative, on the teaching approaches and classroom interactions, and student achievement, and students' views of mathematics. Although students' learning experiences ultimately happen on the classroom level, they are shaped and organized by factors in the broader context, such as curriculum design, course sequencing, and departmental collaboration. Consequently, we sought to work across multiple levels to understand the organization of instruction on the classroom level.

We report our results in two parts. The first set of results is more quantitative, describing broader trends and documenting differences. We offer more statistical detail than is perhaps necessary in this section, so that the interested reader is provided more information. The statistics, however, need not be read in detail to understand the overall results and the story of Railside. The second set of results is more qualitative in nature, with descriptions and quotes from the students, which helped to show *how* the documented differences came about.

The Teaching Approaches

Most of the students in Hilltop and Greendale high schools were taught mathematics using a traditional approach, as described by teachers and students—the students sat individually, the teachers presented new mathematical methods through lectures, and the students worked through short, closed problems. Our coding of lessons showed that approximately 21% of the time in algebra classes was spent with teachers lecturing, usually demonstrating methods. Approximately 15% of the time teachers questioned students in a whole-class format, 48% of the time students were practicing methods in their books, working individually, and students presented work for approximately 0.2% of the time. The average time spent on each mathematics problem was 2.5 minutes, or an average of 24 problems in one hour of class time. Our focused analysis of the types of questions teachers asked, which classified questions into seven categories, was conducted with two of the teachers of traditional classes (325 minutes of teaching). This analysis showed that 97% and 99% of the two teachers' questions in traditional algebra classes fell into the procedural category (Boaler & Brodie, 2004).

At Railside School the teachers posed longer, conceptual problems and combined student presentations with teacher questioning. Teachers rarely lectured (for approximately 4% of the time), and students were taught in heterogeneous groups. Approximately 9% of the time teachers questioned students in a whole-class format, 72% of the time students worked in groups while teachers circulated the room showing students methods, helping students and asking them questions of their work, and students presented work for approximately 9% of the time. The average time spent on each mathematics problem was 5.7 minutes, or an average of 16 problems in a 90-minute class period—less than half the number completed in the traditional classes. Our focused analysis of the types of questions teachers asked, conducted with two of the Railside teachers (352 minutes of teaching), showed that Railside math teachers asked many more varied questions than the teachers of traditional classes. Sixty-two percent of their questions were procedural, 17% conceptual, 15% probing, and 6% fell into other questioning categories (Boaler & Brodie, 2004). The broad range of questions they asked was typical of the teachers at Railside, who deliberately and carefully discussed their teaching approaches, a practice that included sharing good questions to ask students. We conducted our most detailed observations and analyses in the 1st-year classes when students were taking algebra, but our observations in later years as students progressed through high school showed that the teaching approaches described above continued in the different mathematics classes the students took.

Student Achievement and Attainment

At the beginning of high school we gave a test of middle school mathematics to all students starting algebra classes in the three schools.[3] At Railside, all incoming students were placed in algebra, as the school employed heterogeneous grouping. Comparisons of means indicated that at the beginning of Year 1, the students at Railside were achieving at significantly lower levels than students at the two other schools using the traditional approach ($t = -9.141$, $p < 0.001$, $n = 658$), as can be seen in Table 2.2. At the end of Year 1 we gave all students a test of algebra to measure what students had learned over the year. The difference in means (1.8) showed that the scores of students in the two approaches were similar (traditional = 23.9, Railside = 22.1), a difference that was significant at the 0.04 level ($t = -2.04$, $p = 0.04$, $n = 637$). Thus the Railside students' scores were approaching comparable levels after a year of algebra teaching. At the end of Year 2 we gave students a test of algebra and geometry, reflecting the content the students had been taught over the first 2 years of school. By the end of Year 2 Railside students were significantly outperforming the students in the traditional approach ($t = -8.309$, $p < 0.001$, $n = 512$).

There were fewer students in the geometry classes in Railside due to the flexibility of Railside's timetable, which allowed students to choose when they took geometry classes (as will be described in the next section). The students in geometry classes at Railside did not represent a selective group; they were of the same range as the students entering Year 1.

Before proceeding, we describe in more detail the type of information presented in Table 2.2. Table 2.2 reports the mean score, or the average of the students' scores on the assessment, for each group of students (Traditional, Railside).

Table 2.2. Assessment Results

	Traditional			Railside			
	Mean score	*Std Deviation*	*n*	*Mean score*	*Std Deviation*	*n*	*t* (level of significance)
Y1 Pretest	**22.23**	8.857	311	**16.00**	8.615	347	−9.141 ($p < 0.001$)
Y1 Posttest	**23.90**	10.327	293	**22.06**	12.474	344	−2.040 ($p = 0.04$)
Y2 Posttest	**18.34**	10.610	313	**26.47**	11.085	199	−8.309 ($p < 0.001$)
Y3 Posttest	**19.55**	8.863	290	**21.439**	10.813	130	−1.75 ($p = 0.082$)

Along with the mean scores, Table 2.2 reports Std Deviation, which is the standard deviation of those scores. This value indicates how "spread out" the scores were. The higher the standard deviation, the wider the range of the scores. A standard deviation of 8.8 indicates that about 70% of the students' scores were between 8.8 points below and 8.8 points above the mean score. (Note that one uses a standard deviation on data that are assumed to be normally distributed.) The "*n*" represents how many students, or the sample size. Finally, the "*p*" value in the last column is the "level of significance," and it indicates how likely the observed differences are to be the result of random chance. In the case of $p < .0001$, it means that these observed differences between mean scores, given the spread of the data, are likely to happen by chance less than 1 in 10,000 times. A *p* value of .05 means that the observed differences from the given populations are likely to happen by chance 1 in 20 times. By convention, we set the bar at this .05 level (1 in 20), and when observed differences are less likely than this to have occurred by chance, we say that the difference is statistically significant, represented by *t*.

The scores in Table 2.2 were for all assessments taken by students. In order to determine whether student attrition impacted the mean scores, we also compared the scores for students in both approaches who took all three tests. We wanted to know if scores in later years were artificially inflated by students who transferred or dropped out of high school. These results show that the Railside students taking all three assessments started at significantly lower levels and ended Year 2 at significantly higher levels (see Table 2.3). (These analyses include only those students who went straight from algebra to geometry in each school [a smaller number] and do not capture students who repeated a course or took time off from math.)

Interestingly, the students most advantaged by the teaching approach at Railside, compared to those in traditional, tracked classes, appeared to be those who started at the highest levels. These students showed the greatest achievement advantage in Year 2 when compared with students in tracked classes, a finding that should alleviate concerns that high-attaining students are held back by working in heterogeneous groups. Interview data, reported in the next sections, suggest that the high-attaining students developed deeper understanding from the act of explaining work to others.

Table 2.3. Scores of Students who took Y1 Pretest, Y1 Posttest, and Y2 Posttest

	n^a	Y1 Pretest		Y1 Posttest		Y2 Posttest	
		Mean	*SD*	*Mean*	*SD*	*Mean*	*SD*
Railside	90	20.58	8.948	29.19	11.804	24.96	10.681
Traditional	163	23.44	8.802	25.86	10.087	16.58	8.712
t (level of significance)		2.463 ($p = 0.014$)		2.364 ($p = 0.019$)		6.364 ($p = 0.000$)	

[a] *n* is number of students taking all three tests.

In Year 3 the students at Railside continued to outperform the other students, although the differences were not significant ($t = -1.75$, $p = 0.082$, $n = 420$). The Railside students' achievement in Year 3 classes may not have been as high in relation to the traditional classes, as the Year 3 Railside curriculum had not been developed as much by the department, and the classes were taught by teachers in their first 2 years of teaching. In Year 4 we did not administer achievement tests. However, more students at Railside continued to take higher-level math courses. By their senior year, 41% of Railside students were taking advanced classes of precalculus and calculus, compared to about 27% of students in the other two schools.[4]

The Railside mathematics teachers were also extremely successful at reducing the achievement gap among groups of students belonging to different ethnic groups at the school. Table 2.4 shows significant differences among groups at the beginning of the 9th-grade year, with Asian, Filipino, and White students each outperforming Latino and Black students ($p < .001$).

At the end of Year 1, there were no longer statistically significant differences between the achievement of White and Latino students, nor the Filipino students and Latino and Black students. The significant differences that remained at that time were between White and Black students and between Asian students and Black and Latino students (ANOVA $F = 5.208$; $df = 280$; $p = 0.000$). Table 2.5 shows these results.

In subsequent years the only consistent difference that remained was the high performance of Asian students, who continued to significantly outperform Black and Latino students. Differences among White, Black, and Latino students' scores on our tests were not present. At the other schools, achievement differences between students of different ethnicities remained. At Railside there were also no gender differences in performance on any of the tests, and young women were well represented in higher mathematics classes.

Student Perceptions and Relationships with Mathematics

In addition to high achievement, the students at Railside also enjoyed mathematics more than the students in the other approach. In questionnaires given to the students each year, the Railside students were always significantly more positive about their experiences with mathematics. For example, 71% of Railside students in Year 2 classes ($n = 198$) reported "enjoying math class," compared with 46% of students in traditional classes ($n = 318$) ($t = -4.934$; $df = 444.62$; $p < 0.001$). In the Year 3 questionnaire students were asked to finish the statement "I enjoy math in school" with one of four time options: all of the time, most of the time, some of the time, or none of the time. Fifty-four percent of students from Railside ($n = 198$) said that they enjoyed mathematics all or most of the time, compared with 29% of students in traditional classes ($n = 318$), which is

Table 2.4. Railside Year 1 Pretest Results by Ethnicity

Ethnicity	n	Mean	Median	Std Dev.
Asian	27	22.41	22	8.509
Black	68	12.28	12	6.286
Hispanic/Latino	103	14.28	12	7.309
Filipino	23	21.61	22	8.289
White	51	21.20	21	9.362

Table 2.5. Railside Year 1 Posttest Results by Ethnicity

Ethnicity	n	Mean	Median	Std Dev.
Asian	27	29.44	30	12.148
Black	68	18.21	16.50	10.925
Hispanic/Latino	103	21.31	21	11.64
Filipino	23	26.65	26	10.504
White	51	26.69	28	13.626

a significant difference ($t = 4.758$; $df = 286$; $p < 0.001$). In addition, significantly more Railside students agreed or strongly agreed with the statement "I like math," with 74% of Railside students responding positively, compared with 54% of students in traditional classes ($t = -4.414$; $df = 220.77$; $p < 0.001$).

In Year 4 we conducted interviews with 105 students in the three different schools. Most of the students were seniors, and they were chosen to represent the breadth of attainment displayed by the whole school cohort. These interviews were coded, and students were given scores on the categories of *interest, authority, agency,* and *future plans for mathematics.* The categories of *authority* and *agency* (Holland, Lachiotte, Skinner, & Cain, 1998) emerged as important, as students in the different approaches varied in the extent to which they believed they had authority (the capacity to validate mathematical methods and ideas using their own knowledge rather than the teacher or textbook) or that they could work with agency (having the opportunity to inquire and use their own ideas; see Boaler, 2009). Significant differences were found in all of these categories, with the students at Railside being significantly more interested in mathematics ($x^2 = 12.806$, $df = 2$, p $= 0.002$, $n = 67$) and believing they had significantly more authority ($x^2 = 29.035$, $df = 2$, $p = 0.000$, $n = 67$) and agency ($x^2 = 22.650$, $df = 2$, $p = 0.000$, $n = 63$). In terms of future plans, *all* of the students interviewed at Railside intended to pursue more mathematics courses, compared with 67% of students from the traditional classes, and 39% of Railside students planned a future in mathematics, compared with 5% of students from traditional classes (x^2 = 18.234, df = 2, p = 0.000, n = 65).

Because of the challenges of accessing individual student data and confidentiality issues, we are unable to report anything beyond school scores for the students on state-administered tests. Despite this limitation, these school-level data are interesting to examine and raise some important issues with respect to testing and equity, as Railside students performed higher on our tests, district tests, and the California Standards Test of algebra but did not fare as well on the CAT 6, a standardized test, nor on indicators of Adequate Yearly Progress (AYP), which are determined primarily by standardized tests.

In contrast, the California Standards Test, a curriculum-aligned test taken by students who had completed algebra, showed the Railside students scoring at higher levels than the other two schools (see Table 2.6). Fifty percent of Railside students scored at or above the basic level, compared to 30% at Greendale[5] and 40% at Hilltop. Students at Hilltop and Greendale scored at higher levels on the CAT 6, and these schools had higher AYP numbers, as seen in Tables 2.7 and 2.8.

The relatively low performance of the Railside students on the state's standardized tests is interesting and may be caused by the cultural and linguistic barriers provided by the state tests. The correlation between students' scores on the language arts and mathematics sections of the AYP tests, across the whole state of California, was a staggering 0.932 for 2004. This data point provides strong indication that the mathematics tests were testing language as much as mathematics. This argument could not be made in reverse, as the language tests do not contain mathematics. Indeed, the students at Railside reported in open-ended interviews that the standardized tests used unfamiliar terms and culturally biased contexts that our tests did not use (see also Boaler, 2003). Tables 2.7 and 2.8 also show interesting relationships between mathematics and language, as the Greendale and Hilltop students were more successful on tests of reading and language arts, a trend that held across the state, but the Railside students were as or more successful on mathematics. Another interesting result to note is that 40% more White students scored at or above the 50th percentile than Latino students at Hilltop

Table 2.6. California Standards Test, Algebra, 2003: Percentage of Students Attaining Given Levels of Proficiency

	Greendale	Hilltop	Railside
Advanced	0	0	0
Proficient	10	10	20
Basic	30	30	30
Below basic	60	40	40
Far below basic	10	20	20

Table 2.7. CAT 6, 2003, STAR, Grade 11 (Year 3): Percentage of Students at or Above 50th Percentile

	Railside	Hilltop	Greendale
Reading	40	60	70
Language	30	50	70
Mathematics	40	50	70

Table 2.8. AYP (Adequate Yearly Progress), 2003: Difference Between Percentage of Students Scoring at "'Proficient" Level in Language Arts and Mathematics (Data Rounded to Nearest Whole Number)

	Difference (% proficient in language arts—% proficient in mathematics)	"Similar schools" average difference
Railside	1	13
Hilltop	9	11
Greendale	15	12

(the only other sizeable group of ethnic minority students in the study) on the CAT 6. At Railside the difference between the same two groups was only 10%. The data in Tables 2.6–2.8 may indicate the inability of the state standardized tests to capture the mathematical understanding of the Railside students that was demonstrated in many other formats.

Summary Comments

The students at Railside enjoyed mathematics more than students taught more traditionally, they achieved at higher levels on curriculum-aligned tests, and the achievement gap between students of different ethnic and cultural groups was lower than those at the other schools. In addition, the teachers and students achieved something that Boaler (2006b, 2008) has termed *relational equity*. In studying equity most researchers look for reductions in achievement differences for students of different ethnic and cultural groups and genders when tests are taken. But Boaler has argued that a goal for equity should also be the creation of classrooms in which students learn to treat each other equitably, showing respect for students of different cultures, genders, and social classes. Schools are places where students learn ways of acting and being that they are likely to replicate in society, making respect for students from different circumstances an important goal. It is not commonly thought that mathematics classrooms are places where students should learn about cultural respect, but students at Railside reported that they learned to value students who came from very different backgrounds to themselves because of the approach of their mathematics classes (for more detail, see Boaler, 2006b, 2008).

ANALYZING THE SOURCES OF SUCCESS

I. The Department, Curriculum, and Timetable

Railside had an unusual mathematics department. During the years of our study, 12 of the 13 teachers worked collaboratively, spending vast amounts of time designing curricula, discussing teaching decisions and actions, and generally improving their practice through the sharing of ideas. Unusually for the United States, the mathematics department strongly influenced the recruitment and hiring of teachers, enabling the department to maintain a core of teachers with common philosophies and goals. The teachers shared a strong commitment to the advancement of equity, and the department had spent many years working out a coherent curriculum and teaching approach that teachers believed enhanced the success of all students. The mathematics department had focused their efforts in particular upon the introductory algebra curriculum that all students take when they start at the school. The algebra course was designed around key concepts, with questions drawn from various published curricula such as College Prepatory Mathematics (CPM), IMP, and a textbook of activities that use Algebra Lab Gear™ (Picciotto, 1995). A theme of the algebra and subsequent courses was multiple representations, and students were frequently asked to represent their ideas in different ways, using math tools such as words, graphs, tables and symbols. In addition, connections between algebra and geometry were emphasized even though the two areas were taught in separate courses.

Railside followed a practice of block scheduling, and lessons were 90 minutes long, with courses taking place over half a school year, rather than a full academic year.[6] In addition, the introductory algebra curriculum, generally taught in one course in U.S. high schools, was taught in the equivalent of two courses at Railside. The teachers spread the introductory content over a longer period of time partly to ensure that the foundational mathematical ideas were taught carefully with depth and partly to ensure that particular norms—both social and sociomathematical (Yackel & Cobb, 1996)—were carefully established. The fact that mathematics courses were only half a year long at Railside may appear unimportant, but this organizational decision had a profound impact upon the students' opportunities to take higher-level mathematics courses. At Greendale and Hilltop (as in most U.S. high schools), mathematics classes were 1 year long and a typical student began with algebra. Consequently, students couldn't take calculus unless they were advanced, as the standard sequence of courses was algebra, geometry, advanced algebra, then precalculus. Furthermore, if a student failed a course, the level of content he or she would reach is limited. In contrast, a Railside student could take two mathematics classes each year. Consequently, students could fail classes, start at lower levels, and/or choose not to take mathematics in a particular semester and still reach calculus. This relatively simple scheduling decision was part of the reason why significantly more students at Railside took advanced-level classes than students in the other two schools.

Because the teachers at Railside were deeply committed to equity and to heterogeneous teaching, they had worked together over the previous decade to develop and implement a curriculum that afforded multiple points of access to mathematics and comprised a variety of cognitively demanding tasks. The curriculum was organized around units that each had a unifying theme such as "What is a linear function?" The department placed a strong emphasis on problems that satisfied the criterion of being *groupworthy*. Groupworthy problems are those that "illustrate important mathematical concepts, allow for multiple representations, include tasks that draw effectively on the collective resources of a group, and have several possible solution paths" (Horn, 2005, p. 219). The Appendix to this chapter includes an example of a problem that the department deemed groupworthy.

An important feature of the Railside approach we studied that cannot be seen in the curriculum materials was the act of asking follow-up questions. For example, when students found the perimeter of a figure (see the Appendix) with side lengths represented algebraically, as $10x + 10$, the teacher asked a student in each group, "Where's the 10?," requiring that students relate the algebraic expression to the figure. Although the tasks provided a set of constraints and affordances (Greeno & Middle School Mathematics Through Applications Project, 1997), it was in the implementation of the tasks that the learning opportunities were realized (Stein, Smith, Henningsen, & Silver, 2000). The question of "Where's the 10?," for example, was not written on the students' worksheets, but was part of the curriculum, as teachers agreed upon the follow-up questions they would ask of students.

Research studies in recent years have pointed to the importance of school and district contexts in the support of teaching reforms (McLaughlin & Talbert, 2001; Siskin, 1994; Talbert & McLaughlin, 1996). Railside, however, is not a case of a district or school that initiated or mandated reforms. The reforms put in place by the mathematics department were supported by the school and were in line with other school reforms, but they were driven by the passion and commitment of the mathematics teachers in the department. The school, in many ways, was a demanding context for the reforms, not least because it had been managed by five different principals in 6 years and had been labeled an "'underperforming school" by the state because of low state test scores. The department, under the leadership of two strong and politically astute co-chairs, fought to maintain their practices at various times and worked hard to garner the support of the district and school. While the teachers felt well supported at the end of our study, Railside does not represent a case of a reforming district encouraging a department to engage in new practices. Rather, Railside is a case of an unusual, committed, and hardworking department that continues to grow in strength through its teacher collaborations and work.

II: Groupwork and "Complex Instruction"

Many teachers use groupwork, but groups do not always function well, with some students doing more of the work than others, and some students being excluded or choosing to opt out. At Railside the teachers employed strategies to make groupwork successful. They adopted an approach called *Complex Instruction*, designed by Cohen and Lotan (Cohen, 1994a; Cohen & Lotan, 1997) for use in all subject areas. The system is designed to counter social and academic status differences in classrooms, starting from the premise that status differences do not emerge because of particular students but because of group interactions. The approach includes a number of recommended practices that the school employed that we highlight below.

Multidimensional Classrooms. In many mathematics classrooms one practice is valued above all others—that of executing procedures correctly and quickly. The narrowness by which success is judged means that some students rise to the top of classes, gaining good grades and teacher praise, while others sink to the bottom. In addition, most students know where they are in the hierarchy created. Such classrooms are unidimensional—the dimensions along which success is presented are singular. In contrast, a central tenet of the Complex Instruction approach is what the authors refer to as *multiple ability treatment*. This treatment is based upon the idea that expectations of success and failure can be modified by the provision of a more open set of task requirements that value many different abilities. Teachers should explain to students that "no one student will be 'good on all these abilities' and that each student will be 'good on at least one'" (Cohen & Lotan, 1997, p. 78). Cohen and Lotan provide theoretical backing for their multiple ability treatment using the notion of multidimensionality (Rosenholtz & Wilson, 1980; Simpson, 1981).

At Railside, the teachers created multidimensional classes by valuing many dimensions of mathematical work. This was achieved, in part, by implementing open problems that students could solve in different ways. The teachers valued different methods and solution paths, and this enabled more students to contribute ideas and feel valued. When we interviewed the students and asked them, "What does it take to be successful in mathematics class?," they offered many different practices, such as asking good questions, rephrasing problems, explaining well, being logical, justifying work, considering answers, and using manipulatives. When we asked students in the traditional classes what they needed to do in order to be successful, they talked in much more narrow ways, usually saying that they needed to concentrate and pay careful attention. Railside students regarded mathematical success much more broadly than students in the traditional classes, and instead of viewing mathematics as a set of methods that they needed to observe and remember, they regarded mathematics as a way of working with many different dimensions.

The multidimensional nature of the classes at Railside was an extremely important part of the increased success of students. Put simply, when there are many ways to be successful, many more students are successful. Railside students were aware of the different practices that were valued, and they felt successful because they were able to excel at some of them. Given the current high-stakes testing climate, teachers may shy away from promoting the development of practices outside of procedure execution because they are not needed on state tests, but the fact that teachers at Railside valued a range of practices and more students could be successful in class appears to have made students feel more confident and positive about mathematics.[7] This may have enhanced their success in class and their persistence with high-level mathematics classes.

The following comments given by students in interviews provide a clear indication of the multidimensionality of classes:

Back in middle school the only thing you worked on was your math skills. But here you work socially and you also try to learn to help people and get help. Like you improve on your social skills, math skills and logic skills. (Janet, Y1)

J: With math you have to interact with everybody and talk to them and answer their questions. You can't be just like, "Oh, here's the book, look at the numbers and figure it out."
Int: Why is that different for math?
J: It's not just one way to do it. . . . It's more interpretive. It's not just one answer. There's more than one way to get it. And then it's like: "Why does it work"? (Jasmine, Y1)

It is not common for students to report that mathematics is more "interpretive" than other subjects. The students at Railside recognized that helping, interpreting, and justifying were critically valued practices in mathematics classes.

One of the practices that we found to be particularly important in the promotion of equity was justification. At Railside students were required to justify their answers at almost all times. There are many good reasons for this — justification is an intrinsically mathematical practice (Martino & Maher, 1999; RAND, 2002), but this practice also serves an interesting and particular role in the promotion of equity. The practice of justification made space for mathematical discussions that might not otherwise be afforded, particularly given the broad range of students' prior knowledge in the Railside mathematics classes. Students had both the right to receive a justification that satisfied them, and the obligation to provide a justification in response to another's question. Justifications then were adapted to the needs of individuals, and mathematics that might not otherwise be addressed was brought to the surface.

The following excerpt gives an indication of how two students viewed the role that justification played in helping different students:

> *Int*: What happens when someone says an answer?
> A: We'll ask how they got it.
> L: Yeah, because we do that a lot in class. . . . Some of the students—it'll be the students that don't do their work, that'd be the ones, they'll be the ones to ask step by step. But a lot of people would probably ask how to approach it. And then if they did something else they would show how they did it. And then you just have a little session! (Ana & Latisha, Y3)

The following boy was achieving at lower levels than other students, and it is interesting to hear him talk about the ways he was supported by the practices of explanation and justification:

> Most of them, they just like know what to do and everything. First you're like "why you put this?" and then like if I do my work and compare it to theirs. Theirs is like super different 'cause they know, like what to do. I will be like—let me copy, I will be like, "Why you did this?" And then I'd be like: "I don't get it why you got that." And then like, sometimes the answer's just like, they be like, "Yeah, he's right and you're wrong." But like—why? (Juan, Y2)

Juan also differentiated between high and low achievers without referring to such adjectives as "smart" or "fast," instead saying that some students "know what to do." He also made it very clear that he was helped by the practice of justification and that he felt comfortable pushing other students to go beyond answers and explain why their answers are given. At Railside the teachers prioritized the message that students had two important responsibilities—both to help someone who asked for help, but also to ask if they needed help. Both are important in the pursuit of equity, and justification emerged as an important practice in the students' learning.

The Importance of Student Roles. A large part of the success of the teaching at Railside came from the complex, interconnected system in each classroom, in which students were taught to take responsibility for one another and were encouraged to contribute equally to tasks. When in groups, students were given a particular role to play, such as *facilitator, team captain, recorder/reporter,* or *resource manager* (Cohen & Lotan, 1997). The premise behind this approach is that all students have important work to do in groups, without which the group cannot function. At Railside the teachers emphasized the different roles at frequent intervals, stopping, for example, at the start of class to remind facilitators to help people check answers or show their work. Students changed roles at the end of each unit. The teachers reinforced the status of the different roles and the important part they played in the mathematical work that was undertaken. These roles contributed to a classroom environment in which everyone had something important to do and all students learned to rely upon one another.

Assigning Competence. An interesting and subtle approach that is recommended within the Complex Instruction literature is that of assigning competence. This practice involves teachers raising the status of students who may be of a lower status in a group, for example, by praising something they have said or done that has intellectual value, and bringing it to the group's attention; asking a student to present an idea; or publicly praising a student's work in a whole-class setting. For example, during a classroom observation at Railside a quiet Eastern European boy muttered something in a group that was dominated by two outgoing Latina girls. The teacher who was visiting the table immediately picked up on what Ivan said, noting, "Good, Ivan, that is important." Later, when the girls offered a response to one of the teacher's questions, the teacher said, "Oh, that is like Ivan's idea; you're building on that." The teacher raised the status of Ivan's contribution, which would almost certainly have been lost without such an intervention. Ivan visibly straightened up and leaned forward as the teacher reminded the girls of his idea. Cohen (1994a) recommends that if student feedback is to address status issues, it must be public, intellectual, specific, and relevant to the group task (p. 132). The public dimension is important, as other students learn about the broad dimensions that are valued; the intellectual dimension ensures that the feedback is an aspect of mathematical work; and the specific dimension means that students know exactly what the teacher is praising. This practice is linked to the multidimensionality of the classroom, which values a broad range of work and forms of participation. The practice of assigning competence demonstrated the teachers' commitment to equity and to the principle of showing what different students could do in a multifaceted mathematical context.

Teaching Students to Be Responsible for One Another's Learning. A major part of the equitable results attained at Railside came from the serious way in which teachers taught students to be responsible for one another's learning. Groupwork, by its nature, brings an element of responsibility, but Railside teachers went beyond this to encourage the students to take the responsibility very seriously. In previous research on approaches that employ groupwork, students generally report that they prefer to work in groups and they list different benefits, but the advantages usually relate to their own learning (see Boaler, 2000, 2002a, 2009). At Railside, students' descriptions of the value of groupwork were distinctly reciprocal, as they also voiced a clear concern for the learning of their classmates. For example:

> *Int*: Do you prefer to work alone or in groups?
> A: I think it'd be in groups, 'cause I want, like, people that doesn't know how to understand it, I want to help them. And I want to, I want them to be good at it. And I want them to understand how to do the math that we do. (Amado, Y1)

Students talked about their enjoyment of helping others and the value in helping one another:

> It's good working in groups because everybody else in the group can learn with you, so if someone doesn't understand—like if I don't understand but the other person does understand they can explain it to me, or vice versa, and I think it's cool. (Latisha, Y3)

One unfortunate but common side effect of some classroom approaches is that students develop beliefs about the inferiority or superiority of different students. At Railside the students did not talk in these ways. This did not mean that they thought all students were the same, but they came to appreciate the diversity of classes and the different attributes that different students offered:

> Everybody in there is at a different level. But what makes the class good is that everybody's at different levels so everybody's constantly teaching each other and helping each other out. (Zane, Y2)

The students at Railside not only learned to value the contributions of others, they also developed a responsibility to help one another.

One way in which teachers nurtured a feeling of responsibility was through the assessment system. Teachers graded the work of a group by, for example, rating the quality of the conversations groups had. The teachers also gave both individual and group tests. A third way in which responsibility was encouraged was through a practice of asking one student in a group to answer a follow-up question after a group had worked on something. If the student could not answer, the teacher would leave the group and return to ask the same student again. In the intervening time it was the group's responsibility to help the student learn the mathematics he or she needed to answer the question. This move of asking one member of a group to give an answer and an explanation, without help from his or her group mates, was a subtle practice that had major implications for the classroom environment. In the following interview extract the students talk about this particular practice and the implications it holds:

> *Int*: Is learning math an individual or a social thing?
>
> G: It's like both, because if you get it, then you have to explain it to everyone else. And then sometimes you just might have a group problem and we all have to get it. So I guess both.
>
> B: I think both—because individually you have to know the stuff yourself so that you can help others in your groupwork and stuff like that. You have to know it so you can explain it to them. Because you never know which one of the four people she's going to pick. And it depends on that one person that she picks to get the right answer. (Gisella & Bianca, Y2)

These students made the explicit link between teachers asking any group member to answer a question and being responsible for their group members. They also communicated an interesting social orientation that became instantiated through the mathematics approach, saying that the purpose in knowing individually was not to be better than others but so "you can help others in your group." There was an important interplay between individual and group accountability in the Railside classrooms.

The four practices described—multidimensionality, group roles, assigning competence, and encouraging responsibility—are all part of the Complex Instruction approach. We now review three other practices in which the teachers engaged that are also critical to the promotion of equity. These relate to the challenge and expectations provided by the teachers.

III. Challenge and Expectations

High Cognitive Demand. The Railside teachers held high expectations for students and presented all students with a common, rigorous curriculum to support their learning. The cognitive demand that was expected of all students was higher than other schools', partly because the classes were heterogeneous and no students were precluded from meeting high-level content. Even when students arrived at school with weak content knowledge well below their grade level, they were placed into algebra classes and supported in learning the material and moving on to higher content. Teachers also enacted a high level of challenge in their interactions with groups and through their questioning, for instance, in the earlier example where students found the perimeter of a set of algebra lab tiles to be $10x + 10$ and the teachers asked students to explain where the +10 came from. Importantly, the support that teachers gave to students did not serve to reduce the cognitive demand of the work, even when students were showing signs of frustration. The reduction of cognitive demand is a common occurrence in mathematics classes when teachers help students (Stein et al., 2000). At Railside the teachers were highly effective in interacting with students in ways that supported their continued thinking and engagement with the core mathematics of the problems.

When we interviewed students and asked them what it took to be a good teacher, students demonstrated an appreciation of the high demand the teachers placed upon them, for example:

> She has a different way of doing things. I don't know, like she won't even really tell you how to do it. She'll be like, "Think of it this way." There's a lot of times when she's just like — "Well, think about it" — and then she'll walk off and that kills me. That really kills me. But it's cool. I mean it's like, it's alright, you know. I'll solve it myself. I'll get some help from somebody else. It's cool. (Ana, Y3)

The following students, in talking about the support teachers provided, also referred to their teachers' push for understanding:

> *Int*: What makes a good teacher?
> J: Patience. Because sometimes teachers they just zoom right through things. And other times they take the time to actually make sure you understand it, and make sure that you actually pay attention. Because there's some teachers out there who say: "You understand this?" and you'll be like, "Yes," but you really don't mean yes you mean no. And they'll be like, "OK." And they move on. And there's some teachers that be like — they *know* that you don't understand it. And they know that you're just saying yes so that you can move on. And so they actually take the time out to go over it again and make sure that you actually got it, that you actually understand this time. (John, Y2)

The students' appreciation of the teachers' demand was also demonstrated in our questionnaires. One of the questions started with the stem: "When I get stuck on a math problem, it is most helpful when my teacher . . . " This was followed by answers such as "tells me the answer," "leads me through the problem step by step," and "helps me without giving away the answer." On a four-point scale (SA, A, D, SD), almost half of the Railside students (47%) *strongly* agreed with the response: "Helps me *without* giving away the answer," compared with 27% of students in the traditional classes at the other two schools ($n = 450$, $t = -4.257$; $df = 221.418$; $p < 0.001$).

Effort Over Ability. In addition to challenging students through difficult questions that maintained a high cognitive demand, the teachers also gave frequent messages to students about the nature of high achievement in mathematics, continually emphasizing that it was a product of hard work and not of innate ability. The teachers reassured students that they could achieve anything if they put in the effort. This message was heard by students and communicated to us in interviews:

> To be successful in math you really have to just like, put your mind to it and keep on trying—because math is all about trying. It's kind of a hard subject because it involves many things. . . . but as long as you keep on trying and don't give up then you know that you can do it. (Sara, Y1)

In the Year 3 questionnaires we offered the statement "Anyone can be really good at math if they try." At Railside, 84% of the students agreed with this, compared with 52% of students in the traditional classes ($n = 473$, $t = -8.272$; $df = 451$; $p < 0.001$). But the Railside students did not only come to believe that they could be successful. They developed an important practice that supported them in that—the act of persistence. It could be argued that persistence is one of the most important practices to learn in school—one that is strongly tied to success in school as well as in work and life. We have many indications that the Railside students developed considerably more persistence than the other students. For example, as part of our assessment of students we gave them long, difficult problems to work on for 90 minutes in class, which we videotaped. The Railside students were more successful on these problems, partly because they would not give up on them and continued to try to find methods and approaches even when they had exhausted many. When we asked in questionnaires: "How long (in minutes) will you typically work on one math problem before giving up and deciding you can't do it?," the Railside students gave responses that averaged 19.4 minutes, compared with the 9.9 minutes averaged by students in traditional classes ($n = 438$, $t = -5.641$; $df = 142.110$; $p < 0.001$). This response is not unexpected, given that the Railside students worked on longer problems in classes, but it also gives some indication of the persistence students were learning through the longer problems they experienced.

In the following interview extract, the students link this persistence to the question-asking and justification highlighted earlier:

> A: Because I know if someone does something and I don't get it I'll ask questions. I'm not just going to keep going and not know how to do something.
> L: And then if somebody challenges what I do then I'll ask back and I'll try to solve it. And then I'll ask them: "Well how d'you do it?" (Ana & Latisha, Y3)

CONCLUSION

Railside is not a perfect place—the teachers would like to achieve more in terms of student achievement and the elimination of inequities, and they rarely feel satisfied with the achievements they have made to date, despite the vast amounts of time they spend planning and working. But research on urban schools (Haberman, 1991) and the experiences of mathematics students in particular tells us that the achievements at Railside are extremely unusual. There were many features of the approach at Railside that combined to produce important results. Not only did the students achieve at significantly higher levels, but the differences in attainment among students of different ethnic groups were reduced in all cases and disappeared in some.

We have attempted to convey the work of the teachers in bringing about the reduction in inequalities as well as general high achievement among students. In doing so we also hope to have given a sense of the complexity of the relational and equitable system that the teachers implemented. People who have heard about the achievements of Railside have asked for the curriculum so that they may use it, but while the curriculum plays a part in what is achieved at the school, it is only one part of a complex, interconnected system. At the heart of this system is the work of the teachers, and the numerous different equitable practices in which they engaged. The Railside students learned through their mathematical work that alternate and multidimensional solutions were important, which led them to value the contributions of the people offering such ideas. This was particularly important at Railside, as the classrooms were multicultural and multilingual. It is commonly believed that students will learn respect for different people and cultures if they have discussions about such issues or read diverse forms of literature in English or social studies classes. We propose that all subjects have something to contribute to the promotion of equity, and that mathematics, often regarded as the most abstract subject, removed from responsibilities of cultural or social awareness, has an important contribution to make. The discussions at Railside were often abstract mathematical discussions, and the students did not learn mathematics through special materials that were sensitive to issues of gender, culture, or class. But through their mathematical work, the Railside students learned to appreciate the different ways that students saw mathematics problems and learned to value the contribution of different methods, perspectives, representations, partial ideas, and even incorrect ideas as they worked to solve problems. As the classrooms became more multidimensional, students learned to appreciate and value the insights of a wider group of students from different cultures and circumstances.

The role of multidimensionality in the promotion of equity is not one that has reached the attention of many researchers in the United States. Multidimensionality is encouraged by open curriculum materials that allow students to work in different ways and bring different strengths to their work. The use of open materials in mixed-ability classrooms is something Boaler (2009) also found to promote equity in her study of English schools. Freedman, Delp, and Crawford (2005) also noted many aspects of a teacher's work that promoted equity and that are consistent with our findings, including learners being taught to be responsible for their own learning, a learning community that appreciates diverse contributions, opportunities for different ways of learning, and high challenges for all students. In Freedman et al.'s study they also found that equitable teaching did not rely on culturally sensitive materials, nor on the groupwork that the teachers in our study used, reminding us that there are many different routes to equity. In our study we found that mathematical materials and associated teaching practices that encouraged students to work in many different ways, supporting the contributions of all students, not only resulted in high and equitable attainment, but promoted respect and sensitivity among students.

The mathematical success shared by many students at Railside gave them access to mathematical careers, higher-level jobs, and more secure financial futures. The fact that the teachers were able to achieve this through a multidimensional, reform-oriented approach at a time in California when unidimensional mathematics work and narrow test performance were all that was valued (Becker & Jacob, 2000) may give other teachers hope that working for equity and mathematical understanding against the constraints of the system is both possible and worthwhile.

APPENDIX: GROUPWORTHY TASK

Figure 2.1. Graphic from Groupworthy Task

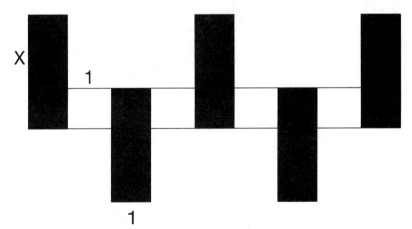

Figure 2.1. Graphic from Groupworthy Task (continued)

Explanation of figure:

There are two types of tiles used to create the above configuration. The dark
 tiles are x by 1 in dimension. The light square tiles are 1 by 1 in dimension.

Task prompt:

Build the arrangement of Lab Gear™ blocks (shown in the diagram given to
 students), and find the perimeter of the arrangement.

Result (which students derive in groups):

The perimeter is $10x + 10$.

Teacher follow-up question as she moves from group to group:

Where's the 10 in the $10x + 10$?

Students must discuss "where" the 10 is, and all students must be able to explain this to the teacher.

Chapter 3

Working Toward an Equity Pedagogy

Carlos Cabana, Barbara Shreve, and Estelle Woodbury

To begin to illustrate how the principles that shaped mathematics teaching and learning at Railside High were woven into the daily teaching and learning practices in classrooms, we invite you into a scene from a typical day[1] in a Railside mathematics class:

"Hi, Mr. C.! What are we doing today?"
"We have a quiz today, Glenda. Aren't you excited?"

"Mr. C., I didn't understand my homework. Can I turn it in tomorrow?"
"Of course, Mariela! Thanks for telling me. Do you want to come in at lunch for help?"

"What smells funny in here? Is it you, Mr. C.?"
"Yes, Luis, it's me. I didn't want you to be the only one."

Thirty-two 9th- and 10th-grade students roll into their Algebra I classroom, playfully greeting each other and their teacher. As the start bell gets close to ringing, the teacher turns on the projector and asks the class to follow the directions on the screen (see Figure 3.1). When the bell rings, students finish up their chatter as the teacher says, "I see Team 2 is ready. Team 1 is ready. Team 3, did your Resource Manager do his job? Team 4 is almost ready . . .

"Okay, good morning, you guys! It's good to see everyone looking SO happy that we have a quiz later today! But before that, I want us to build on our work on slope from yesterday. Marisol has been absent for a few days, so can someone explain to her what you know so far about slope? What does that word mean?"

The teacher records on a transparency as students share their ideas: "It's the grow-by number . . . like, in a *t*-table, it tells how the *y*'s are growing. . . . Yeah, in

Figure 3.1. Quiz Announcement Slide

> *Happy Quiz Day!*
>
> Please be ready by
> the time the bell rings:
> - HW in your
>   team folder
> - Tables clear except
>   for graph paper
>
> Resource Managers,
> please get color
> pencils for your team.

a pile pattern too. It tells how many squares the piles grow by. . . . It's the m in $y = mx + b$."

"Great list," the teacher says. "I love how you guys explained slope in everyday words, and also using multiple representations. Marisol, are there any of these ideas you're not sure about yet?" Marisol says no, and the teacher probes the class further:

The teacher replaces the slope brainstorm transparency with one that has three problems (see Figure 3.2). He says, "Please copy each problem and work together to find the slope. Be sure everyone can explain, because at least three of you will come up to the overhead to discuss your ideas."

As teams get to work, Mr. C. surveys the class for a few moments before beginning to circulate around the room. Some teams begin by sharing ideas right away, while others quietly copy the problems. One team seems to be doing nothing, so after a few moments Mr. C. goes over to them to intervene. "How are you guys going to get started? Do you all want to copy the problems first or discuss how to get the slope first?"

After 10 minutes, the teacher pulls the class together to begin a discussion. He moves to the back of the room to facilitate the debrief as a member of the class. "Who wants to go up to show what your team did? You can start with any problem you want, and it's okay if you aren't quite sure yet. In fact, it would help us all out if someone went up who didn't really get it yet and wants to learn."

Figure 3.2. Slope Warm-up

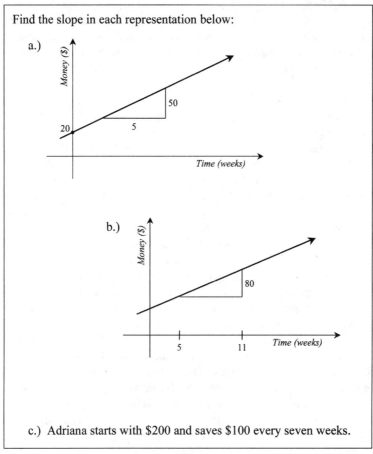

Find the slope in each representation below:

a.)

Money ($)

50

20   5

Time (weeks)

b.)

Money ($)

80

5   11   Time (weeks)

c.) Adriana starts with $200 and saves $100 every seven weeks.

"I think we're missing a representation. Does anyone see what we missed? . . . Yes! What about graphs? What does 'slope' mean in a graph? You and your team will need to discuss this to make sense of today's warm-up, because the warm-up will help you on the quiz."

After a few moments, Ana says, "I'll go! But I'm not sure I'm right."

"That's perfect!" says Mr. C. Ana goes up and sits on the stool waiting expectantly. "Which one would you like to do?" asks the teacher. Ana picks the first one, and the teacher asks her questions to help her makes sense of the numbers in the problem, following each response with another question to help her share her thinking: "What is this graph about? What story is it trying to tell? What do each of the numbers represent in the graph's story? What are you supposed to be finding?"

As Ana answers questions and begins to think out loud, the teacher praises her ideas and her persistence while also asking her to justify: "Yes! Perfect answer, Ana! How did you decide that?" When Ana is stuck, Mr. C appeals to the class to help her make sense of the problem. He asks her to color-code her work, so that the numbers she uses in her calculations match both the numbers and dimensions in the graph. This helps him see whether Ana is understanding where the numbers come from rather than writing down guesses she thinks may be right. When Ana finishes, Mr. C. asks her if she has any questions about her work, or if anyone else in the class has questions. Seeing none, he asks for a volunteer to solve another problem. When no one offers, Mr. C. tells Ana to "pass the pen." Ana and the class know that this means she can pass the pen to anyone (except her tablemates) to be the next presenter. Ana looks around, and Mr. C. suggests she pass it to someone who she thinks is good at explaining clearly. Ana settles on Eric, who groans a little for dramatic effect but nevertheless moves quickly to the overhead. He presents his answer to the second problem smoothly and tries to also color-code like Ana did, but makes a mistake: He labels the change in x-values "11." The teacher lets him finish and asks the same question he used when Ana finished: "Do you have any questions about your work, Eric? Does anyone else?" Several students raise their hands, and Mr. C. is pleasantly surprised to see that Alex is one of them, since Alex is usually insecure about his understanding. "Alex, what's your question?" Alex asks, "Why did you use eleven? Shouldn't it be six?" Alex's question isn't very clear, but Mr. C asks, "What do you think, Eric?" Eric looks at his work for a moment and then asks Alex, "Why six?" The two boys exchange ideas back and forth until Eric is convinced. Mr. C says, "Alex, that was a terrific question, but even better was that you were able to explain your reasons so that Eric could figure out that he agreed with you. And Eric, the fact that you organized your work so clearly I think made it possible for Alex to see where he disagreed. The mistake you made is a really common one. Did anyone else make the same mistake? I bet I'll catch some of you making that common mistake on today's quiz, so make sure you understand!"

This debrief has gone on much longer than Mr. C. anticipated, so he cuts off the discussion and moves to the front of the class. "That discussion was so good that I think we should stop there. I wish we had more time to talk about the last problem and the decisions you make to find slope based on the information given in different representations, but we have discussed in depth two of the problems and that will still be enough to get you warmed up for our quiz!"

"Okay, so our quiz is an explanation quiz, which means you will get to work with your team. In the warm-up, you found the grow-by, or the slope, starting from graphs and from a situation. In the quiz, you will start from coordinates. On the activity card I am passing out you will see three places where your group needs to call me over to check your ideas. Team Captains, it is your job to make sure everyone is ready to explain when your Resource Managers call me over. Team Captains, can you raise your hands? What is your job for today?

"Facilitators, please get your group started by having someone read the directions. Use the colored pencils to show where your numbers come from like Ana and Eric did. Ready? Okay, get started. Facilitators, I need to hear you asking, 'Who wants to read?'"

Mr. C. has passed out two copies of the activity card per team and again surveys the class to see how teams get started. This time every team seems to be on task, so he just watches from a corner of the room. Marisol frowns and raises her hand, but without leaving his corner Mr. C. says, "Marisol, are you the Resource Manager? Ask your team first, okay, and then have your Resource Manager call me if you still have doubts." She asks, and the team handles the question. Mr. C. watches and then goes over to say, "Nice work, Marisol! Your question was exactly what you guys needed to be discussing to help you be successful." He starts circulating around the room to get a sense of how teams are starting. As he glances at students' work, he makes quick suggestions: "Hey, remember to color-code. . . . Are you guys sticking together? How come you have different answers for number three?"

As Resource Managers begin to call him over, Mr. C tries to ensure quickly that teams are not only getting the right slopes but also understand why they need to subtract coordinates. He also asks how they know which dimension is the numerator and which is the denominator. The class has not learned "rise" and "run" yet, so many teams use the language of "dollars" and "weeks" from the warm-up to explain their thinking. When he is satisfied with a team's responses, Mr. C puts a big A+ in his trademark purple pen on students' papers, saying, "You all get A-plusses because you not only figured out a strategy for how to find the slope for these problems, but you also color-coded and everyone was able to explain your reasons clearly." Occasionally he says, "I can't quite give you an A-plus yet. Can you guys please talk about why your idea works, and call me back when everyone thinks they can explain? It's really important that everyone understands!"

Five minutes before the end of the period, Mr. C. interrupts the class to thank them for their hard work on today's quiz. He asks them to put their quizzes in their team folders while he passes out homework. When all this business is taken care of, Mr. C. wraps up by saying, "I was so impressed by how much you guys are figuring out about slope no matter what representation we start with. Best of all, you were able to give me solid reasons when I asked you to justify your thinking. We will debrief the math tomorrow so you can see what other teams figured out." There is just a moment left in class, and Mr. C. says, "Mariela, you're coming at lunch to work on your homework, yes? And Luis, let's both remember to smell better tomorrow, okay?" Luis groans and the bell rings.

□   □   □

The warmth, care, and attention to mathematical understanding present in the classroom described above give a glimpse into how teachers and students together created a culture of mathematical learning at Railside. The equity pedagogy that the Railside math department was constantly developing, and that was enacted in our work with students in ways ranging from casual interactions as students entered and left the classroom each day, to more formal student-teacher interactions about mathematics in exchanges at the overhead or with teams, to specific structures through which students engaged with math content such as an explanation quiz (as was described in the vignette). This chapter will highlight five particular aspects of our teaching practice at Railside and connect them to the core principles that shaped Railside mathematics teaching. Those aspects of practice are: (1) structuring lessons to support engagement in *groupworthy tasks*, (2) approaching math concepts through *multiple representations*, (3) organizing curriculum around *big ideas*, (4) using *justification* to push students to articulate their mathematical thinking, and (5) making students' thinking public and valued through *presentations at the overhead*. These features of teacher practice each played a specific role in creating classroom spaces where more equitable student outcomes could be realized.

GROUPWORTHY TASKS

The groupworthy problems used throughout each course at Railside allowed students to see one another as learners and build relationships with their peers as well as with the teacher. Students were often asked to tackle these big tasks from the very first day of a course. For example, "Analyzing Geometric Relationships" was a big groupworthy task used to launch Algebra II. (Figure 3.3 shows the activity card for this task.) This task was designed so that students were required to apply their understanding of math topics from previous classes and their knowledge of multiple representations to make sense of what to do, rather than beginning the course by reviewing content from prior courses. Those skills and ideas were extended in new and challenging directions to help set up the important mathematics in the course. The task design allowed students with different strengths to showcase their ideas and ask questions when needed. The task also provided opportunities for the teacher to recognize student accomplishments and to push students so that they would experience success on a challenging task.

The department identified tasks as "groupworthy" if they met several design criteria: (1) focusing on core mathematical ideas, (2) offering multiple solution paths or requiring multiple representations, and (3) being likely to require the

Figure 3.3. Analyzing Geometric Relationships

Algebra II
Analyzing Geometric Relationships

Team Captain:	Read the directions for your group. Make sure everyone understands what the problem is asking. Make sure everyone stays together, no talking out of group, and **every idea is heard**.
Facilitator:	Keep the conversation moving! Ask questions that push your group further: "How do you know . . . ? What else can we try? How do you see it? How else can you show . . . ?"
Recorder/ Reporter:	Have your group agree on your information before you write it down. Ask clarifying questions like, "What I hear you saying is . . . Does anyone need to hear that again? Did everyone hear that idea?" If you huddle with the teacher, bring back the information to your group.
Resource Manager:	Make sure that everyone's work is A+. Call me over with any group questions. Get all supplies your group needs from the supply table.

Your task is to **generate** data, **analyze** your data, and **explain** your group's findings to the class. As a team, start by choosing a geometric relationship from the task cards provided by your teacher. For the geometric relationship your team chooses, generate data and model it using as many representations as your group can imagine, then write summary statements that explain your observations and justifications. As a team you will explain your geometric relationship data and representations along with your summary statements in the form of a team poster and presentation.

While you are working, use the following questions to further your group's work:

- What patterns or trends can you find in your team's data? Why do they happen?
- What are all the possible inputs for your function? Are there some *x*-values that do not make sense? Why or why not? How do these results end up in each of the mathematical representations you create?
- How can you use a geometric representation to explain what is happening in each of the other representations?

Figure 3.3. Analyzing Geometric Relationships (continued)

(A) *The Sliding Meter Stick*	(B) *Right Triangle – Fixed Hypotenuse*
Lean a meter stick against the wall. Explore the function with inputs that are the measures of the angle formed by the meter stick and the floor and outputs that are the height of the point where the stick meets the wall.	Imagine a right triangle with a hypotenuse of 10 units. Explore the function with inputs that are the height of the triangle and outputs that are its area.
(C) *Right Triangle – Fixed Area*	(D) *String Rectangles*
Imagine a right triangle with an area of 10 square units. Explore the function with inputs that are the length of the base of the triangle and outputs that are its height.	Make a rectangle out of a 40 cm piece of string. Explore the function with inputs that are the measure of one side of the rectangle and outputs that are its area.
(E) *Paper Box*	(F) *Paper Folding*
Cut a sheet of paper so that its dimensions are 15 cm x 20 cm. Cut the same size square out of each corner, and fold the sides up to form a shallow box (with no lid). Explore the function with inputs that are the length of the side of one of the cut-out squares and outputs that are the volume of the box.	Cut a sheet of paper so its dimensions are 15 cm x 20 cm. Take a top corner and fold it down so that it exactly touches the bottom edge of the paper. This creates a small triangle (the shaded one in the diagram). Explore the function with inputs that are the height of the shaded triangle, and with outputs that are its base.
(G) *Meter-Stick Slopes*	(H) *Leaning Ruler*
Place a meter stick flat on a table. Hold down one end and let the other end pivot up (so that the meter stick rises off the table, with one end still touching the table). Explore the function with inputs that are the measure of the angle formed by the meter stick and the table and outputs that are the slope of the meter stick.	Lean a ruler against a stack of books on your desk. Explore the function with inputs that are the measures of the angles formed by the ruler and the desk and outputs that are the length of the hypotenuse of the resulting right triangle.

Presenting your Findings

An A+ Poster:

- Is **big** and **well-organized**. I should be able to see and read everything from the back of the room.
- Uses **color**, **arrows**, etc. to help **explain** your summary statements, reasons and connections.
- Represents the thinking and participation of EVERYONE in the group. **Everyone needs to contribute in important ways** to generate the data and write summary statements, and also to the making of the poster.
- Is a good visual aid for your team's summary statements—the things on the poster should *show* and *explain* your group's ideas.

- Is **signed** by every team member to show that everyone participated, everyone understands, and everyone agrees.

An A+ Presentation:

- Begins with the **Recorder/Reporter** introducing everyone in the group.
- Is clear and interesting, and moves at a good pace—everyone knows what to explain and when.
- Every group member has a **summary statement** to explain. Explanations include reasons and connections: "This is true because . . . ," "You can see this in the graph—look how the graphs . . ."
- Every group member can explain in her/his own words, without reading or getting confused. I will assign (through your team roles) who will be presenting what.
- Every group member can answer any follow-up questions from the audience.
- The group is respectful when others are presenting. This includes asking questions and praising other groups' presentations.

collective resources of the group (see Chapters 2, 8, and 9 for discussions of groupworthy problems). These criteria helped to ensure that tasks would be accessible to all and yet challenging enough to merit extensive discussion within the group. Because each of these tasks was connected to a key mathematical idea that was important for students to understand, students came to see that pushing for clear explanations and understanding was essential to their learning.

Placement of these problems in a course and in a unit was a critical decision. Over time, we found or created groupworthy tasks to launch each unit, to help develop conceptual understanding at various points within the unit, and to push students to synthesize their understanding near the end of the unit. At each stage, these activities afforded teachers the opportunity to showcase all the ways students were smart, and to reinforce that by talking with their team, students could tackle math problems they thought of as difficult. This helped create strong relationships for doing math among students and with the teacher.

Importantly, we realized that building strong relationships with students allowed us to give students challenging tasks and hold each student to high expectations. This was possible because while students knew the problems they worked on were difficult, the relationships that were established allowed students to trust their teachers to provide challenges that they could work through and that would lead to deeper understanding. Difficult problems helped students deepen understanding, make sense of new content, and have reasons to talk together about mathematics. To support students in learning how to work together to make sense of math, we talked together at length as teachers about how to explicitly teach students to be powerful group members, and how to value different ways to be mathematically smart.

MULTIPLE REPRESENTATIONS

We emphasized multiple representations to support students' conceptual understanding of central mathematical topics. Most commonly, "multiple representations" referred to tables, graphs, equations, and situations, which students first encountered at Railside as part of an Algebra I unit on linear equations $y = mx + b$. Figure 3.4 was known among teachers and students as the $y = mx + b$ web, a visual display of the connections among representations. As students moved through the Railside course sequence, the web was adjusted to fit the representations critical to making connections and understanding the mathematics important to the current course.

At the beginning of the slope lesson described in the opening vignette, Mr. C. had students brainstorm all the different things they knew about slope. It was at this point in the class that the idea of different representations of slope entered the conversation; students recognized the concept in tables, in graphs, in equations, and in situations or geometric representations, but they also knew to look for connections between the representation that was presented and other representations when answering questions. While the warm-up questions focused students on slope in situations and in graphs, the explanation quiz later in the period pushed them to connect this thinking to finding slope from coordinates. By asking students to approach a new idea through numbers, geometry, algebraic symbols, graphs, and real-world contexts, Railside teachers sought to push students to develop robust conceptual understanding of important ideas, and so to expand the definition of what it means to be smart in math.

Multiple representations were not used in a fixed sequence—teachers did not consistently introduce concepts starting with symbols, move through other representations, and end with applications or problems situated in contexts. Instead, in some units context was the vehicle for introducing a concept, as when Algebra I teachers introduced solving systems of equations by asking students to analyze when two individuals would have the same amount of money (see Figure 3.5).

Because representations were not sequenced in a consistent order, students came to understand each as a possible entry point to a problem and a useful way of building understanding of a concept. Making sense of ideas presented in a graph or geometric pattern was not positioned by teachers as more or less valuable than using equations, nor was applying math concepts in context viewed as dependent on first understanding how to manipulate symbols or to make sense exclusively from numbers. Different ways of seeing a solution were not assigned different degrees of status, and symbolic representations and strategies

Figure 3.4. Connections Among Representations

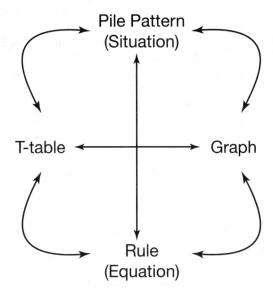

Pile Pattern
(Situation)

T-table ←——————→ Graph

Rule
(Equation)

Figure 3.5. Money in the Bank

> **Money in the Bank**
>
> Jose has $40 in the bank. He just got a job that lets him save $5 per week. Tiffany has $20 in the bank, and with her job she saves $7 per week. Aman is broke, but he just started a job that lets him save $9 per week.
>
> ***Who is the richest?***
>
> 1. Make t-tables for each student to show how much money they have. Decide as a group how many weeks you want to include in your t-table.
>
> 2. Find rules for each student. In your rules, what does the x represent? What does the y represent?
>
> 3. Who has the most money after 20 weeks? Show how you can figure this out.
>
> 4. Who is the richest? Show and explain using multiple representations.
>
> 5. For each of the questions below, explain your answers using your graph and your t-tables.
>
>   (a) When will Jose and Tiffany have the same amount?
>
>   (b) When will Aman and Jose have the same amount?
>
> 6. *Extra for Experts:* How can you answer the questions in #5 using the rules?

were valued but not privileged. Instead, students were asked to make sense of the connections and relationships among the different representations, which made space for multiple ways of thinking and reasoning around an important concept.

For example, early in an Algebra I unit on linear functions, we might ask students to predict the area of pile 10 in a pile pattern such as the one in Figure 3.6.

Some teams would answer this question geometrically (by visualizing what pile 10 would look like), others numerically (by making a t-table comparing pile number to area), and some algebraically (by writing a rule for the area of any pile number). After a student presented one way of explaining his or her answer, teachers might ask, "Did anyone see it a different way?," which suggested that what makes sense to one person is not necessarily what might make sense to another—that mathematical representations are tools to choose from to help solve problems, and that the choice of a different tool is yet another way to be smart at doing mathematics.

After students had experience with the different representations, we could push students to see connections among those representations. One example that illustrates this is an Algebra I activity called "$y = mx + b$ Challenges" that followed tasks with individual representations such as the one in Figure 3.6. In the "Challenges" activity, teams were presented for the first time with mixed representations or missing information (see Figure 3.7). Using the disjointed pieces provided, students needed to work together to generate the missing elements of the table, graph, equation, and geometric representation of the pattern, and be able to explain and justify their ideas. For example, students were given an incomplete graph and one related piece of a geometric pattern, as shown in Figure 3.7.[2]

Typically, it took teams substantial time and conversation to determine the remaining representations and to add missing information to the graph so that the graph and geometric pattern piece would connect. Having made these connections and justified them to the other members of their team, to the teacher, and on paper, students then moved to a very different problem—this time focused on missing information for a new pattern in a different representation (see Figure 3.8).

The mix of representations reinforced the importance of being able to move logically and flexibly among representations, and to recognize and use the connections between them. For students who comfortably understood one representation of a pattern and used that strength to represent all problems, the activity forced them to engage with the same concepts in different representations and pushed them to understand new strategies and connections.

Multiple representations further allowed teachers to broaden students' understanding of what it meant to do and learn math. Specifically, approaching ideas through multiple representations communicated the value teachers placed on multiple ways of being smart. Smartness was not evidenced in answers alone,

Figure 3.6. Predicting the Area in Linear Functions

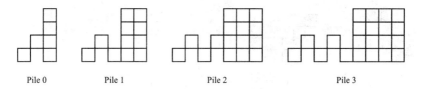

Pile 0   Pile 1   Pile 2   Pile 3

but also in understanding multiple ways of representing and justifying a conclusion. Seeing connections—for example, between parts of an area formula and different ways of decomposing a shape—became a goal that emphasized thinking, justifying, and problem-solving. Students came to understand that they were not done with a task once they had found an answer. They needed to be confident that they knew where the answer came from and why it made sense in their representation, and they also needed to be able to think about the problem using other representations. For example, students who were quick to understand procedures for solving equations were also pushed to justify by representing with Lab Gear[3]; these students recognized that they still had a task that challenged them to stretch their thinking. When studying slope, students who were able to see patterns visually and identify growth in pile patterns could extend that understanding to see how that growth could be represented with an equation, and to see strengths in others who could see the patterns numerically in tables even if those same students were still learning how to represent their understanding symbolically or connect it to the geometric growth.[4]

BIG IDEAS

Part of what facilitated a focus on multiple representations was organizing a curriculum around big, important ideas rather than a sequence of narrow, discrete skills. Railside teachers worked to make the big ideas for each unit transparent to students. In the example at the beginning of the chapter, Mr. C. framed for his students that their work was continuing to focus on the major concept of slope. He got students thinking by asking them to explain what they had learned about slope when he asked, "Marisol has been absent for a few days, so can someone explain to her what you know so far about slope? What does that word mean?" Students knew that this question had an answer based on multiple representations because slope had been treated as a big idea. Rather than define slope in terms of a formula or procedure (such as rise over run, or $\frac{(y_2-y_1)}{(x_2-x_1)}$), Railside Algebra teachers sought to define it more expansively. Slope was defined initially as a rate grounded in growth, which could be represented using geometry (how a pile

Figure 3.7. Solving a Problem with Missing Information

Problem 1:

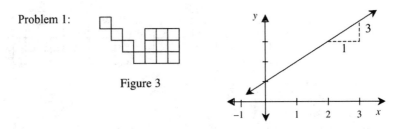

Figure 3

Figure 3.8. Solving Problems with Missing Information and a Different Representation

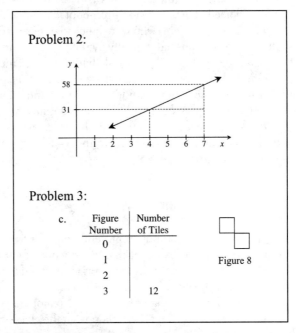

Problem 2:

Problem 3:

c.

Figure Number	Number of Tiles
0	
1	
2	
3	12

Figure 8

pattern is growing) or numbers (in a table) or graphically (using slope triangles) or in situations (such as money being saved over time).

Railside teachers operated with the belief that part of their job was to redefine for students what it meant to do math in school, in an effort to counter some of the negative feelings students often developed about mathematics based on their prior school experiences. Rather than presenting math as a series of discrete topics or procedural steps to be memorized, organizing content around big ideas helped Railside teachers to engage students. This approach opened up opportunities to make sense of topics in different ways and made the diversity of student thinking essential in the classroom. Organizing around big ideas was a first step in changing students' understanding of the discipline of math and created new opportunities for students to learn content they had missed earlier in their schooling. The teacher's job was to help students make connections between different ideas to build a robust and multidimensional understanding of an important concept.

JUSTIFICATION

To engage all students in seeing themselves as active mathematical thinkers, teachers had to broaden and deepen what it meant to be mathematically smart in their classrooms. A central strategy in this effort was to push for students' reasoning and justification. Railside teachers asked students to make their reasoning explicit using standard probing questions: "How did you get that?" "Why do you think that makes sense?" or "How did you decide how to get started?" Teachers implied that a math problem is not finished when a student arrives at an answer, but that instead the goal is being able to understand and communicate the thinking underlying that answer. When Alex asks Eric in the dialogue on page 38, "Why did you use eleven? Shouldn't it be six?," he is asking for reasons to account for a difference in thinking, rather than simply insisting that Eric's answer is wrong. Their subsequent exchange leads to Eric's being convinced to change his answer with minimal intervention from his teacher. This habit of explaining thinking and justifying answers allows students to engage in mathematical debate with a focus on sense-making rather than simply being correct.

School mathematics focused on memorizing and applying formulas and accurately following procedures leads to an unnecessarily narrow definition of what it means to be successful in the discipline. Speed, accuracy, memorization, computation, and the ability to handle abstractions become the hallmarks of smartness, to the exclusion of other strengths. Railside teachers valued those strengths, but also emphasized other abilities central to learning mathematics: explaining ideas, representing concepts, asking good questions that advanced learning, taking intellectual risks, generalizing, reversing processes, and finding connections. Those abilities also connected to the practice of doing mathematics beyond high school.

Insisting on students' justifying their thinking also opened up opportunities to delegate responsibility for learning to the class community, and to share responsibility for leadership with students. By creating the expectation that all

students would be able to explain their thinking and that each person had something genuine and worthwhile to contribute, each student was positioned as a
resource for others in the learning process. "How do you know?" was an authentic question from anyone in the room, one that leveled the playing field between
teacher and student because the teacher genuinely did not know the answer.
Teachers often heard students insist on hearing reasons from one another and
heard them object if another student just told answers. One Railside teacher tells
the story of a new student teacher venturing out to help a group in an Algebra II
class for the first time. After the student teacher left, the group called the regular
teacher over to complain: "We called him over for help, but all he did was give
us answers!" Students expected math to make sense, and demanded explanations
and justifications as a result.

Whether during an explanation quiz like the one on page 38 or during a regular groupwork activity, students were expected to look to one another as resources
for learning. We modeled asking for justification in whole-class discussions and in
teacher interactions with teams to demonstrate the kinds of conversations students
were expected to have with their teammates. When teachers modeled asking,
"How did you get that?," they were trying to communicate multiple things: that
all knowledge and explanation do not need to flow from the teacher, that students
should see one another as resources in the learning process, and that everyone
(teacher included) was engaged in learning.

STUDENT PRESENTATIONS AT THE OVERHEAD

Although groupwork was the primary mode of instruction at Railside, lecturing and direct instruction also had a crucial role—but with distinct differences.
Rather than lectures *setting up* a lesson by front-loading definitions, concepts, or
procedures, our version of direct instruction usually came *after* a lesson, with the
goal of summarizing and consolidating learning. Also, as described in Mr. C.'s
classroom, consolidating class discussions often took place with a student presenting ideas at the overhead. The teacher relinquished both the stage and the voice
of mathematical authority, starting from students' thinking to communicate the
important ideas. Rather than giving notes or leading discussions, teachers usually
participated from the back of the room as audience members and facilitators,
asking questions as necessary to elicit reasoning.

Starting from student presentations provided natural opportunities to push
for higher-order thinking: understanding *why* each method works, and how one
method *connects* to a different one, how each method might be used *in reverse*.
Students heard these ways of being smart in the language of their peers; using
multiple representations became more meaningful because it was applied to
methods students have chosen and shared themselves. Students got attached to

their methods, and so the fact that others chose different strategies was surprising and made students want to know more.

Students were often asked to go up to the overhead when they did not know how to solve a problem. This took time and required vigilance to protect the student taking the risk of going up, but also vividly communicated essential norms to the entire class: that teachers and students are all here to learn, and everyone can learn; that peers will support one another's learning; that risk-taking contributes to learning and it is okay not to understand (yet); that it is okay to be wrong, confused, or stuck; and that seeking reasons and asking questions can help get learners unstuck. These moments of individual learning became a vehicle for deepening understanding in the class. Student responses in these moments served as an informal assessment of student understanding and often sparked questions in other students that led to deeper consideration of the problem.

Another reason why Railside teachers organized their classrooms so that students would articulate important mathematical ideas is that in the same way that students tend to present ideas using language that speaks to their peers, they also present ideas as snapshots of their current thinking rather than as complete little parcels of learning. When teachers lecture, they often try to explain ideas completely and concisely. Students often do not have such fully formed notions yet, and so they present more of their thinking process, their understanding so far, and often their confusions. The gaps in their presentations give the rest of the class space to think along and ask questions, and they give teachers the opportunity to catch students being smart. This is especially important when a solution process is intricate and requires multistep logic.

For example, Algebra I students were asked to find areas of complex irregular shapes similar to the one shown in Figure 3.9. In addition to helping solidify the meaning of area and when it can (and cannot) be found using certain formulas, complex shapes allow for multiple solution strategies and false starts. Some students might begin by dividing the shape into smaller pieces, others might surround the shape with a large rectangle intending to subtract the extra pieces, or students might try a combination of these ideas. While it is common to ask students to work on such problems after the teacher models some examples, at Railside, teachers would typically not model at all. Instead, the task would be framed as one in which team members would need to discuss strategies among themselves, and then later present and justify their approaches to the class. The expectation was that students would ask presenters questions such as, "Why did you add that line? How did you know you had to split the shape up like that? Why did you divide by two for that piece but not the last one?" If students did not probe for reasons and logic in these ways, the teacher stepped out of the facilitator role to model it. Each person in the room shared responsibility for asking questions and offering ideas so that reasons and logical explanations were shared and examined in presentations.

Figure 3.9. Finding the Area of Complex or Irregular Shapes

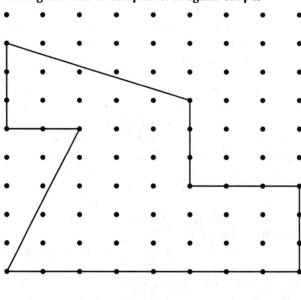

CONCLUSION

The efforts to engage all students in mathematics at Railside had their foundation in the five practices described above: (1) using groupworthy tasks, (2) working with multiple representations of concepts and seeing how those representations are connected, (3) identifying big ideas around which to organize a unit, (4) pushing students to articulate their thinking by justifying their work, and (5) making student thinking central in the classroom through student presentations at the overhead. These aspects were intertwined, and in striving to develop equitable practices, the department consciously worked toward a pedagogy that would engage and support each student's mathematical thinking. Through these practices, teachers created space to push for deep conceptual understanding and served to change students' conception of the discipline of mathematics. They also established and reinforced norms that allowed all students to learn. Teachers' continual work to develop these practices, to build strong teacher-student and student-student relationships, to honor student thinking and contribution, and to push for deeper, more connected understanding were foundational to the equity pedagogy at Railside, and supported students in developing both deep understandings of mathematics and a strong sense of themselves as learners of mathematics.

Promoting Student Collaboration in a Detracked, Heterogeneous Secondary Mathematics Classroom

Megan E. Staples

I conducted this study in the first year of several that I had the opportunity to spend at Railside.[1] I was still learning the ropes, understanding how the teachers organized their classroom learning environments, and learning the culture of the department and school. I was most interested in better understanding *student collaboration.* What was it that teachers did to support students working through problems together, engaging one another, and discussing ideas? These activities are rather rare in math classrooms in the United States and yet were common at Railside. Moreover, this collaboration was realized in heterogeneous classrooms, a feature many teachers find burdensome, but that was seen, and used, as a resource at Railside. My goal was to understand how these teachers, and in this case, specifically Ms. McClure, made their lessons fly.

In this chapter, I offer an analysis of Ms. McClure's geometry classroom, focusing on how she promoted collaboration among students working in heterogeneous groups. The analysis identifies four categories of the teacher's work that supported group collaborative practices. In doing so, I link the teacher's work with principles of complex systems.

It must be recognized that student practices, including collaboration, are *emergent* with respect to the classroom system and teacher's pedagogical strategies. Teachers cannot prescribe collaborative interaction, but can organize the classroom system to promote and occasion opportunities for collaboration. Ms. McClure, the teacher of this geometry class, did this extremely successfully. To help make sense of the teacher's role and the productive learning interactions in this classroom, I draw on principles of complexity science, as this framework became useful in helping me understand how Ms. McClure "designed" the class to support productive collaboration among her groups.

GROUPWORK AND COHEN'S DILEMMA

As teachers work in detracked settings, they face significant challenges in organizing effective instruction. The potential benefits of detracking are well documented (e.g., Boaler, 2002a; Boaler & Staples, 2008; Burris, Heubert, & Levin, 2006), but detracking by itself is unlikely to alleviate the negative outcomes associated with tracking, as students of different initial achievement levels can be offered different learning opportunities *within the same classroom.*

One instructional strategy that is promising for supporting student participation and learning in heterogeneous classes is groupwork (Cohen, 1994a; Lou et al., 1996; Webb, 1991). The research literature identified two principles that govern the design of effective groupwork in both heterogeneous and homogenous settings (Cohen, 1994a): *interdependence* (goal and resource) and *accountability* (group and individual). *Goal interdependence* occurs when each group member can achieve his or her goal only when other group members also achieve their goal, for example, creating a group product whose production requires input from all students. *Resource interdependence* occurs when group members need information or resources from other group members (e.g., a jigsaw situation) to complete their task. *Individual accountability* requires that some product or documentable aspect of the process or outcome can be attributed to an individual, and the individual can be held accountable for it. *Group accountability* requires holding the group as a whole accountable for some process or outcome. Both of these principles promote student-student task-related interaction.

When teachers aim to promote higher-level reasoning skills among their students (e.g., by engaging them in open-ended tasks), some particular challenges arise with respect to organizing effective groupwork. Collaboration requires students to consider others' thinking, adapt their initial approach, represent their thinking, articulate arguments, and so on. None of these practices is routine, and consequently, their work together cannot be overly structured. Students needed latitude in their interactions to engage in the generative exchanges required to solve these problems. For such learning goals, "task arrangements and instructions that constrain and routinize interaction will be less productive than arrangements and instructions that foster maximum interaction, mutual exchange, and elaborated discussions" (Cohen, 1994a, p. 20). This led Cohen to highlight a core challenge in organizing productive groupwork when engaging students in complex tasks:

> Herein lies the dilemma: If teachers do nothing to structure the level of interaction [among group members], they may well find that students stick to a most concrete

mode of interaction. If they do too much to structure the interaction, they may prevent the students from thinking for themselves and thus gaining the benefits of the interaction. (p. 22)

Cohen further explains that supporting collaborative talk requires the delegation of authority. The teacher cannot directly monitor the groups' ongoing work, as this impedes the very talk that is productive. Yet, promoting higher-order thinking and the engagement of all students, particularly those perceived to have lower status academically, requires teacher intervention and direction. The teacher must judiciously use his or her position to enable productive conversations and find a delicate balance between creating structure and opening space for students to collaborate. At first glance, offering structure and affording autonomy may seem contradictory ends, but they need not be, as structure also creates affordances for student interactions, sometimes by restricting options (Greeno & MMAP, 1997).

This analysis of a detracked geometry class at Railside High School addresses Cohen's (1994a) "dilemma" by demonstrating how one teacher fostered collaborative interactions among students as they worked in heterogeneous groups on open-ended problem-solving activities. The dilemma Cohen defines precludes simple analysis of cause-and-effect relationships. It requires careful attention to the interconnectedness among various components within the system and an understanding that student collaboration is an emergent practice embedded within a complex system. For these reasons, it was necessary to use a framework that could conceptualize student interactions within groups as an emergent product of the classroom system. *Complexity science* provided the requisite framework for this task.

USING COMPLEX SYSTEMS TO UNDERSTAND MATHEMATICS CLASSROOMS

Complexity science refers to a family of perspectives that are often based on ecological approaches to learning. They take as the unit of analysis not an individual organism or member, but the collective or system as a whole. A main tenet of these perspectives is that the patterns and practices that result from the interaction among individuals within the system must be understood as emergent. "In effect, a complex system is not just the sum of its parts, but the product of the parts and their interactions" (Davis & Simmt, 2003, p. 138).

The idea of emergence, or emergent behaviors, is a defining feature that sets complex systems apart from simple systems (Barab et al., 1999). In simple systems, certain inputs cause/predict certain outputs. In complex systems, there is constant dynamic change whereby the system adapts and learns. From the constraints or "rules" of the system, noticeable regularities emerge, yet there is always opportunity for innovation. In a classroom, a group's practices are emergent and the innovations produce new ways of interacting and novel approaches to problems. A group's behaviors and solution path are not predictable and cannot be prescribed, but they are bounded, and they emerge in relation to the environment.

Davis and Simmt (2003) identified five overlapping principles of complex systems: *internal diversity, redundancy, decentralized control, organized randomness,* and *neighbor interactions.* These principles are "necessary but insufficient conditions [that] must be met in order for systems to arise and maintain their fitness within dynamic contexts—that is, to learn" (p. 147). I describe each principle, explaining how they are useful in illuminating important aspects of mathematics classrooms. Emphasis is placed on the last three principles, as they do not exist simply by having a heterogeneous group (as is the case with internal diversity and redundancy) and consequently require very deliberate attention by the teacher as he or she plans for and structures the group's work together.

- *Internal diversity.* Internal diversity references the variety of different ways members can contribute. Diversity is a resource for the generation of new practices and solutions. It supports learning and adaptation.
- *Redundancy.* Redundancy enables communication, as group members mutually recognize various cues and meanings of symbols, words, and gestures. It provides a level of coherence and a common basis to support communication. A redundant system also does not uniquely rely on one component to fulfill a role. Having multiple ways to fulfill the same function makes the system resilient and adaptable.
- *Decentralized control.* Control, or authority, in a mathematics classroom can be exercised with respect to mathematical ideas or with respect to the particulars of the interaction. In many classrooms, the teacher maintains a high degree of authority, particularly with respect to identifying preferred methods and determining correctness. In some classrooms, the teacher also maintains control over the kinds of opportunities individuals have to interact. Decentralized control—or distributed authority—offers students and/or groups the authority to devise approaches and mathematical strategies and to regulate their behaviors (within the constraints of the broader system). It invites a broader range of participation. This principle must be balanced by other principles so that the emergent interactions are generative rather than unproductive.
- *Organized randomness.* Balancing and helping to capitalize on decentralized control and internal diversity is the principle of organized randomness. "The structures that define complex systems [must] . . . maintain a delicate balance between sufficient organization to orient

agents' actions and sufficient randomness to allow for flexible and varied response" (Davis & Simmt, 2003, p. 155). Thus, particularly when students are working on open-ended or nonroutine problems, some level of structure is needed to promote student task-related interaction. Structure orients participants within the system so that their individual efforts or ideas can be brought together productively toward some goal or ends. What emerges is patterned or organized.

- *Neighbor interactions.* Neighbor interactions are needed to capitalize on internal diversity. This principle refers to the possibilities of ideas "colliding" with one another, which supports the spreading and exchange of ideas for the purposes of innovation. In a classroom, for ideas to collide, students need to share ideas and listen to and evaluate the validity of others' ideas. Neighbor interactions can also refer to exchanges between groups and not just within groups.

These principles of complexity science described by Davis and Simmt (2003) offer a way to think about Cohen's (1994a) dilemma, which calls for a balance of structure and autonomy in governing student-student interactions with respect to mathematical ideas. Too much structure, and the group will be overly constrained and not have the autonomy to engage in collaborative, generative interactions. Too little structure, and students' individual contributions and efforts may be too random or diffuse to develop a flow or focus. Davis and Simmt describe the need for "a shift in thinking about the sorts of constraints that are necessary for generative activity" (p. 155). It is understanding the constraints "necessary for generative activity" that is pursued in this analysis. Given that the teacher cannot prescribe collaborative interactions, I examine ways the teacher promotes the emergence of such interactions within groups.

UNDERSTANDING HOW COMPLEX INSTRUCTION WAS USED

The teacher, Linda McClure (all names are pseudonyms), was a White female with 3 years of teaching experience at Railside School. Like the other teachers in her department, she grounded her pedagogical approach in Cohen's program of *Complex Instruction* (Cohen, 1994b; Cohen & Lotan, 1997). *Complex Instruction* is a form of groupwork originally designed to address the unequal status of different students in classrooms. Cohen's research consistently has found that for conceptually oriented, high-order tasks, unequal participation among students is linked to variation in learning gains. Unequal participation stems from status differences.

The geometry curriculum was created by Ms. McClure and her colleagues specifically to support groupwork in their heterogeneous classrooms. Evident in the curricular materials was an emphasis on nonroutine problems and developing mathematical understandings via problem solving (Schroeder & Lester, 1989). Curricular tasks were "groupworthy" (see Horn, 2005; Lotan, 2003; as well as Chapters 2 and 8 of this volume)—they focused on core mathematical ideas, were characterized by multiple representations and solution paths, and were likely to draw on the collective resources of a group.

The focal geometry class comprised approximately 31 10th- to 12th-grade students. During class time, students were arranged in heterogeneous groups that rotated approximately every 2 weeks. Classes met daily for one and a half hours for one semester. The analysis presented here is based on observations of 39 lessons during the semester (approximately 58 hours), 26 of which were videotaped. The data corpus also included student and teacher interviews, as well as curricular materials from videotaped lessons.

Four Processes That Supported Group Work

This analysis focuses on how the teacher fostered collaborative interactions within groups. The groups' ways of interacting can be seen as emergent against the backdrop of the constraints and affordances of the system organized by Ms. McClure. Four categories emerged as critical for understanding the teacher's role:

1. Promoting individual and group accountability
2. Promoting positive sentiment among group members
3. Supporting student-student exchanges with tools and resources
4. Supporting student-student mathematical inquiry in direct interaction with groups

These categories are referenced as: (1) the accountability system, (2) positive sentiment, (3) tools and resources, and (4) direct teacher-group interaction. For each category, I describe the relevant aspects of the teacher's work and how these aspects supported a system that prominently shaped the students' interactions during groupwork, especially when the teacher was not working directly with the group. The principles of decentralized control, organized randomness, and neighbor interactions will be apparent in the analysis. I return to these principles explicitly in the discussion at the end of the chapter to understand Ms. McClure's role in supporting a system with these conditions.

The Accountability System

In Ms. McClure's classroom, the accountability system promoted individual and group accountability among students with respect to (a) learning mathematics and (b) enacting good groupwork. Various aspects of this account-ability system promoted group interdependence, a critical feature for productive groupwork (Cohen, 1994a). I discuss both the informal (formative) and formal (summative) assessment systems. (Several of the practices described here were used by other teachers in the mathematics department. See Boaler [2006a, 2008] and Boaler and Staples [2008] for additional discussion of how Railside math-ematics teachers promoted student responsibility and relational equity.)

Accountability System—Enacting Good Groupwork. In all documented lessons in her classroom Ms. McClure used verbal feedback as a mechanism to promote group accountability for enacting good groupwork. She highlighted practices she wanted to see and provided information regarding the degree to which she saw these practices. This feedback was prominent as groups started a new task. Typical comments she made included the following:

"I like how Group 5 is putting the picture in the middle of the table to do the problem. That way everyone can see the pictures."

"Group 8 is reviewing already. Thank you, Group 8."

Ms. McClure believed that if she made clear to the students what doing good groupwork was, they would enact those practices. "If I make explicit what is doing well, they'll act it out." Her verbal commentary made salient productive practices. Her naming amplified them and sanctioned them as appropriate. Simi-larly, at the end of class, Ms. McClure debriefed by recapping the mathematics and commenting on the class's participation that day:

I loved the work I'm seeing. Many of you are really thinking hard about how to approach the problem and coming up with great ideas. I'm a little concerned, however, that not everyone in the group is together always. Sometimes a group member is being left behind. Groups, be sure everyone understands what's going on. And everyone, be sure you ask questions!

You guys are doing fabulous math work in here. . . . But sometimes a few groups are starting to visit a little too much. . . . If you don't stay focused, you will fall behind and get frustrated. You have to govern yourselves.

These comments focused on group processes and the kinds of participation for which groups were responsible. Ms. McClure indicated that she expected groups to monitor and regulate their interactions. In addition, the group collectively was responsible for each member's understanding, and each individual was respon-sible for asking questions.

Participation quizzes further promoted productive group processes and interdependence among group members. To conduct a participation quiz, Ms. McClure put up a blank overhead and listened to the groups as they worked together. She wrote partial quotes or comments that she heard, indicating the group number, to capture group processes. If Ms. McClure evaluated what she observed positively, she wrote the comment up in one color; if it was evaluated negatively and not seen as productive for groupwork, she wrote it up in another color. At the end of the class, she assigned each group a score based on her recorded observations.

Accountability System—Learning Mathematics. The accountability systems also promoted interdependence among group members with respect to their mathematics learning. Ms. McClure administered both group tests and individual tests. A group test was given first, and students worked collaboratively to solve the problems. The students each had their own paper. Ms. McClure collected all four papers and randomly graded one of them. The mark for this paper was the grade for every group member. A few days later, students took an individual test on the same material. It was expected that, in part, the group test would serve as an opportunity to review or solidify each student's understanding of the mathematics.

This assessment system promoted mutual accountability and interdependence among group members, as an individual's work on the group test was consequential for the group as a whole. Furthermore, given the upcoming individual test, individuals were likely to use this as an opportunity to ensure that they understood the mathematics. Importantly, the length of the test permitted time for discussions. Note that the combination of the group and the individual test, graded in the particular manner described, with the appropriate time allotted, created a system that encouraged collaborative interactions around the mathematics and supported the participation of all students.

Another form of assessment was a *content-focused* explanation quiz. As she launched the task, Ms. McClure announced that she would quiz groups on particular problem(s). When the group had completed an indicated problem and felt ready for the quiz, they called over Ms. McClure. Sometimes Ms. McClure chose the member to be quizzed randomly (through shuffling papers); sometimes the speaker was her deliberate choice. The group received points based on this student's response. The student had to explain how the group solved the problem and answer Ms. McClure's follow-up questions. If the student could not satisfactorily respond, Ms. McClure told the group to talk about the problem a little more and then she would return to quiz them again. Sometimes Ms. McClure returned multiple times.

This quizzing practice encouraged student collaboration. Prior to the quiz, groups worked to ensure that all members understood. If a group was unsuccessful on the quiz, Ms. McClure left a group to think about a problem further and then returned to quiz them again. The response of the group was to talk about the mathematics or work with the student(s) who needed more support to fully comprehend or articulate their solution. Of central importance was the nature of Ms. McClure's questions. These were higher-level questions that required justification or clear articulation of a concept and related ideas. Many of her questions pushed for justification, asking students, "How do you know?," or asking them why it was appropriate for them to use a particular procedure.

In a classroom system where students are arranged for groupwork but the assessment system is an individual one, a student need only have the goal of promoting his or her own understanding. There is minimal incentive for group members to respond to a request for an explanation, initiate an explanation to another even when not requested, or demonstrate a lack of understanding by asking a question. In this classroom, the multiple components of the accountability system created structure for the group's interactions. Ms. McClure did not exercise direct control over the groups, but managed a system that promoted or made likely certain kinds of student-student task-related interactions.

This is not to say that students were always engaged in task-related behaviors. There were times when Ms. McClure needed to reduce a group's classwork points or request that one or more students stay after school to discuss their participation with her. Students also did not reach the same level of understanding on each problem. Ms. McClure had to make judgments about how far to push an individual student during a content quiz and what to accept as a sufficient explanation. She held high standards for all students while maintaining a sensitivity to each as a learner. Progress was prioritized and praised as much as the absolute quality or sophistication of the ideas, as Ms. McClure knew that her relationships with students and their confidence working mathematically were critical to their continued effort and engagement, and consequently their learning.

Positive Sentiment

A risk of extensive interdependence is that it can produce intragroup tensions, especially if it is perceived that one member is causing the group to not succeed, or if a member feels that another member's suboptimal performance is affecting his or her grade. If negative sentiments arise through interaction (perhaps because the group is unsuccessful), then the group will be averse to future interactions. Conversely, if group members have positive experiences working together, they will subsequently seek out similar interactions with that group.

Promoting success. Ms. McClure supported opportunities to develop positive sentiment among group members in a variety of ways. First, although not a focus of this chapter, Ms. McClure was quite skillful in selecting and/or designing tasks that were appropriately challenging for students, but that they could complete on some level with reasonable effort. Thus, students had the opportunity to experience success, but this success was the product of effort (see also Horn, 2005). In addition, these tasks could not readily be completed by one student and so drew on the resources of many group members. Consequently, members of a group likely saw their accomplishments as a result of interaction with their group.

Ms. McClure also gave the groups control in deciding when they were ready to demonstrate their understanding on a group quiz. Consequently, there was a high chance that the group would be judged positively. A group presumably would not call Ms. McClure for a quiz until they were ready. She made this practice clear the 2nd day of school. She explained that she might ask if they were ready for a quiz:

> But you guys have the option to tell me, "Wait, Ms. McClure, come back in three minutes. We need to review a little more." And I'll honor that without taking off points. So it's all in your hands.

In addition, Ms. McClure deducted only 1 point out of 10 if the chosen student could not answer the first time and she had to return to quiz the group again. Consequently, a suboptimal initial performance had minimal negative impact on their grade and they still had the opportunity to demonstrate understanding and be successful. Note that Ms. McClure did not support success on quizzes by having low standards. She asked questions that probed students' understanding.

The following excerpt provides a brief example of how Ms. McClure promoted success (positive sentiment) of the group and the influence of the group's accountability for all members' understanding. The problem was from a warm-up activity where two different (fictitious) people had created formulas for the area of a particular parallelogram (see Figure 4.1).

The students had to decide which formula was correct and explain how they knew. After the students worked for a few minutes, Ms. McClure began to interact with groups.

> LM (*approaching Group 8*): So, do you guys get it?
> B: Ye-up.
> LM: Tell me about it, ma'am. *Specifically addresses Tanesha, indicating that she should be the speaker for the group.*
> T: Okay. You take that and put it over there, it'd be a square, and if you put it, in half, but half. . . . *She starts laughing.*
> LM: You want me to come back real quick?
> T: Yeah. (*Laughing.*)
> LM: I want everyone to have it. *Says as she pats T on the shoulder and starts to move away from group.* She's got the right idea. Talk it over with her one more time.

T: I understand, I understand. It's just that I forgot.

LM: But you forgot. Okay. Talk with her about it real quick and I'll come back. *LM departs. Turns over her shoulder and says to the group,* 'Cause you guys are sayin' something cool.

When it seemed that at least one member of the group (Tanesha, a lower-attaining student) did not fully understand the problem yet, Ms. McClure restated that she wanted everyone "to have it." Ms. McClure left the group, explaining that she would come back. She did not identify the initial response as incompetent or wrong, but rather as a work in progress. With more group interaction, Ms. McClure expected, everyone would understand. The idea that not understanding was a transitory state was also conveyed with comments such as "not that it's wrong, it's just incomplete." Such comments prompted groups to continue and build on the work they had already done. When Ms. McClure returned later, the

Figure 4.1. Warm-up Problem and Overhead Instructions

Please take out your materials:

Organize binder. Graph paper. Pencil. Calculator.

Materials manager: Scratch Paper

Discuss the following. Use the scratch paper in the middle for discussion notes.

Show the final work on your own paper.

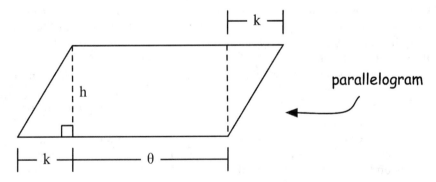

Elizabeth found the area by using $\frac{1}{2}kh + h\theta + \frac{1}{2}kh$

Marisol used $h(k+\theta)$

Who did it correctly?

If they are the same, show how you know.

students generally gave an improved response. Her stance toward their work and her assessment practices supported group success and the development of positive sentiment.

Product differentiation. Another critical feature in promoting positive sentiment was that tasks were deliberately designed and implemented to allow for product differentiation, whereby a range of mathematical solutions could be produced and deemed high-quality work. Particularly given the class's heterogeneity, there was often a variety of solution strategies evincing various levels of sophistication. In general, there was not an identified "end point" that each group had to "get." Ms. McClure valued each group's work and positioned each solution as evidence of competence and productive mathematical work.

In the above lesson, after the groups had worked on the problem, Ms. McClure selected three groups to present their solutions at the overhead. Each approach demonstrated a different level of sophistication with respect to proof. The first group showed a "plug-in" method, using two sets of numeric values that produced the same areas for each formula. The second group demonstrated how each formula described the parallelogram's area by mapping components of the formula to the figure. The third group algebraically demonstrated that the two formulas were equivalent (which showed that either both were correct or incorrect). Each approach was valued as productive mathematical work. Ms. McClure also engaged the students in a discussion of what each method did and did not demonstrate, and she discussed with them a bit more about what comprised a proof.

Ms. McClure's approach avoided direct comparison among groups, where one group might feel they "get it" and another feels inadequate. At the same time, Ms. McClure upheld disciplinary standards for what counted as high-quality work and what was a more or less sophisticated response. For example, with the group that used the "plug-in" strategy for the parallelogram problem, Ms. McClure accepted their response as reasonable and productive, but then pushed them to think about the limitations of the approach.

Ms. McClure's approach likely played an important role in promoting positive sentiment, as each group could experience success. Furthermore, requiring more homogeneity with group products or guiding students towards one end point would affect the nature of the student-student interaction within the groups. It could constrain their talk (and thinking), place unwarranted value on one particular method over others, and make students less inclined to see themselves as producers of mathematical ideas. In addition, guiding students to a particular solution can undermine the development of positive sentiment, as students might not see their solution as a product of their group's thinking.

Enthusiasm for Student Thinking. A final way Ms. McClure promoted positive sentiment was by expressing genuine enthusiasm for the ideas that a group generated. In the excerpts above, she talks about students' ideas as "cool" and notes that "plugging in is a great idea." In general, she expressed interest in their formulations and positively reinforced strong efforts and good thinking even when the problem did not fully yield to the group. The group's effort and mathematical thinking were valued highly. Along this dimension, all groups had the opportunity to be successful.

Group members' positive sentiment toward one another has an indirect, but potentially very significant, impact on the nature and quality of group interactions. Such sentiments prompt interactions that are above and beyond the "letter of the law" in the classroom. Group members are more likely to extend an important conversation or persist on a challenging problem after having found past success (Forsyth, 1999). From a complex system perspective, where the system always adapts and evolves, these developing relationships can be understood as feedback loops. Some feedback loops have a dampening effect, whereas positive feedback loops can have an amplifying effect, enhancing subsequent activities in a particular direction.

Tools and Resources

Tools are practices or objects (physical or conceptual) that a group can use to accomplish its work together (Wenger, 1998). The particular tools available, including those tools whose use is required, create a set of constraints and affordances that shape a group's interactions. They are resources that can be used to support a group's work. I focus on two tools and resources that figured prominently into a group's work together, the physical space and group roles, which were other means by which Ms. McClure promoted student collaboration.

Structuring the Physical Environment. Ms. McClure structured the physical environment to make it conducive to groupwork. The classroom desks were arranged in groups of four or five. When introducing a new activity, Ms. McClure asked groups to clear their "table" of all backpacks, books, and so forth, for example, "I want you to have lots of space because you will have to talk in the middle." This practice set up a common work area accessible to all group members.

This phrase "in the middle" was used repeatedly by Ms. McClure. It focused students on the physical space in the middle of their desks where they should work together on the mathematics. After handing out the problem, Ms. McClure would often go around and put scrap paper in the middle. This act helped to orient students, moving them away from the mindset of an individual working at her own desk to the group working on the problem in the middle, where their ideas could be represented and shared. Ms. McClure also reinforced this idea during lessons. In this excerpt from the same lesson, one student, Paj, has just offered an incomplete explanation.

LM: But why do they both work? Danesha, did he convince you that they both work?

P: They're the same thing, just put in different words.

LM: Could you show your group members that they are the same thing, but put into different words?

P: (inaudible)

LM: Oh, puh-lease. Maybe you have to try defining better. You know, that's why you have this big piece of paper in the middle, so you can talk about it. And when you can convince them, I want to hear it. (*She leaves the group.*)

In addition to demonstrating Ms. McClure's emphasis of the space in the middle, this excerpt shows how Ms. McClure maintained the interdependent task goal that all students understood.

Another way Ms. McClure created common physical focal points within the workspace was by handing out only two assignment sheets per group. This made it more difficult for students to work on their own. Ms. McClure's organization of their physical environment made certain behaviors and interactions more likely. It limited the students' ability to work individually and made readily available a collective workspace.

Student Roles. Assigning student roles is a standard strategy for supporting the work of a cooperative group (Cohen, 1994b). The roles used in Ms. Mc-Clure's classroom were adapted from Complex Instruction (Cohen & Lotan, 1997): team captain, materials manager, reporter/recorder, and facilitator. These social roles had ramifications on the nature of the group's interactions. Depending on the exact task, Ms. McClure varied the specific responsibilities for the role. In general, the team captain kept the group on task; the materials manager retrieved and returned necessary supplies and raised his or her hand to ask group questions, the reporter/recorder kept track of the group's ideas, and the facilitator made sure all voices were heard and checked for understanding.

In this excerpt, Ms. McClure restated the roles and indicated specifically how those roles would play out as they discussed the homework problems due that class period.

And of course you're going to use your roles. Team captain, you're going to be sure that there's no direct copying. If I see direct copying, those papers go away. Zero points. Facilitator, you're going to make sure that all the answers are compared. That could be reading out loud, that could be papers in the middle. . . . Materials manager, you have the most important job. Your job is to make sure that all discussions happen in the middle of the table if there's a question. So suppose that in this group, (inaudible) got one answer and Michael got something totally different, it's the materials manager's responsibility to make sure that gets discussed and that everyone agrees in the end. And lastly, recorder/reporter, you're going to keep track of time. So if I say 2 minutes, you're going to make sure your group is ready in 2 minutes. And you're also going to tell me the questions your group absolutely has to see on the board. Once again, you don't have a question unless the whole group is stuck.

These roles, as implemented, shaped how each group carried out its collective work together. From my analyses, the role (and role procedures) most significant to the group's interactions with respect to mathematical collaboration was materials manager. The materials manager was responsible for raising his or her hand to ask any "group questions"—a question of which everyone in the group is aware and that no one can answer. Ms. McClure regularly noted that she would entertain only group questions. When Ms. McClure responded to the materials manager's raised hand, she often asked the group, "Is it a group question?," or she asked someone other than the materials manager what the question was. If the person she asked could not state the question, or if the group indicated that they did not know if it was a group question, she departed, commenting that they could call her back when they had a group question.

This technique was effective in helping to structure student-student interaction and group collaboration because it made necessary exchanges around a specific issue prior to asking Ms. McClure. For example, during one lesson a group of students was working on a warm-up problem. Three of the group members were working well together, and two boys seemed to be a little more on the fringes. As the materials manager raised her hand, another group member asked the two boys if they had heard the question, which would be necessary to have Ms. McClure talk with them about it. They responded no. The question was repeated for them. Hearing the question, one of the boys answered it, and the group continued on with its work. This interaction emerged within the context of the system that Ms. McClure had established. Apparent in this example are the elements of organized randomness (orienting) and neighbor interactions in support of student collaboration.

Direct Teacher-Group Interaction

This analysis has focused on how student-student interactions within their groups were influenced by the characteristics of the systems Ms. McClure established, particularly when Ms. McClure was not directly working with the group. For example, although Ms. McClure reinforced the idea of working in the middle when she directly interacted with groups (as in the example with Paj above), equally important was the influence of this move in shaping the group's interactions when she was not present and directly monitoring their activities. As part of this fourth category, *direct teacher-group interaction*, I describe how particular choices Ms. McClure made when directly interacting with groups around mathematical ideas kept authority and responsibility for thinking with the students and encouraged productive student-student interactions both during the interaction and when Ms. McClure was subsequently not present.

One noticeable feature of Ms. McClure's interactions with groups was her choice of when to leave a group. Ms. McClure generally first listened to understand what the group was thinking. Next, as appropriate, she helped them gain more clarity on their point of confusion or focused their attention on an aspect of their logic that was incomplete. Then she would leave them to continue their work as a group.

For example, in one lesson, students were working to prove (or disprove) the following statement: The quadrilateral created by bisecting the angles of a parallelogram is always a rectangle. One group correctly explained to Ms. McClure that a set of four congruent angles was created by bisecting opposite angles of the parallelogram, but they made some assumptions in claiming that opposite sides of the new quadrilateral were then parallel. They had referenced alternate interior angles as part of their explanation. Ms. McClure responded to their explanation.

> LM: You've proven that [the two pairs of angles are congruent] to me, but your argument for why those lines have to be parallel, I am feeling a little lost on.
>
> S1: Well also, so this, so this is aa (*he points to one of the angles created by a bisector*), and this is aa, and when you (inaudible) do it the same kind of thing. . . .
>
> S3: Because, because they're the same angles, like over here to over there (*points*). Because it's the same angle, it's going to set these lines the same angle apart.
>
> LM: So, if you can show to me that they are alternate interior angles, then lines are parallel, then that's cool. If you can show me that they are corresponding angles and they're equal, then the lines are parallel. So, you guys are definitely on the right track, but you're going to need a few more angles to be able to say that they're parallel. So look for them. You guys are definitely on the right track.
>
> LM *leaves group. Group continues discussion.*
>
> S2 (*Pointing to a figure in the middle of the desks*): You see this triangle right here and this one? Then there's this one in here without this line and then there's this one in here without this line. . . .

In this brief segment, as is typical of many interactions with groups, Ms. McClure listened to the group's argument, identified a place that needed further elaboration, listened to students' initial responses (in part to be sure they understood what she was bringing to their attention; in this case S3 offers a reasonable but informal argument), and then indicated an aspect of their thinking they needed to continue to pursue to support their argument. As in this excerpt, Ms. McClure often included encouragement or demonstrated her excitement for their thinking. Note that Ms. McClure did not remain with the group to help construct the needed justification. This work was for the group to do. With this approach, Ms. McClure supported the group in moving beyond their current position, gave them responsibility for generating the ideas, and allowed them to continue the conversation unconstrained by her presence. The duration of this interaction was also important because there were eight groups in the room. Even with her concise interactions with groups, groups often had to wait for her attention.

Another important feature, already noted above, was that Ms. McClure's manner of interacting with each group respected each group's intellectual journey. She did not impose a particular method, and only rarely suggested approaches she thought would be easier or more efficient. Her feedback was primarily in terms of responding to and extending their thinking.

EXAMINING THE CLASSROOM SYSTEM

I have presented an analysis of one teacher's organization of collaborative group-work in a geometry class in a detracked mathematics program by examining four aspects of her role: the accountability system, positive sentiment, tools and resources, and direct teacher-group interaction. The analysis focused on how the teacher organized a classroom system that supported collaborative interaction among students as they worked in heterogeneous groups on open-ended, nonroutine tasks. It offers some insights into how teachers might address the dilemma stated by Cohen (1994a), whereby teachers must carefully create some structure to support student collaboration, but not overly constrain interactions, as students need autonomy to productively work on nonroutine problem-solving tasks. This analysis emphasized the classroom as a system with interrelated components that provided a set of constraints and affordances for student interaction.

Complex Systems

Returning to key principles of complexity science, we can see how the system created by Ms. McClure can be characterized by decentralized control, organized randomness, and neighbor interactions.

Decentralized control, with respect to generating mathematical ideas and, perhaps to a lesser degree, group processes, was supported in a variety of ways.

Groups generated their own paths toward problem-solving and were not required to use a particular approach or produce a solution at a given level of sophistication. By strategically choosing when to leave the group (usually after she helped them identify a line of thinking that they could continue to pursue), Ms. McClure kept the group developing their mathematical ideas. In terms of process, groups chose when they would be quizzed and Ms. McClure interacted with groups generally only with their permission (offering them uninterrupted space to think) or under certain conditions. Although students had assigned roles, these were not scriptlike, and all members had the opportunity and responsibility to contribute ideas.

Decentralized control, however, can lead to a lack of productivity or quality thinking if there is no coordination of individual efforts. Complementing decentralized control were elements that promoted organized randomness. To help structure and capitalize on the range of contributions students might make, Ms. McClure made the expectations for group processes very clear and reinforced and supported them through verbal feedback, her interactions with the group, and the assessment system. Each group member was held accountable for explaining the group's solutions and articulating the group's questions, which required communication among group members. Ms. McClure's interactions with the groups and the questions she asked them also helped focus their collective efforts, offering them feedback on their mathematical thinking and logic as they developed their solution. Furthermore, group unit tests and group quizzes created a collective goal and promoted interdependence.

For the purposes of prompting collaboration on nonroutine tasks, part of organizing randomness is also promoting the colliding of ideas, or neighboring interactions. Many of the above-mentioned strategies promoted neighbor interactions and the exchange of ideas. In addition, the use of the workspace and scrap paper "in the middle" helped make public individual ideas for group consideration. The positive sentiment fostered within groups further strengthened neighbor interactions among group members.

In Ms. McClure's classroom, although groups were given autonomy in their thinking and many aspects of their group interaction, there were a large number of rules and structures that influenced the groups' activities. The constraints helped organize the potentially unconnected contributions and enable a certain set of possibilities for interaction. This reconceptualization of the role of constraints or rules might represent a fundamental departure from how teachers often think about their classrooms and the choices they make in an effort to promote students' mathematics learning.

It is important to recognize that one aspect of this classroom system did not undermine other aspects of it. For example, each group was expected to develop an approach to solving a problem, and there was no expectation that the groups would use the same method, learn a "best" method, or complete the same amount of work. Any of these expectations could have undermined the groups' collaboration and the commitment to all students' understanding. From a complex systems perspective, such homogenization of approaches or products would undermine the principle of decentralized control (regarding intellectual ideas) and would reduce the meaningfulness of, and need for, neighbor interactions.

Ms. McClure's teaching of this geometry class seems to represent a successful case of addressing the dilemma posed by Cohen (1994a). Cohen highlighted the challenge of identifying a productive level of structure for student collaboration. Reframed, the challenge is to find a judicious balance between decentralized control and organized randomness. There is a tendency to want to prescribe—to offer to students an efficient method or to specify how they should talk with one another. However, it is not possible to prescribe collaborative interactions or students' intellectual engagement with a problem-solving activity. These practices must emerge—and they emerge against (or in conjunction with) the properties of the complex system. The role of the teacher then shifts: "A key element in effective teaching is not maintaining control over ideas and correctness, but the capacity to disperse control" (Davis & Simmt, 2003, p. 153). It is the group that ultimately identifies the specific mathematics they will work on and where they can more fluidly revisit and connect the diverse contributions and address gaps in understanding as needed. Ms. McClure's practice seemed to strike a balance whereby groups were provided latitude to collaborate and govern their problem-solving process and yet were held accountable to high-quality thinking and adhering to certain group processes.

Complex Systems and Implications for Teaching

It is daunting to determine how to offer effective instruction when faced with attending to the range of needs of 30 students. Our typical models for teaching— particularly in mathematics—assume a level of homogeneity across students and are organized around specific daily learning goals. Diversity (of student thinking, dispositions, etc., or of learning goals) disrupts this model. Minimizing diversity seems to lead to greater efficiency, as, theoretically, fewer approaches are needed, or the response to a given approach is less variable. These models are based on cause-and-effect relationships between what the teacher does and what the students learn. They do not explicitly account for the fact that students exercise a high degree of agency with respect to their participation in any given setting.

The shortcomings of this model are apparent when one poses the question "How do you teach problem solving?" or "How do you get all students to participate?" These defy cause-and-effect analysis. Indeed, everyday classroom life often defies such analysis, as teachers throw up their hands wondering why something that worked one day does not another. To understand teaching, we must think about how students are participating in the classroom. Thus, we must consider the full complement of actions, tools and resources, accountability systems, and so on that the teacher utilizes to establish a classroom system that supports these forms of participation.

Future and current teachers would profit from understanding and being able to analyze the classroom as a complex system, where multiple components mutually influence one another to produce some emergent patterns and structures. On the most basic level, when analyzing a lesson or students' participation, it is important for teachers to consider the interrelated set of factors that supported and undermined the desired outcomes. While potentially useful for all aspects of teaching, using a complex systems perspective may be particularly important or beneficial for specific aspects of the teacher's work such as supporting student collaboration (as discussed in this chapter), establishing norms for a productive learning environment, or promoting other, less routine kinds of thinking, such as modeling and adapting procedures.

Take, for example, the establishment of norms. This teacher task can be conceptualized fairly simplistically, where the teacher states expectations and then positively reinforces the behaviors when they arise and discourages any breaches of the stated expectations. (This may seem to work in some settings.) A complex systems perspective, by contrast, implores teachers to consider how the broader classroom system is making it more or less likely that the desired ways of interacting may emerge. Teachers must ask questions like: What resources are available to students so they can act in ways consistent with the stated expectations? Are there incentives or disincentives, structural or otherwise, that promote or impede such ways of interacting? How is the assessment system, nature of the tasks, or any other component of the classroom influencing a system that supports these norms? Are there components that are undermining the desired outcomes?

Conceptualizing a classroom as a complex system foregrounds different resources and aspects of the environment. Complex systems thrive on diversity—it is the grist for the mill. The teacher does not play a gatekeeper role, restricting passage until she deems it appropriate. Her role is gate-opener, encouraging all students to be drawn into the process through her interactions with groups and the systems she establishes and continues to monitor and shape over time. The teacher's goal, then, is to determine the productive constraints and affordances to prompt the emergence of the desired generative activities at the individual and group level.

CONCLUSIONS

This case provides an important example of teaching in a heterogeneous mathematics class and begins to unpack the role of the teacher in organizing a classroom system that supports productive student collaboration. Further research is needed to better understand other aspects of the teacher's role and their relation to the emergent patterns of group interaction in, for example, how the teacher promotes more equal participation among group members. Further research is also needed to better understand the degree to which classrooms can be understood as complex systems and how such a framework can be usefully used by teachers to support their thinking, planning, and decision-making in relation to the classroom.

APPENDIX: DATA COLLECTION AND ANALYSIS

Data were collected from multiple sources. I observed 39 lessons during the semester (approximately 58 hours), for which I recorded fieldnotes and wrote up more detailed notes and reflective memos following most lessons. Twenty-six lessons were also videotaped, which provided the opportunity to return to the lessons for more detailed analyses. In each lesson, I recorded all whole-class activities and public discussions. During groupwork, I used two strategies: I followed the teacher as she moved from group to group, or I focused on one group. In addition, I collected curricular documents and other materials, and I conducted interviews with a majority of students (18 total, in pairs) and with the teacher (3x). The analysis presented here draws primarily on the video data and fieldnotes.

Data analysis followed standard qualitative techniques. In the first phase of analysis, I used *open coding* (Glaser & Strauss, 1967; Strauss & Corbin, 1998) on fieldnotes, looking for emerging themes in relation to the research questions. These fieldnotes comprised documentation of the lessons (content, tasks, major segments), reflective notes, and records of conversations with Ms. McClure regarding the class and the mathematics program. This analysis was conducted concurrently with the fieldwork, thus providing the opportunity to compare and refine emerging patterns against subsequent classroom events. The result of this process was a preliminary set of themes related to the constraints and affordances the teacher organized to support student collaboration.

In the second phase, 10 focal lessons were selected for more detailed analysis. The initial four lessons were chosen because the video recordings had significant periods of time when the camera was focused on a particular group, so the students' interactions when the group was not under the direct purview of the teacher could be analyzed, as could the influence of the teacher's interactions with the group when she directly worked with them. Video content logs, which recorded activities at 30-second intervals, were prepared for each lesson and were analyzed in relation to the codes/themes developed in the first phase of analysis to further document how the groups' work together was organized and supported.

The other six videos were chosen to represent lessons early and late in the semester. Segments related to students' collaborative work and the teacher's interactions with groups were transcribed. Building on the identified themes, a graduate research assistant and the author prepared an analytic memo for each lesson. These analytic memos were synthesized to produce a final document regarding the teacher's work that supported the group collaboration around mathematics. Two additional videos were selected to review for disconfirming evidence. At the same time, we conducted a parallel analysis on a second high school teacher at another school (Staples & Colonis, 2006). This second classroom provided a point of contrast and comparison that helped illuminate particular features of Ms. McClure's classroom.

Two forms of triangulation enhanced validity. I conducted a *member check*, whereby Ms. McClure read an earlier version of this paper. She confirmed that the portrayal of her practice was accurate, and she recognized various elements of her practice that I identified as important to her work with groups. I also triangulated the video analysis with information gleaned from interviews.

In the final step, the results were considered in light of the literature on heterogeneous groupwork and complex systems. This led to further refinement of the relationship among categories, as the literature highlighted aspects of the classroom system that were likely critical to the organization of productive groups. The four categories reported in this paper were identifiable elements of the teacher's practice that were connected with the patterns of interactions observed across the groups.

Part II

STUDENT EXPERIENCES AT RAILSIDE

Section 1 primarily focused on describing the practices that comprised the Railside signature pedagogy. In Section 2, we took a closer look at students in Railside classrooms, exploring how students experienced math classrooms, and how the math classrooms provided a space for mathematical identity development for young people.

Chapter 5 begins this section. In it, Railside alumna Maria D. Velazquez and Nicole Louie analyze data from a focus group that Velazquez conducted with other Railside alumni. They argue that three overarching themes emerged from the focus group: the ways in which Railside math classes taught students to understand the nature of mathematics (and mathematics learning) in expanded ways, what they learned about their peers and appreciating multiple kinds of contributions, and what they learned about their own and others' learning processes. They also reflect on how all of this occurred with a classroom that provided a supportive learning community.

Chapter 6, by Victoria Hand, looks closely at how Railside students who did not have strong mathematical identities at the beginning of the school year used the participation structures in the classroom to become active, engaged learners of mathematics. Hand's analysis shows that Railside math classrooms provided unique opportunities for potentially marginalized learners to "take up their space," by which she means that they were able to be themselves in the math classroom, and thus engage learning in ways they could not do elsewhere.

In Chapter 7, Lisa M. Jilk offers another case study of how Railside math classes made identities of learning available. She explores the ways in which an immigrant Latina student was able to construct Railside math classes as a place where she could "be somebody," providing the opportunity for identity consistency between home and school.

An important contribution of the chapters in this section is that they hone in on the lived experiences of students from marginalized groups in the mathematics classroom. In these chapters, Railside mathematics classrooms are viewed as interacting with the individual and community experiences that students bring to the classroom and the unique ways in which they provide spaces where young people feel welcome, find community, and are viewed and treated as mathematical thinkers.

Chapter 5

What You Can't Learn from a Book
Alumni Perspectives on Railside Mathematics

Maria D. Velazquez and Nicole Louie

In this chapter, we consider the experience of learning mathematics at Railside from the perspective of Railside alumni. We explore alumni thoughts on the nature of mathematics teaching and learning at Railside, through their reflections on their experiences in mathematics classes. The first author, Maria Velazquez, is herself an alumna. The editorial team asked Maria to organize fellow alumni to reflect on what it was like to be a mathematics learner at Railside, and on what they have carried with them beyond high school from that experience. Maria was excited to undertake this work because of her history at Railside: She entered the school as a freshman from another school district, and she felt that the mathematics classes eased her transition into the school. After high school, Maria attended a local university, and in her studies there, she learned about the research done at Railside. She was intrigued by what she learned and went on to do her own research on equity in mathematics education for her senior honors thesis.

For this chapter, Maria and a former classmate, Julie, gathered Railside alumni for a 2-hour focus group. They deliberately worked to include alumni with a wide range of experiences in and after high school. The focus group involved seven Railside graduates (including Maria and Julie) who had completed different levels of mathematics courses at Railside and pursued a variety of paths upon graduation. Participants were asked to reflect on features of teaching and learning that stood out to them as salient aspects of their time at Railside. We begin this chapter with a description of the alumni who participated in the focus group.

RAILSIDE ALUMNI

The focus group involved seven alumni who graduated from Railside between 2003 and 2007.

Maria graduated from Railside High in 2006. The highest level of math she completed at Railside High was AP Calculus. Upon graduation, Maria attended the University of California (UC), Berkeley, working while continuing her studies. In 2010, she graduated with a B.A. in Ethnic Studies and a minor in Education. She is currently working at an education-related nonprofit. She identifies as Chicana.

Julie graduated from Railside High in 2006. The highest level of math she completed at Railside High was AP Calculus. Upon graduation, Julie attended UC Berkeley. She graduated with a B.A. in Integrative Biology in 2010 and is currently working as an administrative assistant. She identifies as Chinese American.

Alex graduated from Railside High in 2003. The highest level of math he completed at Railside was Algebra II. Since graduation, Alex has been working as a metal fabricator and wheel builder. He identifies as Latino.

Camilo graduated from Railside High in 2004. The highest level of math he completed at Railside was Precalculus. Upon graduation, Camilo went to work. After being out of school for 7 years and working in a laboratory warehouse, Camilo recently signed up for his first math class at his local community college. He identifies as Latino.

Brooke graduated from Railside High in 2006. The highest level of math she completed at Railside was AP Calculus. Upon graduation, she attended the University of California, Davis, and a local community college. She is currently working as an office clerk. She identifies as White.

Lacy graduated from Railside High in 2006. The highest level of math he completed at Railside was AP Calculus. Upon graduation, Lacy attended the California Polytechnic State University, San Luis Obispo, where he earned a B.S. in Electrical Engineering. He now works as an engineer. Lacy identifies as African American.

Ashley graduated from Railside High in 2007. The highest level of math she completed at Railside was AP Calculus. Upon graduation, Ashley worked while attending UC Berkeley, where she double-majored in Legal Studies and Gender and Women's Studies. She recently completed her bachelor's degree and is planning to go to law school. Ashley identifies as White.

The meeting, held at the home of one of the alumni, felt like a high school reunion. As people came in, they greeted one another or introduced themselves enthusiastically. As facilitators, Julie and Maria posed guiding questions to lead the conversation, and it became obvious early on that everyone had a lot to say. As soon as the facilitators introduced each topic—such as initial reactions to math classes, groupwork, or relationships with teachers—someone was quick to answer. The conversation flowed easily from one person to another, each speaker elaborating on what had already been said with her or his own recollections and anecdotes. The conversation was full of laughter, jokes, and stories. The focus group conversation was audio-recorded and transcribed, and the transcripts were analyzed with the goal of identifying key themes that emerged during the conversation.

FOCUS GROUP THEMES

Four major themes emerged from the focus group. Alumni pointed to three types of learning as they reflected on their experiences in Railside mathematics: *learning about the nature of mathematics, learning about peers,* and *learning about learning itself.* An additional theme was the *sense of community* that enabled deep learning to occur.

Learning About Mathematics

Railside mathematics classes challenged the views of mathematics that alumni had previously held. Several alumni contrasted their experiences learning math in middle school with their experiences at Railside, highlighting the ways that Railside taught them that math could be engaging and personal, that the process of solving problems is just as important as the solution, and that there is more than one way to work through a problem.

Mathematics as Personal and Engaging. School mathematics can sometimes feel rigid and impersonal. Alumni reported that Railside's approach was strikingly different. Camilo illustrated the stark differences in teaching between his middle school and Railside High:

> I remember in junior high it was different. [Teachers would say] "Book, and chapter blah blah, today is going to be about this." But when I went [to Railside High] and I had Ms. Woodbury and all [the other teachers] it was just like they were [teaching math] out their minds, with no book. . . . They got to speak.

Math teaching prior to high school for Camilo was based on the school's text-book. Teaching at Railside High was different. Teachers taught in a way that was interactive; they didn't read from a book and expect students to be able to learn math concepts simply by reading and following example problems. Instead, they engaged students with hands-on projects and problems that connected to students' lives. Lacy remembers problems as being "really personalized a lot of times . . . [where] you would see your name on the problem so it made you interested in actually solving it." Curriculum included not only students' names, but phrases that students were known for, their interests and possessions, and incidents that occurred in class. For example, Maria remembered a peer named Guadalupe who became famous for taking an unusually long and complex route to solve a problem at the board one day. Most of her classmates had found a much shorter way, and they were impressed by Guadalupe's process. Mr. Cabana, the teacher, titled her approach the "Guada Method," and the following week, he introduced a new topic by having students figure out whether this method would work or not in a new context. This simultaneously engaged students with their classmate's thinking and with unfamiliar mathematics, in a way that strengthened the community by creating space for both good-natured teasing and compliments toward Guadalupe.

Brooke explained how Railside math involved projects that were creative and connected to the real world—projects that engaged her and made her re-think what it meant to learn math:

> One doesn't really think of math as having projects or group projects. It's more like, "This is how you learn, this is how you take a test," and that's it. [But at Railside High] they would always have us do projects, like the Transamerica Building Project, the Flagpole Project, the Barbie Project. We always had these projects . . . you wouldn't think [you] would do something like that in math.[1]

At Railside, Brooke found that her understanding of mathematical concepts—not just her memory of formulas—was pushed, as she worked with peers to integrate classroom mathematics topics and the real world. For example, students deepened their understanding of ratios through the Flagpole Project, in which the assignment was to find the height of the flagpole in front of the school. Together with their teachers, students brainstormed a list of geometric tools and techniques that might be useful. Then, in teams, they devised and executed plans for determining the height of the flagpole, using meter sticks, clinometers (tools for measuring angles of sight), and one another as resources. Each team was required to develop two methods and then compare the results. In this way, the project and others like it pushed students to solve problems in nonalgorithmic ways, inventing and analyzing multiple approaches. Projects like these were designed in part to change students' perspectives on what it meant to learn math.

Math as a Process. Alumni vividly recalled how teachers pushed them to focus on processes and explanations, not just having the right answer. Ashley remembered teachers saying things like, "Here is a problem, talk to each other, create an answer and tell me why or argue for it"—contrasting this with the more typical, "Here is the answer, here is how you do it." Students not only had to show their work, but they also had to justify it. Several alumni said this emphasis on being able to explain caused them to see math differently. It also caused them to interact differently with their peers, expanding students' opportunities to learn mathematics content and to see one another as capable learners and thinkers.

Math as Multimethod. At Railside, students learned that there were multiple ways to work through and understand a math problem. One way this occurred was through groupwork, a point all the alumni agreed on. As Camilo explained, in doing groupwork, students got to see that "you can do [math] differently compared to your partner but you guys still get the same answer. . . . [We would compare, saying,] 'Okay, so they did it this way,' or 'This is shorter than my version.'" The process of comparing strategies allowed Camilo and his peers to see the many ways to work through a math problem or concept and helped them learn to evaluate alternative methods for solving problems.

The Railside approach to mathematics teaching and learning sought to transform students' ideas of mathematics. Instead of viewing the discipline as rigid and impersonal, where right answers were all that counted, alumni described coming to see mathematics as a field in which process was just as important as product, and where there was room for projects, personality, and most importantly, for themselves as learners. This perspective in turn helped them to learn more mathematics content by increasing their engagement with math and by expanding access. Alex explained how this supported him, outlining a typical peer response when he was stuck. He described another student saying something like, "Check it out, do it this way, and if you don't understand it talk to this guy. He does it differently, he takes longer to get to the answer, but he's like figured it out." These multiple methods gave him and others access to concepts that a traditional, "strictly textbook" approach may not have.

Learning About Peers

Set in a detracked department, Railside mathematics classes provided a unique opportunity for students to work with and get to know one another. This prompted students to rethink their assumptions about one another, teaching them that everyone had valuable mathematical contributions to make—no matter their status in other classes or initial appearances regarding who was good at math. In some cases, this was a hard lesson. For example, Lacy recalled:

> I didn't know how to work in teams when it came to math. So it was really different. I didn't like the math program when I first got to Railside. . . . [I thought,] "Why do I have to work with these people, I already know this stuff, and I have to explain this to other people . . . why do I have to do this?"

He went on to describe how he changed his mind about working with others, shifting from seeing groupwork as a chance for "stupid" kids to get help from smart ones, to viewing it as an opportunity for everyone to benefit by combining forces:

> For a while you just hate your group members and you're thinking, "He's stupid, they're stupid," and they're thinking the same thing about you, you know. But eventually you come to an answer and you realize what you were doing was wrong and what they were doing was wrong. But if you had put your heads together you would have known exactly what to do. By the time I had got to my senior year, like I had learned how to work within groups and listen to my group members . . . despite what you think, how you think their grades are, and all that. You actually have to put faith in your group members 'cause everybody knows something. You put four minds together and it's better than just one.

Brooke was even more explicit in describing how math classes taught her that everyone, not just her peers in AP and honors classes, was smart:

> In [Railside] you had a lot of people who were in AP classes, in the higher-up classes like AP English, AP U.S. History, you would be in the classes together. But in the math [classes], sometimes you would see people who [you] hadn't seen in those [higher-up] classes, and that's the only time you would see them . . . you think, "Oooh, they might not know what we know," but then they come in and they're actually really smart and they know what they're talking about.

As students who were not in honors classes outside of mathematics, Camilo and Alex also noticed that students saw one another's value differently in math than in other classes. As Camilo said in response to Brooke's comment, "[S]ome of them had those high classes, but when you were in math you were the same. They didn't treat you differently. But in English classes, some of them, they thought they were [better]."

The relative absence of hierarchy in Railside math classrooms was directly connected to the ideas about mathematics that we have described. In particular, it was difficult to make assumptions about who was "smart" because assignments were complex, multidimensional, and multimethod. They were deliberately written so that everyone would have something to contribute and no one could succeed on his or her own. Teaching emphasized working together to understand complicated concepts, not just getting the right answer, and each student was held accountable for the learning of his or her peers.

Lacy summarized the impact that Railside mathematics had on him in terms of how he saw—and continues to see—others:

> I don't just shut off. Just because someone is failing the class doesn't mean they don't know anything. . . . I always put in my head, "He knows something that I don't," and that is what Railside High taught us. Always be open to your group members and always keep that open mind. . . . We learn[ed] life lessons. . . . You can read in a book, or even somebody can sit down and teach you [math], but no one can sit you down and teach you something about respecting others.

The structure of Railside classes required students to work together and rely on one another for support. These circumstances enabled students to overcome their assumptions about what their peers could or could not contribute and achieve, as well as come to value the ways that a peer could contribute to the larger group's learning.

Learning About Learning

Through the process of transforming their ideas about mathematics and about their peers, these alumni also came to see learning itself in a different light. Several alumni described learning strategies that they adapted from their Railside mathematics classrooms to their studies and careers after high school. For example, Alex described how working with others in the classroom helped him learn from his co-workers in building motorcycles:

> 'Cause all the group[work] stuff, when I started working with the motorcycle stuff it was like, "I want to do this by myself," but then I understood, "This guy did the same thing but he did it different." It was the same thing with Mr. Cabana's class. Everybody did [the math work] a different way. . . . [There are] twenty different guys that do the same thing I do, and each one of them has their own way of forming and shaping metal on a motorcycle. So now, every now and then we get together and be like, "How'd you do this one? I did it this way and I made this tool."

As Alex described, he started out being closed off and focused on his own work. But as he came to see the value of learning how others formed and shaped metal, he created a workplace that paralleled the group work environment in mathematics classrooms at Railside, where he could learn from what other people did.

Lacy similarly described how he was able to apply cooperative learning strategies to his studies after high school. When he first started college, he "tried to do everything on my own," which "didn't work too well." He developed study groups and found that, as at Railside, "get[ting] like four or five people to share their knowledge on what they learned . . . [helped us] start putting pieces together, then all of a sudden we solved this problem, and we're ready for the exam." He argued that his experiences with groupwork at Railside prepared him to create and take advantage of opportunities to learn from and with other students when he encountered difficulties on his own, instead of giving up or being too embarrassed to seek help.

In addition to transporting the lessons of groupwork to college, Lacy described another learning strategy from Railside that he used in his college engineering program: constructing physical models to illustrate abstract concepts. He vividly recalled a Railside lesson that taught him this technique, in which the teacher (Mr. Cabana) introduced integrals not by lecturing or presenting a formal definition, but with a concrete activity:

> [Cabana] put a lemon on everyone's desk. . . . [He said,] "Slice it, slice it, slice it up into little pieces. As small as you can get 'em. Come on, smaller!" You know? I was like, "Why? Why are we slicing up lemons right now?" You know? And that's how he taught us, like, integrals is that you try to slice up the lemons into infinite pieces and you can measure the area and so . . . that's how I learn now. It's like whenever I learn something new in school, I'll always try and relate it to some sort of physical thing . . . I just come up with these analogies on how to exactly model things.

Having a tactile example helped Lacy visualize and conceptualize the meaning of an integral. As he described, this learning approach helped him so much that he continued to use it in his college classes.

A Supportive Community

In addition to the ways their experiences provided new ways of thinking about learning, alumni also highlighted the importance of their *relationships* with one another and their teachers. In their remarks, two ideas stand out: the sense of accountability students felt toward one another, and the sense of safety they had in Railside math classrooms.

Accountability. Alumni described how feeling responsible for the learning of their peers motivated them to come to class prepared, to participate actively, and to stay focused. One participation structure that they pointed to was the "group quiz" (see also Staples, Chapter 4). During these quizzes, teachers would designate checkpoints. To move past each checkpoint, the group would call over the teacher, who would then ask a randomly selected student—and that student only—to explain the group's work on the checkpoint problem. In order for the group to proceed to the next problem on the quiz, the selected student had to be able to provide an adequate explanation. This structure encouraged students to support one another, since it was uncertain who the teacher would select. It also pushed students to work hard on their own understandings and explanations. As Brooke described, "You didn't want to let down your team, your group members. ... Everybody had to get the answer and had to understand it."

Ashley similarly described the impossibility of avoiding participation in Railside mathematics classes, and how the regular demand to contribute kept students accountable for doing work both inside and outside of class:

> For [Railside] students, pride is a big thing and if you go into class the next day and you don't have anything to provide for groupwork from homework, or if you didn't prep yourself, you look like you didn't do shit. You're just the odd one out if [you] don't have anything to contribute or if you don't have anything to say. So it motivated you to do the homework.

Groupwork held students accountable for both their own learning and that of their peers. Students held a sense of responsibility to be prepared to work with their peers or contribute to the classroom environment. The alumni argued that this motivated students to be on top of their classwork.

Safe Space. The accountability structures described above put a constant spotlight on students' thinking. This was paired with an ethic of caring that kept the spotlight from being intimidating and overwhelming. All the alumni remember mathematics classrooms as safe spaces where they weren't afraid to admit they needed help or to make mistakes. They didn't worry about being put down or having their peers talk down to them. Ashley pointed out how teachers helped students develop trust by emphasizing the value of asking for help:

> If we didn't have groupwork at [Railside], I would have been hesitant to ask [for help]. . . . [But the teachers taught us that] asking for help isn't a bad thing, it's a good thing. In a lot of ways, it's how you learn more. It's how you learn from each other.

Powerfully, Alex described how his initial anxieties about the gaps in his understanding were soothed by classmates who offered explanations and advice instead of contempt:

> Say a person that's really into math and me [who] has no idea what math is . . . [he would say,] "You didn't understand it?" and I was like, "Here we go, he is going to give me some crap about it." But [no, he would say something like,] "Well, check it out, do it this way, and if you don't understand it, talk to this guy. He does it differently."

Julie's experiences in college contrast sharply with this picture, highlighting the safety of Railside mathematics classrooms and how consequential it could be for students. In college math courses, Julie found interactions with her peers to be quite difficult. While she was able to adjust to the lecture- and textbook-based style of teaching and learning, the competitive and unfriendly environment was problematic for her—despite her many talents and successes as a high school student and as a biology major at a prestigious research university: "I actually tried to ask my fellow classmates how to answer [questions]. They were snobby. . . . I felt like an idiot . . . as if I couldn't ask any questions. I felt as if I wasn't good enough for the rest of this class." Feeling intellectually shut off from her peers made classes uninviting and uncomfortable for Julie. As a result, despite her ability to engage well with the new learning and teaching styles, she didn't "go really far in math classes" in college.

At Railside, on the other hand, "in math class you got along with everybody." In making this statement, Alex specifically included students who were very different from himself. Ashley echoed the sentiment, noting that there were many conflicts within the student body that just didn't seem to matter in mathematics classes:

> I think the groupwork in the math department at [Railside] was like a catalyst for everyone opening up to each other, because there were issues at [Railside]. There was so much tension between certain groups and the [math] classroom is what really broke it down, like everyone was cool with each other in math class.

In math, students were required to work together and expected to get past their differences. This became easier as students got to know one another on more personal levels through collaborating to learn mathematics.

In addition, teachers helped students feel safe and included by developing their own relationships with students. Alex talked about how teachers "noticed" him and his struggles in mathematics, and how they supported him by pairing him with another student with similar struggles so that they could work together to figure out a big idea. Neither student was treated as "smart" or "slow." The teachers also offered one-on-one help. Both of these actions made Alex feel cared for and valued.

Alumni also described how teachers' treatment of off-task discussions supported their learning while strengthening teacher-student relationships. For example, Camilo described how Ms. Woodbury would make students' personal issues public in ways that were sometimes embarrassing, but that students knew came from her concern for their learning. The message to students was, either focus on mathematics, or be prepared to discuss whatever you're gossiping or passing notes about with the whole class. Similarly, Lacy discussed how teachers worked with students to address personal issues:

> They weren't afraid, they didn't live in a fantasy world where all students are only going to focus on school. Like they weren't afraid to put us on blast for non-curriculum-related things. [They would say,] "Okay, well, this is the real world, so let's address this." [That response] makes you focus even more, I feel.

Thus, teachers didn't expect students to just be *students* in their classrooms. They got to know students as whole people and made room for students to bring up issues that were influencing their lives. This environment helped students learn by making them feel welcome and allowing them to bring parts of themselves into the learning environment.

While we have presented alumni responses in a qualitative way, it is important to note that the alumni substantially agreed on what made learning mathematics at Railside a special and important experience. To ensure that our analysis represented each person's perspective fairly, we shared the themes we saw in the focus group transcript with the participants and asked them to comment. As Table 5.1 shows, the alumni agreed that the themes we identified matched their experiences at Railside.

CONCLUSION

Other chapters in this volume identify several critical aspects of the Railside mathematics department's pedagogy. Many of these were also salient from the students' perspective, in particular the multimethod approach to mathematics, groupwork and other student-to-student accountability structures, and relationships between teachers and students. As a departure from the mathematics learning that students had previously experienced, these features took some getting used to, but years later, alumni described their ongoing use of the collaborative

Table 5.1. Individual Participants' Agreement with Focus Group Themes

Statement	*Yes, this matches my experience*	*Somewhat matches my experience*	*No, this doesn't match my experience*
Railside math taught me that math could be personal and engaging (for example, through group projects).	7/7		
Railside taught me that the process of solving for a math problem is just as important as the solution.	5/7	2/7	
Railside math taught me that there is more than one way to work through a math problem.	7/7		
Railside math classes provided us with opportunities to interact and work with students we wouldn't have gotten to know otherwise.	6/7	1/7	
Interactions with some of my peers caused me to rethink the assumptions I had of them. I came to see that they had valuable mathematical contributions to make—no matter their status in other classes or initial appearances regarding who was good at math.	6/7	1/7	
I have been able to see the importance of groupwork and apply it either in my studies or career after high school.	7/7		
In Railside math, I had a sense of accountability toward my peers. I felt like I had come to class prepared, participate actively, and stay focused.	4/7	3/7	

Table 5.1. Individual Participants' Agreement with Focus Group Themes (continued)

Statement	*Yes, this matches my experience*	*Somewhat matches my experience*	*No, this doesn't match my experience*
I felt that Railside math was a safe space where I could admit if I needed help, make a mistake and not worry about being put down or have peers talk bad about me.	6/7	1/7	

learning practices they encountered at Railside in their postsecondary studies and jobs. They also described the lasting impact of Railside math classes on less tangible aspects of their lives. As they told it, alumni carried the life lessons they learned through mathematics at Railside—about the nature of mathematics, about valuing other people, and about learning itself—far beyond high school.

Chapter 6

"Taking Up Our Space"
Becoming Competent Learners in Mathematics Classrooms

Victoria Hand

I entered graduate school with the intent of studying the role that learners' identities play in their school engagement.[1] I was deeply concerned that many of the Latino and African American students with whom I had worked in and out of school had bought into the story that they were neither cut out for nor interested in mathematics and thus would not pursue college. I was curious about whether the opportunity to make sense of mathematics—to "own it"—would create sufficient momentum to dislodge these entrenched narratives. Dr. Jo Boaler introduced me to Railside High School, where she was conducting a longitudinal study. Three Railside mathematics teachers generously invited me into their classrooms to study their craft, get to know their students, and look closely at the kind of mathematics learners the students were becoming. I am deeply indebted to these teachers, their classes, and three adolescent students in particular–two of whom share the spotlight in this chapter.

WHAT IT MEANS TO "TAKE UP THEIR SPACE"

The mathematics classroom is so often a place where it is difficult for many students to "take up their space." This phrase was introduced to me by one of the math teachers at Railside High School. It describes a phenomenon in which students make a choice to participate in a mathematics classroom because doing so allows them to get what they need *to become the people they want to be.* For many students, becoming a math learner means having to accept a view of oneself as unintelligent or unmotivated. This is due in part to practices within and for mathematics education, such as tracking and asking students to recall a solution to a problem quickly and without making any mistakes, which position students within an explicit and racialized status hierarchy. For groups of students from nondominant ethnic, racial, and cultural backgrounds, becoming a math learner can even require accepting a view of one's community and family as mathematically inferior to the dominant White culture, as deficit-laden rhetoric around the "achievement gap" persists (R. Gutiérrez, 2008; Martin, 2009). These framings and practices mean that numerous students from nondominant backgrounds elect to sit on the sidelines of the mathematics community, watching their chances to *take up their space* in an increasingly STEM-driven[2] society slip away.

The mathematics classrooms at Railside provide an important contrast. Chapter 2 of this volume, by Boaler and Staples, presents compelling evidence that students from a range of backgrounds chose to take up their space within them. This chapter is devoted to exploring one such occurrence involving supporting students' practice-linked identities (Nasir & Hand, 2008).

This chapter is formed around case studies of the students themselves. Too often, reports on what I call a *participation gap* (Hand, 2003) in mathematics come to us in the form of broad national, state, or district statistics on students' test scores across racial, ethnic, or first-language lines. Within these reports, the voices and narratives of students on the ground who are experiencing success or failure, privilege or marginalization, are lost. This chapter attends explicitly to students' experiences by delving deeply into the stories of two math learners, in two different Railside math classrooms, who, despite the odds, took up their space to learn mathematics. It is not a success story, since the students' experiences of competence and belonging in Railside math classrooms came and went, and were not necessarily representative of their experiences in other school contexts. The point is that mathematics classrooms *can* be places where students get what they need to become who they want to be.

The two adolescents selected as focal students in this research study were nominated by their teachers for their weak identities as math learners, which, as predicted by research on mathematics learning, should have impaired their classroom engagement (Kilpatrick, Swafford, & Findell, 2001). But the ways these students came to participate in the Railside mathematics classrooms were quite complex. I chose to focus on patterns in the students' participation, instead of their test scores, in order to draw out this complexity. I studied the nature of their participation around mathematical tasks, their peers, and the teacher, as well as their participation in other classes and school contexts. This type of research—examining *trajectories of participation* (Dreier, 1999) across life contexts—has been particularly fruitful for understanding how individual participation shifts in relation to the way that activity is structured within and across contexts (Nasir & Hand, 2008). I also studied features of the classroom activity system that shaped the opportunities students had, individually and collectively, to participate in mathematics learning and the classroom community. Gresalfi, Martin, Hand, and Greeno (2008) define an activity system as "a social organization that may contain learners, teachers, curriculum materials, software tools, and the physical environment" (p. 50). Features of a classroom system such as classroom tasks, pedagogical practices, and participation structures afford very different opportunities to learn for different groups of learners. Of relevance to exploration of "taking up space," classroom features shape what constitutes a productive contribution, what it means for learners to be competent (or not), and how members of the community come to be accountable for both (Boaler & Greeno, 2000; Gresalfi et al., 2008).

As described in previous chapters, features of the activity system organized by the Railside teachers were markedly different from those one might encounter in typical mathematics classrooms. What students were authorized and held accountable to do in the classroom and what they ended up doing mathematically were atypical. Features defined by Boaler and Staples that supported students in taking up their space included *multidimensionality, group roles, assigning competence,* and *encouraging responsibility* (Chapter 2, this volume). In addition to these, I identified another that I call *promoting dialogical learning* (Alrø & Skovsmose, 2002; Hand, in press). I draw heavily on the descriptions provided by Boaler and Staples of the first four features to illustrate how they supported powerful student participation. The final feature, *promoting dialogical learning,* entails inviting participants to share and draw upon their sociocultural histories as they relate to their negotiation of learning experiences. It is consistent with the notion of *third space* (K. Gutiérrez, 2008; Gutiérrez, Baquedano-López, & Tejada, 2000; Soja, 1996) in that distinctions between cultural and mathematical activity are blurred in classroom discourse. It can also involve reframing students' mathematical learning experiences to locate them explicitly within the system of mathematics education, and identifying this system as aligned within broader power structures and hierarchies (Foucault, 1980). For the Railside teachers highlighted in this chapter, promoting dialogical learning primarily involved actively seeking clues to students' ongoing experiences and restructuring classroom social arrangements to promote solidarity with and among the students.

It is important to mention that features of the classroom activity system identified above were intertwined with and undergirded by ones at the institutional level such as the detracked mathematics program and extended or "block" class periods (Chapters 9 and 12, this volume). These classroom and institutional features functioned symbiotically as an ecological system (Bronfenbrenner, 1979; Lee, 2008), through which the Railside teachers supported students as they forged powerful trajectories of participation around mathematics.

To capture students' trajectories across school contexts, I observed three students for one semester and shadowed them for a second. As a methodological approach, shadowing moves beyond simple observation in that the researcher attempts to gain increasing proximity to the lived experience of the participant. This entails developing an *emic* perspective (Goodenough, 1970) through intensive observation, spontaneous and structured conversations, and to some degree participating in the subjects' daily activities. Thus, in addition to their math classes, I observed the focal students in other classes at least eight times over the semester. I spent time with (or near) the students at lunch and during breaks, and to some extent became a concerned friend and mentor to them.

The next two sections present cases of two of these students—Lucia and Santiago. Each section focuses on one student and comprises a brief description of the student, excerpts of classroom interaction illustrating patterns in the student's participation, and analyses of how the student negotiated forms of participation with respect to features of their mathematics classrooms.

LUCIA

A vibrant and outgoing Latina, Lucia came from a working-class family that resided near the school. Her parents immigrated from Mexico when they were first married and spoke primarily Spanish at home. She had a good relationship with her mother, who, according to Lucia, was very smart. Lucia had long wavy hair and often dressed in jeans, trendy but simple tops, a red sweatshirt, and heels. She was not as fashionably dressed as her girlfriends (a group of Latinas) and she often appeared a bit tired and disheveled.

At the time of the study, Lucia was in her freshman year at Railside (despite being older than her peers, having had to repeat two grades). She was enrolled in 1st-year mathematics (a course required for all incoming freshmen), health, biology, PE, and an elective business class. Despite her lackluster school record, Lucia was a curious and engaged learner. She was rather adultlike in her interactions and approached all people (her teachers included) in a casual and confident manner. While the leader in her peer group, Lucia was not a popular student and was sometimes quietly mocked when attempting to direct her group mates during math class.

She enjoyed her math class, often arriving early (before school started), and she had a strong relationship with her teacher. She eagerly worked on math problems with her peers in groups—when she could get their attention—and didn't hesitate to ask for help when she needed it. She also volunteered solutions to problems in class discussions, even if she was unsure about them. She was less diligent about turning in her homework, but generally managed to complete classwork and tests.

Lucia voiced her ideas and opinions in other classes as well (when she attended them). However, they were less likely to be treated as productive to her or classmates' learning. The other classes were generally organized around fact recall and worksheet completion, which did not move Lucia toward a deep understanding of the content. A number of teachers from these classes lamented to me that Lucia was very smart and engaged but did not pass their classes due to lack of attendance and follow-through. When I asked Lucia about this, she stated that the other classes were boring, and even unfriendly to her.

When asked about her plans for the future, Lucia exclaimed that she loved science and wanted to be a scientist. When I spoke to her math teacher several years later, I found out that Lucia had dropped out of Railside High School and was attempting to get back on track at an alternative high school.

Lucia Takes Up Her Space

Two patterns in Lucia's participation across school contexts appeared to play a prominent role in her engagement in her mathematics class. One was her tendency to *demand to understand* what was occurring in the world around her (including making sense of school subject matter). The other was her inclination to *assert her leadership* over groups of people with whom she interacted. The sections that follow explore these patterns and their relation to opportunities for Lucia to take up her space in the mathematics classroom. Excerpts of classroom interaction illustrate how the classroom activity system opened up these opportunities and how they were negotiated by Lucia.

Demands to Understand. Civil rights leader and mathematician Robert Moses argues that access to a high-quality mathematics education is a civil right (Moses & Cobb, 2001), and that most students from nondominant backgrounds do not have this access. The way change will occur, he contends, is similar to the 1960s Civil Rights Movement when young people who were being disenfranchised demanded access to the vote. In this case, demanding to understand mathematics aptly describes the engaged, purposeful, and empowered way in which Lucia participated in class. Consistent with the disposition she enacted across contexts, Lucia was explicit about her desire to make sense of what she was learning in mathematics. Her inquisitiveness was made productive by a mathematics curriculum that afforded reasoning about mathematical concepts and procedures in various ways (i.e., multidimensionality), and by classroom structures that held students accountable for making sense of one another's ideas (i.e., group roles and encouraging responsibility). Thus, it was her job to understand what she and her peers were doing mathematically, and this intertwined productively with her disposition toward learning. I view this as an opportunity to be able to demand to understand the material, and Lucia's enactment of this opportunity.

I provide two excerpts of Lucia's participation in class to illustrate this process. In the first, Lucia is working on an activity with her group that involves interpreting t-tables (tables of coordinate points that illustrates a pattern between the dependent and independent variables), and advocates for herself with the teacher.

Excerpt 1: "What did you just do?" The students are starting a worksheet that asks them to graph several equations, including $y = 4x - 8$. They are instructed to start by making a t-table. The teacher approaches the group, and Lucia begins to speak. Transcription conventions across the excerpts include: " = " for latched speech, and "[" for overlapping speech (L = Lucia; T = the teacher; D = Danny).

L: It looks like a pattern to me. This looks like all they are all going to
     be lines. (*referring to the three equations given; begins counting the*
     numbers in the first table aloud)
T: Why would you say that they all look like they are going to be lines?
L: Because there is a pattern. (*looks at her paper and takes on a less*
     confident tone)
The teacher continues to press Lucia to explain her pattern.
L: The numbers go right after each other.
D: They're equal.
T: What's equal?
D: Between each number there is an equal amount of numbers . . . grows
     by the same number. (*he raises his arm up with his hand bent flat and*
     palm down in fairly even increments until it is fully extended)
T: How many? How much?
D: By four.
T: Can you show it to me? (*addresses Danny*) Do you remember using the
     little carrot sticks to show me the difference between the numbers?
L (*to Danny*): You need graphing paper. (*Bends down to her backpack. The*
     teacher and Danny continue to discuss how the graph grew. Lucia re-
     emerges.)
L: What did you just do? (*gazes toward the teacher*)
T (*to Danny*): Yes, you need graphing paper.
L: What did you just do?
T: Aww . . . my bad. We talked about this little carrot thing that shows you
     =
L: = Oh yeah
T: = that from –4 to 0 you have to add 4
L: So how come I didn't get that?
T: I don't know. How come you didn't get that?
L: That's what I want to know. (*The teacher walks away from the table.*)
     Four. Eight. Twelve. I don't know, you are probably right. (*unclear who*
     she is addressing)

Lucia was clearly struggling to describe the concept of a linear equation in this episode. However, she was the first person in her group to contribute an idea when the teacher walked over. She continued to offer up her reasoning even when she was unsure about the correct mathematical justification. This can be viewed as an indirect form of demanding to understand. Later on, in a more direct way, Lucia held the teacher accountable for making mathematical concepts available to her when she resurfaced from another task (getting graph paper). Finally, she announced her intention to figure out Danny's solution on her own.

There are several classroom norms that supported Lucia in these moves. One was the norm that students are expected to reason about the mathematics they are working on individually and in group tasks. Lucia demonstrated her compliance with this norm when the teacher walked over and she offered a conjecture about a pattern among the numbers in the table. The second norm was that any work that gets done by a member of the group has to make sense to all of the other members (i.e., encouraging responsibility). Thus, it was reasonable for Lucia to request that the teacher review the conversation that had occurred while she retrieved the graph paper for Danny. In both cases, Lucia pursued mathematical sense making through structures that supported her in this process.

Excerpt 2: *"Lead me through one and I can get the rest."* In this second episode, Lucia and a new group are making what are called "guess and check charts." This is a chart in which students systematically record their guesses and resulting solutions until they reach the desired outcome. They are working as a group, but on individual charts, for the following problem: *Thaddeus's new car costs $14,000. Each month the price will go down $100. When will the car be worth under $12,000?* In this brief excerpt, Lucia again advocates for the group's help in making progress on her work (L = Lucia; SH = Shalina; J = Jerome).

L: How did you set up your column? Where do I minus the 100? (*to Jerome*)

J: Mine's bull****! I'm just doing it weird, but I don't think you should do it like that. (*Lucia proceeds to ask Shalina for help. Jerome and Shalina tell her what and what not to write down for a minute or so.*)

SH: You don't have to write that 31 hundred . . . what you are writing. The second column is going to be 14,000. So, you have to write that.

L: What do you mean? (*shoves her paper toward her*)

SH: You have to write 14,000, because they are all going to be that. (*pointing at Lucia's chart*)

L: So I put 31. (*short pause*) Let's start from the beginning. You guys lead me through one and I can get the rest of it.

For nearly 2 minutes, Lucia continually requested her teammates' help in making sense of the guess and check chart. At first, instead of walking her through their reasoning, they tried to tell her exactly what to write. Lucia was frustrated by this and requested that Shalina start from the beginning, so that she could understand how to fill in the first row well enough to complete the remaining rows herself. As in the previous episode, it is the classroom norms of sense-making and accountability that support Lucia in seeking the understanding she desired.

Asserts leadership. A second theme in Lucia's participation was the leadership role she attempted to enact when with other people. In most of her classes, leadership opportunities did not arise. Science and math class were the exceptions.

During science class, students were often split into groups to complete worksheets through lab experiments. Lucia would normally partner with her friends and dole out instructions on how to proceed. Sometimes her instructions helped the group make progress; at other times, they would lead them astray. In other words, the norms for groupwork in the science classroom supported giving explicit instructions on how to complete a task. One student could authorize herself as the expert and take over, as I observed Lucia do on a number of occasions. As described in Chapter 2, the different roles for members of a group in the math classes supported group functioning in ways that promoted *collective* meaning-making. Thus, in enacting a leadership role in one area, Lucia served as one of several resources for her group's progress on a task. Examples of the way Lucia negotiated her leadership skills in the math classroom are provided below.

Excerpt 3: Getting organized. This episode takes place 10 minutes prior to Excerpt 1. Lucia and her group have just received a worksheet that asks them to graph three functions (L = Lucia; T = the teacher; SH = Shalina).

> L: Anybody needs rulers? (*starts to go over to cabinet*) Who needs rulers? Shalina, do you need one?
> SH: Yep. (*Lucia retrieves rulers for her group and joins in on their conversation, which is unrelated to the task at hand.*)
> L: Today is the 10th, you guys. (*Writes this on her paper; looks over at overhead. Shalina continues to chat with another student about the other conversation.*)
> L: So, they're going to be four graphs, right? (*looks toward overhead*)
> T: Um, how about three? (*calls out from front of class*)
> L: I mean three. That's what I meant. Damn, you guys! I'm hella horrible at making *t*-tables . . . trying to figure them out. So . . .

Lucia was the team captain for her group that day. As team captain, Lucia had the responsibility and authority to ask her group to justify their mathematical statements and to look for connections across mathematical ideas. Since her group was slow to move, she usurped the roles of Resource Manager and Facilitator as well, and attempted to prod the group forward (e.g., getting rulers, announcing the date, and requesting confirmation of the problem space). In contrast to the leadership role she enacted in science class—where she *told* her peers how to complete the worksheet—here she was orchestrating the group such that they would accomplish the task together. Her last line, in which she remarked that she was not very good at making *t*-tables, was again a subtle bid for the group's involvement.

Another leadership move that Lucia enacted, illustrated across all three excerpts, was to refocus the group back on their work together when individuals started to trickle off into working independently or socializing. She might do this by proposing an idea, asking a series of task-related questions, or comparing her answers with those of others. She generally addressed the group as a unit, instead of students individually, positioning the group as the source of mathematical progress. Sometimes she succeeded in leading the group toward productive conversation; at other times, her bids were ignored. Thus, while the mathematics classroom was organized for Lucia to take up various kinds of leadership roles within it, it was not necessarily the case that the other students consistently acted in concert with the norms and practices that created these opportunities.

What these excerpts show is that in being able to participate in mathematical activity in ways that she was disposed to do generally, Lucia had an opportunity to become a full participant in her mathematics classroom. Instead of being treated as irrelevant, or taking her peers off course, her bids to guide groupwork often led to productive mathematical activity.

By the time of an interview with her at the end of the school year, Lucia's view on mathematics and her capabilities with it had made a dramatic turn:

> I hated math my whole life, and for the first time ever I actually am interested, and doing it, and she [the teacher] explains it. . . . There are times when I've been out with friends or at home when I did things that I would never believe before in the past related to math . . . and it makes sense to me at that time when it comes to my head, and I'm like, "Oh. Okay."

This shift in her identity as a mathematics learner and its relation to her ability to take up her space in the classroom will be discussed at the end of the chapter.

SANTIAGO

Santiago was an outgoing, playful boy who identified himself as Latino although he was of mixed descent. He was not forthcoming with information about his home life, but he did not have the same material resources as many of his peers (e.g., clothing, school supplies, lunch, etc.), which suggests that his family did not have much income. He also mentioned that it was rare that anyone was available at home to help him with his homework.

Santiago's appearance was similar to that of the other Latino boys at Railside. He wore baggy jeans, T-shirts, shiny athletic shoes, and a baseball cap—often the same clothes repeatedly—but they were generally clean and neat. He may have been somewhat self-conscious about his appearance because of his girlfriend—also a student at the school—with whom he spent most of his free time. At one point I asked him why always wore red, and if this indicated his membership in one of the Latino gangs. He laughed and said that he was only in a clique—that his uncle and brother were the true "gangbangers." I asked him if it was difficult to quit a gang, and he said that it was expected that everyone in his family would join.

Santiago was enrolled in 1st-year math, English, science, and PE (which he despised). He was constantly joking around with his peers and teachers during class and had difficulty focusing on his work. His social behavior garnered different results, depending on the class. If the teacher was amused by his antics, he could sometimes be coaxed into getting to work. However, in his more traditionally structured biology class, the teacher often became extremely frustrated and angry with Santiago's animated behavior.

His participation in the mathematics class was markedly different. He was highly engaged in the classroom community and only a bit less so in the mathematics work. Although he rarely volunteered answers in class discussions, he helped his group make progress on mathematical problems in a variety of ways (i.e., multidimensionality). He came to class every day that I was there, even when he could have stayed home after a medical appointment. As was the case with Lucia, he developed a strong bond with his teacher, which was highlighted by a set of playful rituals. Santiago relished this attention, and the teacher appeared to enjoy his sarcastic and humorous nature. When I asked Santiago about his plans for the future, he said that he'd like to be a professional baseball player.

Santiago's participation across school contexts was similar to Lucia's in that he struggled to keep up with his work. However, there were two prominent features of his trajectory that were different from Lucia's and, in some respects, could be viewed as detrimental to his learning. The first was his struggle to stay focused on work, and the second was his strong desire to cultivate relationships with the people around him. In the sections that follow, I illustrate how features in his math classroom encouraged him to request structure around his work (i.e., encouraging responsibility) and to develop the bonds he needed in order to feel like he belonged within the community (i.e., promoting dialogical learning).

Demands Accountability

One of the most powerful features of the instantiation of mathematics reform pedagogy within the Railside classrooms was the high level of accountability for students to make sense of mathematical ideas and concepts. This was a primary means through which opportunities to learn were distributed among the students, and it fostered what Boaler (2006b) calls *relational equity*. At first, the teachers held the students accountable for contributing meaningfully to group and class inquiry. My findings and those of the other authors in this book indicate that over time the students took greater responsibility for managing themselves individually and collectively in learning mathematics.

This was true for Santiago as well, which I argue is an important way that he managed his space in the mathematics classroom. Given his tendency toward distraction and clowning around, the fact that he attempted to rein himself in to maintain focus was significant. In the excerpts that follow, I illustrate how Santiago engages the teacher, his peers, and his willpower to sustain his mathematical engagement.

Excerpt 1: "Be the mover." In this first vignette, the class is working in groups on problems that involve modeling equations with Lab Gear™. The teacher walks over to Santiago's desk and examines the group's work for a minute or so before she addresses Santiago (S = Santiago; T = the teacher; J = Julie).

T: Okay, Santiago, I want you to build this one, and I want you to be the mover.
S: Huh?
T: Instead of you waiting for Julie to do it.
S: All right. (*pulls the Lab Gear™ toward him*)
T: Right, Julie, put him to work.
S: Julie—she doesn't do the work! (*Julie flashes him a look of disbelief*)
J: What? (*smiling*)
T: You know how untrue that is. (*looks around the room*)
S: No, it's very true. (*grabs for blocks*) Hey, you know what the problem is, you tell me to be the mover, and you leave, and then I don't move anything.
T: I'm not . . . I'm waiting for you to dig around. (*A student is frantically waving his hand in the background.*)
S: You so lie as you leave! (*She turns to walk to over to the student. Santiago's group laughs.*)
T: So you keep digging. Don't touch it. I'm going right here. But Santiago, I'm watching you. (*After a few seconds she comes back over and watches him build the equation.*)

It wasn't news to Santiago that his behavior in his classes wasn't helping him achieve good grades, or the respect of his teachers. When confronted by his teachers about this fact, though, he would often respond with a snappy retort, or simply shut down. The vignette above starts to follow the path of the former, but then makes a drastic turn when Santiago explicitly addresses his problem. He complains to the teacher that after giving him instructions, she leaves, and he doesn't get anything done. It's not that he wants her help or anticipates getting confused; rather, he knows that he has trouble staying focused without supervision, and needs her to *hold him accountable* for following through. Here, Santiago was attempting to engage resources available to him in this math classroom (the teacher) to manage a challenging aspect of his participation. There is another important aspect of this vignette, which I briefly mention here, but will elaborate on in a section that follows. There was a fair bit of sarcasm in the exchange between Santiago and his teacher. This sarcastic banter was treated as playful, rather than derogatory, and served to strengthen their relationship.

Excerpt 2: "Getting hooked." In this second vignette, Santiago again attempted to a devise a situation to help him stick to the mathematics at hand. In this case, he did not need any prompting to do so. When the teacher came over to see how his group was doing, Santiago kept his head bent over the work. As this was uncharacteristic, the teacher decided to check in with him (S = Santiago; T = the teacher; J = Julie).

T: Are you doin' okay?
S: Yeah. (*looks up at the teacher and gives a halfhearted chuckle*) I just don't want to start talking.
T: You don't have to talk. Just keep writing. (*laughs and says in a clandestine way, putting her hand up to her face*) Why? Cuz you're miked?
J: Don't talk cuz he's gonna get hooked.
T: He is gonna get what?
J: Don't talk cuz he's gonna get hooked.
T: Oh.
S: Yeah!
T: Ahh, that's good self-control! (*Taps Santiago on the shoulder as she smiles. She turns around as if to walk away again, but turns back around and laughs.*) I was really worried about you when you came to this classroom. You're doing well!

Instead of relying on the teacher to maintain his focus this time, Santiago disengaged from the activity around him by keeping his head low. Julie appeared to be in support of this strategy, since she warned the teacher not to get Santiago "hooked" into a conversation. That he could enlist Julie's help to stay on task is reinforced by the class norm for group accountability, where group members are expected to help one another stay on task.

The teacher praised Santiago for his self-control, and what's more, told him that she had noticed a positive shift in his participation. This was in fact the *only* class in which he succeeded at times in gathering the resources he needed to engage constructively in schoolwork.

These two excerpts provide a window into a key feature of Santiago's trajectory of participation that was dealt with productively in his mathematics classroom. Unlike in Lucia's case, where aspects of her participation were *enhanced* by the classroom features, Santiago was able to *mitigate* his tendency toward distraction through them.

It is noteworthy that Santiago was willing to speak so publicly in class about his difficulty staying on task. Students with low confidence often try either to conceal their weaknesses or to attribute them to a problem with their surroundings. There are two factors that appeared to play an important role in Santiago's willingness to expose his vulnerability. One is that the discussions around Santiago's distractibility were usually marked by sarcastic and playful interactions. The second factor relates to another aspect of Santiago's participation across contexts: his attempt to cultivate relationships with those around him.

Cultivates Relationships. As suggested in the excerpts above, Santiago loved to tease everyone (e.g., the teacher, students, the researcher), and did so in saucy and humorous ways. This behavior was different from the silly and immature antics common for boys his age. Santiago was interested in endearing himself to others so that he could connect with them personally. His desire to cultivate relationships with others was another prominent feature of his participation across contexts.

Typically, the relationships that develop between the teacher and students in a mathematics classroom revolve around showing respect to the teacher, keeping students on task, and helping them make progress on mathematics work. While true for the Railside classrooms as well, the type of social arrangements that were organized around these goals were notably different. In contrast to classrooms where the norms for productive, respectful behavior mirror those of the dominant (White) culture, these were open to negotiation by the teacher and students at Railside.

Negotiability of norms for respectful and productive behavior important to *promoting dialogical learning* appeared to support Santiago's desire for acceptance and intimacy at school. As mentioned above, one of the ways that Santiago displayed his affection was through playful and sarcastic behavior. Researchers who study patterns of everyday discourse argue that this form of "permitted disrespect" is common to close friends or family and can evoke a sense of kinship and rapport among interlocutors (Straehle, 1993). The ritual teasing that went on among Santiago, his teacher, and his peers provided an opportunity for him to cultivate a sense of belonging in the classroom, and to reveal his struggle with focus.

Excerpt 3: "Take off your hat." The excerpt that follows illustrates the permitted disrespect and ritual teasing that took place at times in the mathematics classroom. While less focused on task-related mathematical activity, the episode provides evidence of the social bonding that underpinned Santiago's participation in the previous excerpts (S = Santiago; T = the teacher; J = Julie).

> T: Take your hat off! The principal was just in here. (*Makes a gesture like an upward "shooing" motion and an upward "you're out" motion with her left-hand thumb up. Santiago lifts his light blue hat.*)
>
> S: I know, that's why I took it off. (*takes his hat off, tipping it forward, and then places it back on his head*)
>
> T: No, take it off.
>
> S (*takes off his hat and curls it in his hand*): You want to hear about the principal?
>
> J: Tell her! Tell her! (*laughing loudly*)
>
> S: Do you want to hear it? (*smiles, holding his hat in his hand close to his lap*)
>
> T: Is it making fun of me? Is it something I did?
>
> S: It's nothing about you. It's the principal. While you were talking he was going to sleep. He was like this . . . (*pretends to nod off and then scratches his throat, forcing his eyes open*)
>
> J: He was like . . . he was like . . .
>
> T (*laughs*): That means he wasn't really paying attention. That's a good thing. That means he wasn't listening.

Several characteristics of this episode offer evidence of this particular form of rapport-building and learning within a dialogic space. First, the hat-off/on exchange that occurs at the beginning of the vignette alludes to a playful ritual that had developed between Santiago and the teacher. Santiago often entered the classroom wearing a hat, only to be lightheartedly chastised by the teacher. They would pretend to argue about it until one of them would eventually give in. The ritual was telling; hat-wearing in class was banned by the school, making the exchange a sign of resistance to authority, and in part revealing discrepancies between local and broader power structures. The teacher's utterance that "The principal was just in here" reinforces the spin on hat-wearing in this class.

This episode also depicts an unusual aspect of the relationships being forged by the teacher and her students. In it, there is a twist of roles, where the students exert a form of authority over the teacher. When Santiago suggests that he has information about the principal that the teacher might want to hear, he does so the way a friend might tell secrets to another friend. Julie's laughter-filled fervor for Santiago to "Tell her!" suggests that Santiago's information is both valuable and potentially inappropriate. The teacher's concern about the embarrassing nature of it further signals the role reversal, in which the teacher places herself in a vulnerable position with respect to the students. The teacher takes the bait and learns (from Santiago's playacting) that the principal fell asleep while observing her class. This could be viewed as a form of derision. Instead, the teacher's comment that it was good that the principal wasn't listening expands her vulnerability. The classroom social arrangements organized in this excerpt disrupted predominant power hierarchies between the teacher and students, and between the class and school, which cultivated community solidarity.

This series of episodes demonstrates that the classroom features of *encouraging responsibility* and *promoting dialogical learning* supported Santiago in taking up his space in the classroom. He was valued both for his mathematical prowess and for his humanness, to which he responded in kind by organizing a mathematical learning environment that met his most basic and guarded needs.

HOW "TAKING UP THEIR SPACE" WORKS

Together, these scenarios demonstrate aspects of Lucia and Santiago's participation within the Railside mathematics classrooms that honored features of their participation across contexts. They also provide interesting points of contrast. Features of Lucia's trajectory of participation—her tendency to demand to understand and to take a leadership role in group activities—were aligned with the norms of the Railside mathematics classrooms for mathematical sense-making and groupwork processes. Lucia was the kind of student who, if given the chance, was disposed to take charge of her learning (Gresalfi, 2009). Santiago, on the other hand, was disposed to lose his focus during class and to engage in non-task-related activity. Classroom features involving being accountable for contributing mathematically to groupwork and co-constructing norms for respectful and productive behavior provided the means for him to negotiate what it meant to have these tendencies and to learn mathematics at the same time. Santiago co-designed a learning environment that held him accountable for making progress in class activities and that revolved around kinship norms that promoted his sense of trust and affinity. In essence, both students were able to muster the support they needed from within the classroom community to participate actively in learning mathematics, and as such, they exemplify the notion of taking up space (Hand, in press).

Why is it important for students to take up their space in the mathematics classroom? What is the relation between taking up space and becoming a mathematics learner? Research on the notion of a *practice-linked identity* provides some insight into these questions. Practice-linked identities are defined as "identities that people come to take on, construct, and embrace that are linked to participation in particular social and cultural practices" (Nasir & Hand, 2008, p. 147). Developing a practice-linked identity, then, means that engaging in a particular social and cultural practice (such as learning mathematics) allows a person to be more fully oneself. Studies of out-of-school learning have found that youth from nondominant backgrounds who participate in community-based activities (Polman & Miller, 2010), sports (Nasir, 2008), or youth activism organizations (Kirshner, 2007) often prefer these activities to school-based learning because they perceive their participation in these activities to be aligned with who they want to become. As a result, they are more likely to engage deeply and in a sustained way.

To negotiate a practice-linked identity with respect to an activity requires in part that an individual is accepted (even affirmed) by the community and has the opportunity to participate in ways that matter to him or her. This is consistent with the notion of taking up space, and may explain why Lucia and Santiago came to participate more fully in their mathematics learning at Railside than they had in the past. We also see evidence of Lucia's practice-linked identity in the way that she came to mathematize aspects of her everyday life.

Features of the Railside mathematics classrooms that supported practice-linked identities were related to the features described earlier in specific ways. The *multidimensional* forms of mathematical activity deemed productive for classroom mathematics learning expanded the likelihood that students would be able to contribute significantly to class learning. This process was enhanced by the teachers' attention to opportunities to *assign competence* to students who might normally remain on the margins of classroom mathematical activity, and signal that mathematical competence was not confined to the dominant cultural group. The *group roles* permitted students to reinforce and try on identities as learners, and to limit the potential for particular students, or groups of students, to be privileged or marginalized in groupwork. The roles work in synergy with *encouraging responsibility* to promote *relational equity*, and to support students in demanding access to a key component of educational and professional success. Finally, I found that by *promoting dialogical learning*, students were recognized and celebrated for their humanness. Classroom power structures were also further disrupted in ways that brought the teachers and students together as a community.

Stories like those of Lucia and Santiago suggest that to begin to grapple with the participation gap, mathematics education has to broaden the lens on what it means (and takes) to learn mathematics. Based on research on practice-linked identities, learners must feel invited to participate in classroom mathematics communities, and to extend this invitation, classroom norms must be flexible enough for students to take up their space around mathematics learning in a variety of ways (Hand, in press). Findings from this chapter dovetail with research on *third space* (K. Gutiérrez, 2008; Gutiérrez, Rymes, & Larson, 1995), *funds of knowledge* (González, Moll, & Amanti, 2005; Gonzalez et al., 1993; Moll, Amanti, Neff, & Gonzalez, 1992), and *social justice education* (Gutstein, 2005; Moje, 2007), but speak directly to the relationship between equity and reform-based mathematics pedagogy.

Chapter 7

"Everybody Can Be Somebody"

Expanding and Valorizing Secondary School Mathematics Practices to Support Engagement and Success

Lisa M. Jilk

It is common for young women who come from Spanish-speaking countries to enter U.S. schools with big ambitions and a strong drive to achieve in an effort to create lives that are better than what they experienced in their home countries. They very often assume that education is *the* key for this success. Secondary math plays a role in this endeavor, because math knowledge supports access to higher education, workforce preparation, and the ability to critically engage in society and change the conditions of one's life (Martin, 2009). However, traditional school mathematics is often constructed very narrowly, privileges few ways to "do math," and valorizes speed and accuracy above other important mathematical skills and understandings. With so few ways to be mathematically successful, few students are. In fact, too few students choose to engage in secondary math and often fail to achieve their larger life goals. When this happens, students' quests to achieve greatness and better lives are often left unrealized.

The following case of Sandra, a young woman from Nicaragua, contributes to a discussion about students' mathematical experiences, especially those who are often marginalized by traditional school and classroom practices. Sandra's stories make visible issues of equity that emerge from her life as an immigrant woman and affect her engagement and success in secondary mathematics. In this chapter, I highlight how Sandra interpreted particular pedagogical practices used in her math classes at Railside through the lens of her salient "somebody" identity, specifically a version of school math that supported a broad array of mathematical practices and collaborative groupwork and teachers' practice of publicly assigning competence to students' mathematical strengths. I then use Sandra's case to illustrate how the intersection of her salient identity and Railside pedagogies supported Sandra's belief that she was intellectually capable of mathematical success, fueling her desire to engage with mathematics and furthering her development as "somebody" who could also achieve in life.

SECONDARY MATHEMATICS AS A MEANS TO A BETTER LIFE

It is common in the immigrant literature to hear of students who come to the United States from their home countries with dreams of "becoming somebody" (Flores-Gonzalez, 2002; Portales & Portales, 2005; Suárez-Orozco, 1997). Their goals often include lifting themselves and their families out of poverty and creating lives filled with quality education, good jobs, new homes, and happy and healthy families. Research shows that immigrants from Mexico or from countries in Central America strongly believe that education is the key to this better future (Cammarota, 2004; Suárez-Orozco, 1997; Weiler, 2000). It is *the* social capital assumed necessary to move up and out of poverty and often motivates young Latino/as to achieve academically at all costs, no matter the hardship. Stories such as these are often used to justify an argument that places sole responsibility for educational achievement on students, obscures the effects of structural factors on student outcomes, and assumes that hard work is the sole determinant of success.

This argument is pervasive in secondary schools, where the subject of mathematics enjoys particularly high status and is considered by many as a "powerful vehicle for social access and mobility" (Schoenfeld, 2004, p. 255). Students' lack of mathematical achievement is often blamed on their laziness, poor work ethic, or lack of family involvement. However, what many fail to consider is that U.S. secondary school mathematics is often very narrowly defined through available curriculum and teaching and learning practices that are socially and culturally constructed through lenses that position Latino/as near the bottom of the hierarchy of mathematical ability (Boaler & Staples, 2008; Civil, 2002; Ladson-Billings, 1994; Martin, 2007; Moschkovich, 2002). Hence, many students are pushed to the periphery of their mathematical learning communities when both content and learning processes are restricted, significantly impacting how they think about their abilities to achieve in life and become the "somebodies" they aim to be. If math education is assumed necessary for students' success, but students are unable to access it or feel driven away by teaching practices and curricula that position them as incapable, then they often come to believe that it is impossible to create the lives they have imagined for themselves and their families.

Sandra's case demonstrates how she made sense of her secondary math experiences and specific teaching practices used by her Railside mathematics teachers. In particular, Sandra focused on the multidimensional nature of school math, a groupworthy curriculum, and the practice of assigning competence in a way that supported and valued a broad range of important mathematical practices. Sandra interpreted these pedagogies to mean that she and her peers were not only equally capable of learning rigorous mathematics but that every student also had the potential to become "somebodies" in their future lives. In turn, as Sandra engaged with learning mathematics as "somebody," she drew from this salient identity as an intellectual resource and simultaneously developed as more of the "somebody" she wanted to become outside of the math classroom and in her life.

SOCIOCULTURAL PERSPECTIVES IN MATH EDUCATION

Research in mathematics education uses identity as a construct to better understand the relationship between learning and culture within mathematical communities of practice (Boaler, 1997a, 2002b; Boaler & Greeno, 2000; Cobb & Hodge, 2002, 2007; Martin, 2000; Nasir, 2002; Nasir & Hand, 2008). This research is important, as attention to the identities students create within the local cultures of mathematics classrooms has the potential to illuminate how students make sense of their math experiences and then make choices about how to act in relation to them. Additionally, understanding learning as a process that encompasses the construction of new ways of being provides for a unique balance between personal agency and influences from the broader communities in which students participate. This perspective prevents us from attributing students' failure or achievement to cultures located outside of school and simultaneously recognizes the role of the individual in academic pursuits.

Research that has been done about identity and mathematics learning has determined a reciprocal relationship between identity and practice. That is, within any learning community, inside or outside of school, students construct identities in practice. They shape self-understandings relative to the cultural activities afforded them, which means that their participation affects the construction of their identities (Nasir, 2002; Wenger, 1998). Simultaneously, identity affects participation. Students enter a practice with ideas about who they are and their purposes for engagement, which are situated in specific cultural contexts. Students understand practices and are then motivated to practice in particular ways because of these identities (Boaler & Greeno, 2000; Jilk, 2007; Martin, 2000; Nasir, 2002).

This chapter builds on previous research about identity and mathematics education by foregrounding the life story of one young woman and her self-understandings relative to her lived experiences in Nicaragua, the United States, and her secondary mathematics classrooms. It considers the communities outside of school in which she participated as critical sites for identity construction and the ways in which identity is privileged and supported within the context of learning mathematics.

I take a sociocultural perspective in this research, which recognizes that people shape identities through a dynamic process of living in the world. I view identities as "self-understandings with strong *emotional resonance* that people tell themselves or others and then try to act in accordance with" (Holland et al., 1998, p. 3). Identities are located in the narratives people tell about themselves. Identities provide direction to one's actions, and they are important sites from which people create new ways of being in the world.

I understand identities to be dynamic and in constant flux. I acknowledge that I never truly capture an identity, but only a snapshot of an identity that is in process of being developed. In my work, I am less concerned with cultural identities, or "identities that form in relation to major structural features of society: ethnicity, gender, race, nationality, sexual orientation" (Holland et al., 1998, p. 7), and more interested in identities that form in relation to practices and activities situated in socially constructed worlds. Therefore, I assert that people may have multiple identities. Identities may overlap and be intertwined, and may not be easily bound or distinguishable, potentially causing "tensions between past histories and present discourses and images that attract them or somehow impinge upon them" (p. 5).

Research often attends to the relationships between students' cultural identities and learning with an assumption that ethnic and gender identities most impact young people and their lives and school experiences. However, Holland et al. (1998) assert that "it is folly to assume that members of a voluntary group or even members of an involuntary — ethnic or racial—group are uniform in their identities" (p. 190). People also develop identities in different degrees of *salience* based on unique social situations, histories, and varying amounts of involvement in particular communities. The salience of an identity affects one's actions.

Therefore, rather than focus solely on ethnicity or gender identity, this research foregrounds the identities that the participants claimed to be the most salient in their lives,[1] the identities each authored "in relation to practices and activities situated in socially constructed worlds" (Holland et al., 1998, p. 3) and described with "emotional resonance" (p. 3), as well as the meanings they assigned to each. This decision to focus on the *salient identities* of young people reflects an assumption that students participate in multiple communities of practice in which they learn and create identities, as well as a decision to begin with the knowledge and voices of my participants so as to honor *their* understandings of their lived experiences (Bernal, 1998).

This case of Sandra is part of a larger 1-year ethnographic project focused on the cultural interpretations of secondary mathematics classrooms by four Latina immigrants who attended Railside High School. These young women immigrated to the United States from four different countries, began high school as English language learners, and successfully completed 4 years of college preparatory mathematics, including Advanced Placement Calculus. Narrative methods (Lieblich, Tuval-Mashiach, & Zilber, 1998) were used to foreground individual students and their life stories about their home countries, life in the United States, and their experiences in high school math as primary data sources. Other data included focus-group meetings and parent interviews.

WHO IS SANDRA?

I begin this chapter with some information about Sandra, her life in Nicaragua, her family, and her immigration experience. I then describe Sandra's salient identity as "somebody," explaining what this identity meant to her and in which communities she shaped these ideas about herself. I begin Sandra's case in this way because I argue that the identities students create outside of school are critically important for how they make sense of their in-school experiences.

Introducing Sandra

Sandra grew up in a small, poor barrio in Managua, Nicaragua, and lived there until she was 14 years old. She and her parents, her younger sister, Ellie, and her grandmother shared a tiny house that had sheet metal for the roof, cubicle separators to create bedrooms, and a kitchen outside on the back patio. In her barrio, Sandra was surrounded by family. Each of her father's sisters lived within blocks of her home, and she had upward of a dozen cousins nearby. Sandra spent her days going to school, helping in her mother's store, and babysitting her sister and cousins.

> My life when I was over there [in Nicaragua] . . . we went through a lot of economic problems, because it is very poor over there. So, it was difficult, for my mom especially. We had like a store, so we have to wake up early, wake up early and help my mom, then go to school. Then, do homework, like at night. But overall it was good. I had my family support always.

Sandra's parents, Carla and Miguel, never legally married but had lived together since their early 20s, and their families were very intertwined. They met in high school, but neither graduated. Carla was the matriarch of their Managua barrio. "Doña Carla" was how everyone referred to her. Carla ran a small restaurant and business out of the family's home and sold a variety of products that included women's clothing, shoes, and imported liquor. People regularly sought out Carla for advice, financial loans, or care for their children. Sandra's father, Miguel, worked in a coffee factory. He was present in Sandra's life but seemed to take a back seat to Carla's powerful presence.

Carla explained that even at a young age, Sandra's role as a daughter was critically important to the family's financial survival. When she was only 9 years old, Sandra was responsible for going to the market each day to buy food for the restaurant. She helped her mother cook, went to school, and arrived home around six o'clock each night to serve food and manage the money. Sandra was also a budding entrepreneur. She borrowed money from Carla to purchase fingernail polish, perfume, and adornments for women's hair. Then she sold these items for a profit in her mother's small store.

Even with such a meager income, Carla and Miguel managed to put enough money together each year to send Sandra to Catholic schools near Managua. Carla's attitude regarding education was similar to Central American immigrants in other studies who considered education as the key to a better future and therefore the most important thing she could provide for her daughters (Cammarota, 2004; Suárez-Orozco, 1997; Weiler, 2000). Carla explained, "Education is important, because it's valuable everywhere. You feel better as a person, more respected and economically too." Sandra agreed with her mother, and she believed that there was no better way to support her family and eventually become the person she wanted to be. Education was *the* vehicle for her success.

> Education is REALLY[2] important. For me knowledge is REALLY important. To be, to have knowledge is important for me, for my kids in the future. I want to give them a good life, a BETTER life, so that's why education is important. With education, I can be someone. I don't want to stay how I am right now. I want to SUCCEED! You know? So that's why education is important. I think you really NEED education in order to succeed. That's what I think.

Sandra spoke of her schooling experiences in Nicaragua with great fondness. She explained that the public schools in her home country "don't have nothing, no seats and no books." However, the Catholic school Sandra attended was "REALLY good." There, Sandra felt that she had received a high-quality education.

After more than 6 months without work and many attempts to sustain her family and neighbors with personal loans, the pressure to survive financially became too much for Carla to handle. Her debt had piled so high that she was unable to see any options for herself and her family in Nicaragua. As a result, Carla decided to take Sandra and Ellie and move to California. Although it was very difficult to leave her husband's family behind, Carla felt they had no choice. In addition, Carla explained that there were few options for her and her daughters in Managua, and she wanted them to have better educational and career opportunities. Although she expected a difficult transition, Carla felt that the benefits of moving made up for any challenges they would face.

"I Want to Be SOMEBODY!": Establishing a Salient Identity

At the end of an activity used to unearth salient identity in this study, Sandra was left holding a card that read, "college student." She explained that she was "happy that female was taken away." She was willing to let go of her identities as woman, Hispanic, and Catholic to hold onto the one thing that was most important to her, her education. Sandra wanted more than anything to eventually "be SOMEBODY. I want to help my mom, to help my FAMILY, so they can have a better life in the future." Education was assumed to be the key to achieving this "somebody" identity that Sandra desired.

> *Sandra*: It's my dream. It's my goal to have an education, to be in college, to be SOMEONE one day. So, I don't want to give it away for anything.
> *Lisa*: You say this a lot. In your interviews with me you say, I want to be someone. I want to be someone. You say this often.
> *Sandra*: I want to be . . . um . . . I want to have a career. I want to have a good job and so I can HELP people in my society. I want to be someone who can contribute to the society and to help ME and my family as well.
> *Lisa*: So, that's what it means to be someone?
> *Sandra*: Yeah. It doesn't really matter what is my job. I can be a doctor, a social worker, but I want to have a career, a profession so I can *help* people in the future.

While Sandra is simultaneously a daughter, sister, female, Catholic, and Nicaraguan, her "somebody" identity resonated throughout our interviews and was a strong catalyst for her decisions and actions. It was clear from the ways in which Sandra spoke about herself and how her mother spoke about her that Sandra was already a "somebody" when she arrived in the United States. She had been trained by her mother, the neighborhood matriarch, to be a "somebody" and had had many opportunities to hone her skills. When I asked Sandra to describe herself as a girl in Nicaragua, her response indicated that she was well on the road to somebody-ness. She characterized herself as active, responsible, fun, very active in school activities, hardworking, and very responsible:

> *Lisa*: When you think about yourself in Nicaragua, how would you describe yourself?
> *Sandra*: I would say . . . I was really intelligent, smart, but also I was very . . . um . . . I don't know, there was something about me. I was a very outgoing person. I was involved in clubs, helping other people, like teaching, but I had a lot of responsibilities, too.

Lisa: If I asked your cousins to describe you, what would they say about you?

Sandra: Oh, they would say, "Oh, she's fun, happy." I think they would say hard worker, responsible. I was *very* responsible for my age. I was . . . everybody was amazed how I was helping my mom and we were working together.

Carla described Sandra similarly. She seemed genuinely amazed by her daughter and all she had accomplished in her short lifetime:

Even when she was in the first grade, she knew something like twenty songs about chickens, about whatever. She knew so much. She learned the songs from Thalia, Laura Leon, and Gloria Atreve, and regarding things in school, when they did the play for Mother's Day, those things, she always knew how to dance in them. She was such a little one! But she could dance and everything. She was, for example, in the first or second grade and she helped someone who was in the third grade when they didn't understand something. Or when she was in the sixth grade, she helped cousins who were in the first or second grade, and maybe if they didn't know something, she would get down to reading and help them. She also took it upon herself to see that high school students . . . they don't read well. They don't know how to do a certain operation well, and she helped this person. Oh, also she was president of a group in school and they met at home and she held classes and was helping others like always. She got to be seven or eight, she became queen of the school. Doing everything.

When Sandra's story in the United States continued, so did her determination to maintain her salient identity as "somebody." However, Sandra's version of "somebody" shifted when she spoke of herself in the United States. Her stories indicated that she wanted to become a more altruistic "somebody," a person who achieved social status for the benefit of others. As a daughter, Sandra wanted to be "somebody" so she could take care of her mother. As a sister, Sandra hoped her somebody-ness was a model for Ellie. Sandra was thrilled to be "an example" for her younger sister and wanted Ellie to "be BETTER than me," to speak better English, do better in school, and eventually get a better job. As part of her large family, Sandra yearned to be "somebody" so that she could help her family out of poverty and "bring everyone here to find jobs." Being "somebody" drove Sandra's outlook on life. It guided her decisions and actions. She used it to determine her life's direction. This identity had the most salience for Sandra both in the way she talked about herself and in the communities in which she chose to participate.

Sandra's dual frame of reference, her ability to compare her current opportunities in the United States with her past realities in Nicaragua, aided in her creation of this salient identity as "somebody." Sandra's lived experiences in Managua and her periodic trips back to her home country created a point of reference from which she judged the quality of her life and her future aspirations (Ogbu, 1991; Suárez-Orozco, 1991). Sandra often referenced the "poverty" in which she had lived in Managua and the current social and economic conditions with which her father and extended family were still coping. Sandra's awareness of these issues was at the forefront of her mind when she spoke about one of her trips back home.

In addition, Sandra defined her goals and actions relative to the opportunities that she perceived as unavailable to her in Nicaragua. For example, Sandra explained that as a woman in Nicaragua it was unlikely she would ever attend college or earn enough money to support herself. She believed that the social conditions for women were so poor that "they have no choice but to stay with their husband." Sandra also believed that she would never acquire the same material amenities in Nicaragua as she could in the United States. Although Sandra's desires for such things seemed meager, such as her own bed, a bedroom door for privacy, or a telephone in the house, these requests were always constructed relative to what she had known in Nicaragua:

> Here I have things that I think I will NEVER have in Nicaragua. Like driving, like a cell phone. Like we didn't even have a phone in the house! Now, they have, but when I was there we didn't have any. So, here I have a lot of opportunities, a lot! I will never get them if I was in Nicaragua. I KNOW I will never have them.

While Sandra's role as a daughter and older sister took precedence over all else in her life, her "somebody" identity foregrounded how she played these roles. Among many other things, Sandra was a financial provider, role model, translator, co-parent, and chauffeur. She took her sister to school each morning and helped her mom find jobs that did not require much English. Sandra helped to pay the mortgage, sent money home to her family in Nicaragua, and attended college on a full-time basis. Becoming "somebody" was not purely for personal gain. Sandra did not yearn to be a public figure or movie star. She did not talk about owning a large house or jetting around the world in a private plane. Her goals might seem meager to some, but for Sandra, becoming "somebody" was the only way she knew to help her family achieve a better life than they had in Nicaragua.

> *Lisa*: If you could do anything in your life, what would it be?
> *Sandra*: Anything? I would go to Nicaragua and get all of my family here [to the United States] . . . everybody here, so they can work. They can have a better life. I will help all of my family get here. I will get a job

and I will help EVERYBODY to have a good job, my mom, my dad.
If I could do ANYTHING?! I will . . . I don't know *(laughs)*. [Sandra
seems overwhelmed by the idea of thinking about her life without
boundaries.]

Lisa: It's an exciting idea, isn't it?

Sandra: Yeah. Just to think about it. I think I would like to help people.
When I help someone it's a feeling I cannot explain. I would like to go
and to give food to them. I imagine myself traveling around the world
helping people. It's something like, oh my God! It's a feeling that is
hard to explain. I will . . . if I could do ANYTHING, I would get all
the money in the world and help the poor people.

RECIPROCITY IN THE MATH CLASSROOM: IDENTITY AS A RESOURCE FOR LEARNING AND LEARNING MATH TO SUPPORT IDENTITY

In many ways, Sandra's academic and social success paralleled the typical story
that many believe drives immigrant students to work so hard in school and sets
them apart from their U.S.-born peers. One might reasonably argue that Sandra's
dual frame of reference and goals as "somebody" made "present sacrifices in the
United States tolerable" (Valenzuela, 1999, p. 14) and acted as catalysts for her
hard work. While Sandra's situation may seem easy to explain using this argument, it has been shown that it often takes much more than hard work and te-
nacity for immigrant students to achieve academically. Even with the best-made
plans, Herculean efforts, and supportive families, research shows how, more often
than not, Latinas are often forced off their paths by structural and systemic barriers such as tracking (Olsen, 1997; Suárez-Orozco, 1997; Valenzuela, 1999), race
and gender discrimination (Valenzuela, 1999; Weiler, 2000), and negligence and
low expectations among school staff (Cammarota, 2004).

In this chapter, I demonstrate how Sandra used her salient identity as "somebody" as a resource to interpret her math experiences at Railside and support her
participation and learning. In particular, I focus on the use of a multidimensional, groupworthy curriculum and the practice of assigning competence, which
Sandra highlighted throughout her math stories. Through her interpretive lens
as "somebody," Sandra understood the ways in which she practiced school math
to be of great value, and she interpreted the social status she earned as a math
learner to mean that she was also valuable as a person. When the Railside math
teachers recognized and valued students' many ways of being mathematically
competent, Sandra came to believe that she and her peers were equally smart,
were equally capable of learning, and had equal potential for success.

Doña Sandra in the Mathematics Neighborhood

The "multidimensionality" (Boaler, 2004) of both content and practices foregrounded the stories Sandra told about math at Railside. Sandra explained that "doing" and learning mathematics required different ways of thinking and working with content, finding multiple solution paths, reasoning, justifying, and explaining ideas. According to Sandra, there was always more than one way to solve a problem, and she valued finding the "other ways." Sandra understood learning mathematics at Railside as something that required a lot of creative thinking:

> If you don't know how to get the answer, then you have to think of another way. For example, I have to solve a problem where you have to find the factors. If it's hard to do it that way [factoring], I can maybe use the quadratic formula to find the answer and be creative. Find OTHER ways, NEW ways to find the answer. It's not only ONE way. In math there's like DIFFERENT ways to solve a problem. You can actually invent NEW ways to solve problems. So you have to be creative.

This version of school mathematics that Sandra described included an integration of both "everyday" and "academic" mathematics (Moschkovich, 2002, p. 2). It included skills and knowledge both central to the work of mathematicians and touted by the National Council of Teachers of Mathematics (NCTM, 2000) as important process standards necessary for deep understanding of mathematical concepts. In the quote below, Sandra explained that learning "school" mathematics required her to do more than use procedures from a teacher to solve problems. Sandra was expected to "try to make sense" of given information, reflect on her problem-solving approaches, and construct her own understanding about *how* something worked, building from both prior knowledge and new information generated in class. The mathematical practices Sandra described included a balance of activities that included aspects of mathematics reflected in both the practices of mathematicians and those used in everyday life:

> I have to understand, how did the teacher get this? How can I get this for *x*? Things like that. Trying to make sense. How can I get this 3*x*? I don't get it. What happened? I have to know what's going on in the problem. I have to know where I got each number. WHY this 4*x* is negative. I need to know WHY and use it later.

In addition to the multidimensional version of school mathematics that Sandra had access to at Railside, she emphatically recounted the "challenging, fun and interesting" math activities included in her math classes. Sandra remembered the many projects, presentations, "big posters," and Problems of the Week her teachers used as part of their multidimensional curriculum. As a student, Sandra was not privy to the professional decisions that her teachers made about what and how to teach, so it is impressive that her stories about high school math included a central feature of their teaching practice, groupworthy tasks. These "big" problems that Sandra recalled as "fun and interesting" were designed by her math teachers to be "true group tasks" (Cohen, 1994a, p. 22) such that students needed one another as intellectual resources to solve the problem. Groupworthy tasks are "challenging, open-ended, and require many different intellectual abilities and resources" (p. 22; see also Tsu, Lotan, & Cossey, Chapter 8 this volume).

These groupworthy tasks and the multidimensionality highlighted by Sandra necessitated intellectual interdependence among students in order to be mathematically successful. The nature of the tasks and the teachers' expectations for students' processes and final products made it impossible to work alone. To successfully learn mathematics at Railside, students needed to work together such that they built from one another's ideas and prior knowledge, made connections to new strategies, justified their reasoning, and engaged in the intellectual messiness of sense-making. In the following quote, Sandra explained that she enjoyed learning with others. She appreciated the interaction and the opportunities to talk with her peers, and she considered these opportunities supportive of her learning. While these collaborative practices were different from how Sandra had experienced school mathematics in Nicaragua, she believed that it was "really helpful" to work in cooperative groups, because they availed her of alternate intellectual resources, especially her classmates and their math ideas.

> *Lisa*: Were your math classes in Nicaragua different from your math classes at Railside?
>
> *Sandra*: I think I like it here better, the way that they do it, in groups with people. With people like you learn from your mistakes. You can learn from others. Like if I don't get something, other people explain it to you and I can understand it a little bit more. In Nicaragua the teachers explain, and we are all like in rows and if you get it you get it, and if you don't get it you can ask the teacher later or something. But, it's not like a group thing. I really like working with people. So, that's what I really like. In high school, yeah, I think groups are an excellent idea, excellent idea. Like for me it was helpful personally in high school. Being in groups was really helpful.
>
> *Lisa*: What was helpful about it?
>
> *Sandra*: I learned *from* other people. I learned from my friends. I learned from the teacher. And especially I learned that I could help others, too. I felt good helping others and explaining to other people. That makes

you feel good. Like when you help someone, you know, "How do you get this? Can you help me with this?" I want to study more so I can help more.

Sandra understood how working together facilitated a different kind of thinking and learning than was available had she been isolated from her classmates. This was evident in her statement above when she referred to learning "from others," learning "from your mistakes," and hearing different mathematical explanations as she tried to "understand it a little bit more." In addition, the last part of Sandra's quote suggested that she interpreted these opportunities to work collaboratively with her peers as a chance to actualize her identity as "somebody" while she engaged in learning mathematics.

Recall that Sandra had begun constructing her version of "somebody" when she lived in Managua, and a significant part of this identity included helping others. She helped her mother run the family store. She helped care for her younger sister. She helped her grandmother cook, her cousins study, and the older kids at school with their homework. Sandra also learned from her mother, the neighborhood matriarch, how to be "somebody." Her mother, Doña Carla, was "someone important," the woman who took care of her family and her neighbors, the person to whom others turned to in times of hardship and need. Similarly, Sandra wanted to become "somebody" in the United States so she could help her family, send money back to Managua, and use the status of her college education and her future job to take care of others.

In this same way that Sandra's mother had become Doña Carla for her family and friends, Sandra became Doña Sandra in her mathematics classes at Railside High. The construction of school math as multidimensional and the use of collaborative groupwork afforded Sandra opportunities to act as a math learner in ways that aligned well with her identity as "somebody." A more expanded construction of school mathematics lends itself to more exploration and less memorization. It requires less time memorizing and practicing routine problems and more time searching for new strategies and making connections to others' ideas. Railside's version of school mathematics created a need for students to rely on one another and to use one another as intellectual resources in order to be successful.

Sandra not only enjoyed this type of learning community, she thrived in it. Her strengths as "somebody" became intellectual resources that she could contribute to the collective learning process. Sandra knew how to work with others. She knew how to ask for help. She had learned how to bring her ideas to the table so they might be considered by others for the benefit of the group. Sandra's salient identity as "somebody" was necessary for herself and others to be successful with learning math. Additionally, Sandra interpreted this collaborative endeavor of math learning as an opportunity to more fully develop the altruistic version of "somebody" that was salient to her identity. She wasn't only getting something from her peers when they worked together, she was also giving away. Being a math learner at Railside afforded Sandra an opportunity to "learn how to help others, too" as she worked toward being somebody in the world who could eventually help and support others. In this way, participating as a math learner at Railside supported Sandra's salient identity and further enabled her to become the kind of person she imagined herself to be.

"We Are All Equal!"

As part of Sandra's "somebody" identity, she considered all people as "equal" no matter their class, ethnicity, gender, language abilities, or religion, and she had a strong sense of what it meant to be treated "just like everybody else." Sandra's stance against inequality was directed at the forms of injustice she had experienced as a child in Managua and then as an immigrant in the United States, and she used this identity as a lens to interpret new situations she encountered. Sandra often referred to her life in Managua to compare how little people had relative to what was available to her and her family in California. She was adamant that everyone should have enough food to eat and clothing to wear. She believed that children should not have to work in the streets, and that opportunities to work and earn a reasonable financial living should be available to all. These passions for equality extended to school as well. Sandra insisted repeatedly that all students were "equal," and mathematics teachers should assume all of their students to be intelligent and capable of success:

> I want them [teachers] to feel that we [students] are all EQUAL, and that we are all capable of learning. I want them to see ALL the students as equal. Forget about religion. We are all equal and here for the same purpose, to learn, to learn the subject. But some people think that because they are Asian, they are really, really smart. Oh, they're Latino, they're not that smart. It's okay if they get an F. You know? Some people think like that, and it's not right. It doesn't really matter how we look. It doesn't really matter. We are there for the same purpose, to learn math. The same thing, it doesn't matter if we have a ring in our nose or if we are ugly, pretty, it doesn't MATTER. Their JOB is to give the BEST of themselves and be equal with ALL of the students. Because we are ALL capable. We are ALL smart.

Sandra was critically aware of the many ways in which social inequities are often perpetuated in schools. In particular, she recognized how racism and sexism could look and feel and was very astute as to how she might be positioned by her peers and teachers as unequal to her classmates in high school. Throughout our conversations, Sandra consistently spoke about White and Asian students, boys, and native English speakers as the students who were expected to be smarter and more capable, and she recalled several classes where only the "White students" were expected to participate, or the "girls were picked on" by the teacher in an effort to catch them being wrong.

Sandra spoke differently about her math classes at Railside. While she often referred to the racial diversity within these classrooms, she talked about it in a positive way rather than as a tool for pitting students against one another or discerning the smart from the dumb. She also spoke about how she felt "equal" in her mathematics classes. Unlike many immigrant students who are assumed to be incapable of learning math because they cannot speak English or are placed in remedial courses because the classes they took in their home countries are assumed to be less rigorous than those in the United States, Sandra felt positioned "as equal" to her peers. She believed that she had as much potential for success as her White, Asian, male, and English-speaking peers:

> Like they [math teachers] see you as equal, not only Latinos, but also, you know, Indians or people from other parts of the world, not only Asian or White people. Nobody underestimated that I was not smart enough to be in that class. Like everybody looked at me like, "I can do this problem too. YOU can do it. EVERYBODY can do it."

Being "equal" had a particular meaning for Sandra. It did not mean that her teachers were *equally* friendly to all students, or that they spoke Spanish *and* Chinese, or that every student received the same grade. Being equal for Sandra meant that she was positioned as "somebody" in mathematics. She was assumed by her teachers to be intellectually capable of learning, capable of achieving, capable of success. Maybe more importantly to Sandra, she was assumed to be *as* capable as the students whom she thought had high status in mathematics, particularly those who were White, Asian, male, or native English speakers.

In addition to the multidimensional curriculum, assigning competence was a specific pedagogical tool used by Railside math teachers to explicitly value the many intellectual contributions students made while engaged with learning mathematics. Assigning competence is a form of public valorization of diverse mathematical practices. Its purpose is to both increase the intellectual status of all students (Cohen, 1994a) and to expand what is commonly thought of as school math by helping students recognize the myriad valuable ways of thinking and doing mathematics that are interesting and required for success.

Sandra interpreted this practice of assigning competence to mean that her prior knowledge, unique ways of thinking about math, and the skills she used during class had real value. Her "NEW ways to find the answer," the creativity she used to solve problems, the questions she asked and justifications she offered were important and beneficial in these classrooms. This multidimensional curriculum not only provided opportunities for students to use a variety of mathematical skills and understandings, but actually required them in order to be successful. Teachers' assigning of competence to these myriad practices when deemed useful and necessary to the task at hand helped Sandra and her peers recognize their mathematical strengths and important contributions to learning.

In addition to feeling valued as a math learner, Sandra expressed an understanding of equality that went beyond herself and embraced her peers as well. In her math classes at Railside, it was not only the Latino/as who were positioned as equal or as intelligent as other students. It was not only the students who couldn't speak English who were singled out and made to feel good about themselves. According to Sandra, "everybody" was considered smart and capable of learning. There were so many different and valuable ways to "do math" at Railside that Sandra considered everyone equally smart and equally capable of success. She explained,

> I think everybody is smart in math. You just have to work hard . . .
> participate a lot and explain to other people, know how to solve things, be
> able to use your rules, your notes, how to think like, "How can I solve this?"
> That's smart.

This sense of equality that Sandra felt in her mathematics classrooms was so strong that she even suggested that her academic success might have depended on it:

> Maybe that's why I succeed, I think. I went to all the math things, because
> they saw me and all my Latino friends as equal. They saw that I was ABLE
> to succeed, and I was doing good in everything. But other people in other
> schools give more importance to White and Asian than Latino, because
> maybe they are minority people. I don't understand why it is like that. I
> have no idea why.

Everybody Can Be "Somebody"

It is unusual to hear a young person describe secondary mathematics classes as spaces in which all students are considered intellectual equals. Sandra's stories are especially poignant at a time in history when school mathematics more often acts as a gatekeeper than a great equalizer. It is likely that the equality Sandra felt in her mathematics classes stemmed largely from the mathematics teachers at Railside, who "were deeply committed to equity" and made extraordinary efforts to support each student's mathematical success (Boaler & Staples, 2008, p. 627). One might reasonably argue that any young person would benefit from a philosophy and work ethic that put equity at its center. A combination of hard work and a strong commitment from a teacher should lead to academic success. However, it has been shown to take more than a professed stance toward equity, a curriculum aligned with reform efforts, or even a deliberate stance *against* inequity to support students' mathematical achievement (Boaler, 1997b, 2004; Lampert, 2001; Lubienski, 2000).

Current research done by de Abreu and Cline (2007) claims a relationship between the mathematical practices valued in schools and the social identities students assume to be available to them in their futures. When teachers assign more status to certain ways of thinking and doing math in school than others, the identities students construct for themselves and their peers relative to these practices are affected. For example, in de Abreu and Cline's study, "school mathematics" was valued more highly than some "categories" (p. 124) of mathematical practices that students and their families used in their out-of-school contexts. For example, the mathematics used to manage a family farm was assigned less value by teachers than the formal mathematics used in school. Students were not encouraged to use or build from their mathematical resources as farmers when engaged in "school mathematics," and as a result, students assumed that those who excelled in "school mathematics" as opposed to "peasant mathematics" (p. 120) would enjoy higher status in life.

Students also made assumptions about the mathematical abilities of people based on the status of their jobs or the status of their cultures. For example, students believed an office administrator to be more mathematically able than a farmer, because office administrators were more highly valued than farmers in the community where these youth lived. Similarly, a young person from Pakistan was assumed by his teacher and peers to be less mathematically able because Pakistan was not valued as a country relative to the country in which this study was done. In both cases, the link between mastering school mathematics and the social identities that students assumed would be afforded by this mastery was the valorization of certain mathematical practices in school.

Similarly, Sandra understood that if she was good at school mathematics, then she could be "somebody" in life. She interpreted the competence assigned to her mathematical participation to mean that she was intellectually equal to her peers and potentially able to achieve "somebody" status in her future. Sandra could earn a college education, find a good job, and support her family. For Sandra, school math was defined very broadly. It was multidimensional. It required a variety of mathematical practices, such that students could try "different ways" to solve problems and "be creative" with their processes. This multidimensional nature of math and the status it was assigned at Railside literally expanded the definition of "school" mathematics and who could be good at it. So as Sandra used mathematical ideas and practices she had learned as a student in Managua or as a young girl working her family's store, she felt valued as a competent mathematics learner, and in turn she believed that she had value as a person. Sandra interpreted her position as "somebody" vis-à-vis her engagement with multidimensional, groupworthy curriculum and its valorization through teachers' assignments of competence.

According to Sandra, everybody could be good at mathematics. Everybody was "equal." Everybody could be "somebody." She defined mathematical competence very broadly, much like she defined school mathematics itself. Sandra explained that there were a variety of ways to be mathematically "smart." It was "more than doing things fast" or only getting a right answer. In fact, Sandra explained, even smart math people can do things wrong sometimes:

> It's more than doing things fast. You can be smart and do it wrong, too. You don't have to be right all the time. It doesn't mean you aren't smart if you do it wrong. Because in math, sometimes you can be SO smart and you can get the wrong answer, especially in math. So, like, everybody is smart in math I think.

The fact that there were many ways to be mathematically competent given the multidimensional nature of school math at Railside and the public value assigned to the many ways students were mathematically competent contributed to Sandra's understanding that she and everyone around her had status as people. It did not matter whether it was "peasant math" or "farm math" or "school math" that students were using. The range of mathematical practices necessary and valued through the use of the multiple-ability curriculum and the assignment of competence included all of these forms of mathematics and more. Whatever version of mathematics students brought to the task was important. As Boaler and Staples (2008) stated, "When there are many more ways to be successful, many more students are successful" (p. 630). If everyone can be mathematically smart, then everyone is "equal," and everyone can become "someone."

CONCLUSION

People develop identities as a result of participating in communities of practice (Nasir, 2002), but they also enter communities with salient identities through which they translate and assign meaning to new experiences. Sandra entered her secondary mathematics classes with a salient identity as "somebody," which she constructed through her experiences as a child in Nicaragua; a dual frame of reference based on her lived experiences in Nicaragua and the United States; and the strong messages she received from her mother, Doña Carla, about the importance of helping people. Sandra used this salient identity as a lens through which she interpreted her experiences with a multidimensional mathematics curriculum and the valorization of diverse mathematical practices. She interpreted her experiences to mean that she and her peers were equally intelligent and equally capable of success in school mathematics and in life.

In addition, Sandra understood the learning opportunities created by the use of collaborative groups and a multidimensional curriculum as opportunities to develop her "somebody" identity. In her math classes at Railside High, Sandra was given space to further develop the skills and dispositions as a "somebody," because the curriculum and groupwork structures required these strengths. Sandra chose to engage in these opportunities so that she could learn more math and support her peers' learning. In this way, not only did Sandra use her strengths as a "somebody" to help her participate and learn mathematics; simultaneously, her experiences with learning math at Railside supported her to continue developing her salient identity as "somebody." Sandra was "somebody" when she entered her math classrooms, and she was still "somebody" when she left, but a different version, a stronger version, a more capable version, a version that was closer to the "somebody" she wanted to become.

Unfortunately, Sandra's secondary school math experiences are not widely repeated across the United States. Too often students enter schools and classrooms with great intentions to become "somebodies," only to be met with a lack of appropriate resources or opportunities to support these quests. A narrow version of school mathematics and the inability to recognize and value a wide range of mathematical strengths and practices contribute to this problem. As a result, young people too often choose to disengage from learning. What might appear to be stubbornness, laziness, or incompetence on the part of a student to do mathematics might actually be related to the lack of status assigned to students' mathematical practices. It might also be the result of an inability to make connections and build from the knowledge the student constructed elsewhere and the mathematics he or she is trying to do now. A narrow construction of mathematics may in fact alienate the same students we are trying to better serve because the available practices for school mathematics may seem unusual or strange. Sandra's case demonstrates the power of valorizing a diverse range of mathematical practices, such that all students come to believe that they, too, and not only a certain few, are capable of success.

Part III

TEACHER LEARNING AND PROFESSIONAL COMMUNITY

Previous parts of this book have described what mathematics teaching and learning looked like at Railside. This part clarifies that this teaching and learning were not the end product of a few brilliant teachers who had a natural gift for innovative, equitable instruction, but rather a work in progress to which many teachers with a wide variety of strengths contributed over more than 20 years. The chapters in this part illustrate the evolution of the professional community at Railside, the character of moment-to-moment interactions to support both teacher and student learning, and the practices that Railside teachers saw as central in building and sustaining their department. Throughout, there are clear parallels between Railside teachers' views of themselves and of students, all as learners who need and deserve one another's support, respect, and care.

In Chapter 8, former department chair Ruth Tsu, with Rachel Lotan and Ruth Cossey, describes the history of the Railside math department's early engagement with mathematics reform. They tell the story of the department's shift from working in traditional ways (with each teacher teaching in relative isolation) to collaborating, giving teachers the safety, freedom, and responsibility to be vulnerable and take risks in front of one another—in essence, to learn together. Their account shows how the department leveraged teachers' commitment to working together to change practices that did not work for students and to adopt practices that were revolutionary, from taking control of hiring to detracking their mathematics program to observing in colleagues' classrooms to doing challenging mathematics together. As Tsu, Lotan, and Cossey describe, these practices in turn reinforced teachers' rethinking of traditional assumptions about what it meant to be successful in mathematics and who could do it.

Chapters 9 and 10 zoom into conversations between Railside math teachers. Ilana Seidel Horn's Chapter 9 uses conversational episodes to show how teachers at Railside engaged in "transformative learning" in their talk with one another. She compares how mathematics teachers at Railside and another school, South High, either reproduced (at South) or challenged (at Railside) traditional ways of thinking about students, mathematics, and teaching through everyday conversation. Her data show that teachers talked with one another in these professional communities in ways that drew on and reinforced shared values and goals. At Railside in particular, these conversations reveal the ways in which the professional community supported teachers in challenging traditional notions of mathematics teaching, learning, and ability.

In Chapter 10, Ilana Seidel Horn and Judith Warren Little analyze the way in which teachers in Railside's Algebra Group discussed problems that arose in their practice, validating one another's experiences but not stopping there. Using a transcript from an episode in which a new teacher frets over classroom "mayhem" as an example, Little and Horn demonstrate how the Algebra Group made problems of practice objects of collective inquiry. They show that incidents that could have been (and, in their research at other sites, were) treated as "venting" about problems of practice were treated by teachers in the Algebra Group as opportunities to problem solve and learn together.

In Chapter 11, Carlos Cabana, Barbara Shreve, and Estelle Woodbury describe some of the practices that they and their colleagues at Railside developed to support teacher collaboration and learning. They highlight doing math together, working on groupworthy department goals together, distributing leadership, hiring toward a vision, and providing deliberately structured support to new teachers.

All of the chapters in this section can support teachers, administrators, and researchers to reflect on ways in which departments take shape through a combination of structural factors and teachers' everyday conversations with their colleagues. What becomes evident across the chapters is that the departmental community and infrastructure and the continual evolution of the shared vision were critical to the endeavor of providing high-quality math instruction.

Chapter 8

Building a Vision for Equitable Learning

Ruth Tsu, Rachel Lotan, and Ruth Cossey

The purpose of this chapter is twofold. First, it provides some context and history for the department-initiated mathematics reform work at Railside, and second, it describes the principles and processes of Complex Instruction, the set of pedagogical strategies that formed the basis for Railside's equity pedagogy. We begin with the historical context of the reform efforts at Railside, and then describe the core tenets of Complex Instruction, the pedagogical approach that constituted the foundation for the pedagogy the department developed.

HISTORICAL CONTEXT OF REFORM EFFORTS AT RAILSIDE

The Impetus for Reform

In the mid-1980s, Railside mathematics teachers were struggling with the reality that a large number of students were not successful in their learning of mathematics. In the context of the school's going through a routine accreditation process, students spoke candidly and passionately with the visiting school accreditation team. They expressed their frustration with their math classes and complained that they were not learning mathematics. The accreditation committee's final report contained only terse recommendations, beginning with the statement that the department was to "develop an aggressive posture in implementing mathematics reform." There were no specific suggestions about how to do this. It was essential that the mathematics department confront students' lack of learning and make changes. It was work the faculty needed to address as an entire department. Ruth Tsu served as department chair for the first 8 years following the accreditation report, and much of this chapter is written in the first person, from her perspective.

While teachers were unclear about where to begin this work, two things seemed important. First, it was critical to seek information. The full-time math teachers all accepted the responsibility to begin to meet regularly, to share ideas of possible resources, to attend classes and conferences, and to implement what was learned. Second, it was clear that there were some longstanding practices that needed to be changed, such as how teachers were assigned to classes and how new teachers were hired. The teacher assignment issue hindered equitable teaching in two ways: (1) Administrators had often assigned non-math teachers to teach math classes to fill out their schedules, even if those teachers had neither preparation for nor interest in teaching math, and (2) the teachers with the least experience and preparation were those assigned to the low-track classes. With respect to hiring practices, mathematics teachers were hired by the principal from a pool of candidates who came from the district. This practice had failed to elicit highly qualified math teachers, and the department knew it would need to do some specialized recruiting and have more of a say in the hiring process. The administration agreed to work with the math department regarding hiring new math teachers and also teacher assignments. The current department chair wanted to step down, but no one was particularly interested in taking on the leadership. Ruth was amenable as long as the entire department was committed to making serious efforts at reform. Everyone agreed, and the department was ready to move forward—but how?

Learning to Talk and Work Together

We, the math department, knew that we would need to work together differently, yet there was no precedent or set of existing practices to draw upon. Like many mathematics departments, teachers taught on their own, met infrequently, and rarely set foot in one another's classrooms. The normal practice of the prior department chair had been to provide teachers with textbooks and let them know that he was available to answer questions. Luckily, while the accreditation report did not make specific recommendations, it did come with some funding. Because we knew of the 1985 California Math Framework and our former chair knew Lyle Fisher, the director of the Bay Area Math Project (BAMP), the department quickly decided to use some of the money to learn about the framework. We appreciated that the framework prioritized student problem-solving, reasoning, and explanation. This was quite different from the focus on skills and procedures in our then-current math classes—especially the remedial courses we had created with the goal of improving the learning of our struggling math students.

In the 1986–1987 school year, Lyle Fisher led a series of five full-day workshops for teachers in the department. Each workshop included time to work on tasks from one of the content strands of the Framework, and we were encouraged to talk together to solve the math tasks we were given and explain our thinking to one another. The afternoon provided the opportunity to learn how these and similar tasks could be incorporated into our classrooms. Every teacher agreed to implement at least one of these tasks prior to the next workshop and to share what they were learning at department meetings. We began to use department time for conversations about teaching and learning, with teachers sharing what they learned from attending the problem-solving workshops and from using new materials with students. Teachers of low-track classes spoke of their students' positive response to challenging problems. Some were surprised to find that students in the low-track classes were willing to engage in working on complex problems, and very often were successful in solving them and explaining their thinking. Teachers began to realize that there was less difference between the participation and learning of high- and low-track students when using rich tasks with a focus on problem-solving than with problems that were mostly procedural. Following these workshops, teachers began to use a greater variety of instructional practices in their classrooms, and problem solving started to become more central.

As teachers shared both experiences they were proud of and those that troubled them, a culture of trust began to develop. One teacher wrote,

> The camaraderie and support in meetings was stimulating, affirming and energizing. Two important elements of all meetings were food and laughter. (Because of the smell of freshly brewed coffee and the sound of laughter emanating from the classroom where we met, some referred to our meetings as "parties.") The laughter grew out of sharing from our classrooms and our discussions, but it was never derisive or at the expense of our students or each other. (Tsu, 1998, pp. 20–21)

During these meetings, we began to move the desks into a circle so we could see one another and communicate more directly. This also carried over into our classrooms. Because our entire high school was in the process of replacing the old and highly marred classroom furniture, each teacher could choose either individual student desks or tables and chairs. We chose tables, since sitting at tables facilitated student interaction in groups and the larger and flat surfaces also made it easier to use manipulatives, which had been introduced through the workshops. We developed a checkout system of classroom sets of a variety of manipulatives, including pattern blocks, geoboards, four-color tiles, and various geometric shapes. We also made sure that every teacher had a classroom set of materials that were used regularly, and we prioritized funding for additional materials to support learning.

As teachers talked together about specifics, they were beginning to get a sense of the value of talking and working together. At one department meeting, the question arose of how we could better support our students' learning. This question led us to launch a tutoring program, with teachers volunteering to meet with students after school. Thus, teaching math at Railside increasingly became a public activity. Teachers began to see themselves as responsible for the math learning of every student in the school as if they were their own, and students realized they could come to any of the teachers if they had a question or needed extra help. Also, the conversations that started during tutoring time were sometimes taken up in a department meeting. For example, the mention of a concept that many students struggled to better understand led to a discussion of how each of the teachers presented the concept and strategies to support students' learning.

In these ways, a very ordinary department grew into a department that supported a rigorous set of professional practices. When professional development days were scheduled, we arranged for the department to use part or all of the time for the work we were doing together. We also arranged to meet together after school and in the summer. In the late 1990s teachers created and formalized an annual "Algebra Week" summer institute; weekly algebra team meetings; language for talking productively about students; language about teachers' successes and frustrations in supporting student learning; routines for new teacher induction and support; and ways of sharing curriculum, lesson plans, and student work. These structures developed and persisted because they contributed to teachers' effectiveness and sense of both personal and professional support, but they were not created instantaneously nor as a complete package.

Detracking

At the time, Railside contained grades 8 through 12, and mathematics was heavily tracked as students moved through their high school years. Figure 8.1 shows the labyrinthine layers of tracking in place in the math department at the time of the accreditation review, in the spring of 1986.

Figure 8.1. Math Department Tracking in Spring 1986

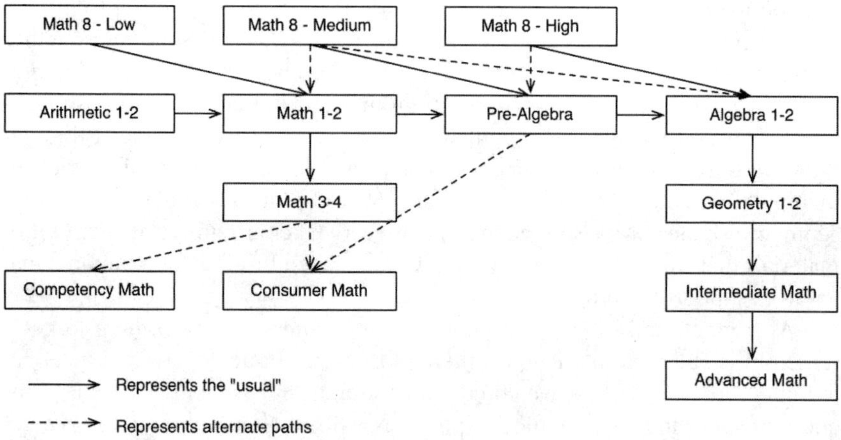

In our first year of intense engagement with the 1985 California Math Framework, we began to consider our tracking practices as a potential source of students' lack of math success. Previously, tracking had been *expanded* as a response to students' lack of success, based on the belief that some students could not handle more advanced mathematics. Now, teachers were able to reassess these assumptions because we had given students challenging mathematical tasks and had seen the results. After a period of reading and discussing articles documenting the negative effects of tracking on nearly all students—combined with teachers' experiences with introducing more problem-solving into the curriculum—the department made the decision to detrack all 8th-grade mathematics classes for a period of at least 3 years, effective the following year.

The decision to detrack was the most far-reaching decision the Railside teachers had made, and there was no way they could anticipate or realize its impact on students and teachers. The conviction that all students can learn—underpinning teachers' need to continue to learn—was not yet a departmental principle. However, this move prompted teachers to realize that they needed one another's ideas and support to make sense of heterogeneous classes and be successful with students. As the professional community grew, teachers were asking tough questions of one another about teaching and learning and becoming more willing to risk exposing areas of vulnerability. As a result, structures and practices were being created not only to help students but also to support teachers. One teacher wrote:

> As we learned together we began to probe deeper, to become more reflective. But our questioning, reflecting and probing was always grounded in our work in the classroom with our students. We came to view our classrooms as laboratories in which we put into practice the theories that we had generated in our meetings. Just as we worked together to develop tasks, assessments, and instructional strategies, so too we sought the assistance of our peers in observing our students as they worked on those same tasks. We were learners together. Inside our classrooms we were learning about our students, what they knew, what they needed to learn, what approaches facilitated their learning. Outside the classroom we were striving to make sense of what we saw in the classroom and to search for further resources which would enable us to more effectively work with our students and support their learning. (Tsu, 1998, pp. 17–18)

Very gradually, teachers began to visit one another's classrooms. Those who shared the responsibility of teaching the new untracked classes quickly realized how interdependent they were—planning the tasks, giving feedback to one another about the questions that were most useful to generate thinking and discussion, and beginning to evaluate their students' work. This practice led to deeper discussions about curriculum, instruction, and assessment choices that would further improve students' learning.

Developing Broader Communities and Partnerships

Another important aspect of our work at Railside was tapping into a range of communities and information networks for support. This included attending at least one mathematics conference each year, for instance the California Mathematics Council Conference at Asilomar, where we met before the conference to share the kinds of information teachers would each be seeking at the conference, and which workshops each planned to attend. A follow-up meeting was scheduled for soon after the conference, where teachers would share their learning and the implications for our students. This shared expectation to go to the Asilomar conference together lasted for over 2 decades and expanded to include more goals than just departmental learning. The department paid for its student teachers to go, both as a recruiting tool and to share the principle that teachers never stop benefiting from also being learners. The evening prior to the conference, department members gathered for a meal to launch the event together. This became a place where friends and colleagues from outside the department could be invited to spend time with Railside teachers, building on a social opportunity to continue to build a professional network.

In addition to getting connected to the Asilomar community, we engaged other partners to support our thinking and learning. The early learning of the department was inspired and supported by the BAMP, its workshops, and especially its director, Lyle Fisher. He shared his vast experience from decades of working with high school students using a problem-solving approach as well as his work with thousands of math teachers throughout California. Many Railside teachers became participating fellows in BAMP or the Northern California Math Project. Through these networks, we met and learned with many teachers who were wrestling with similar challenges.

We also found resources for curriculum development. The first was the *Investigations Mathematics Curriculum Project* (Brutlag, 1994), funded by the National Science Foundation with Dan Brutlag as the project coordinator and primary author. Railside teachers offered to help pilot and revise early drafts of *Investigations* units in the heterogeneous Math 8 course. The Math 8 curriculum went through multiple iterations, but the *Investigations* units remained core elements of the curriculum and helped Railside teachers learn how to craft their own materials. One Railside teacher reported:

> Dan's units completely shaped the way I thought about designing
> curriculum. He taught me to ask myself, "What is the big mathematical
> idea? What are all the mathematical representations that might help
> students make sense of that idea, and how are they all related?" Most of all,
> I remain inspired by the fact that Dan's units always include an ambitious

project that comes a little before students are really ready for it. The fact that it is ambitious means that students know they are doing something big and important, and the fact that it comes a bit too early means that it is a genuine learning and synthesizing opportunity rather than an exercise in repeating what students already know.

The second curriculum source was the College Preparatory Mathematics Educational Program (CPM), first written at the University of California, Davis, by a group of math teachers. Railside teachers were drawn to this project because of the promise of involving teachers fully in planning, developing, using, revising, and introducing to their colleagues the new materials and new teaching techniques (Kysh, 1995). These materials were written expressly assuming that students would talk and work together in groups. They provided an essential starting point for Railside teachers to extend the work being done in 8th grade. Because all the evidence indicated that students learned more in CPM classes and they had more confidence in their learning than in the traditional classes, CPM was soon adopted as the district high school core curriculum, and Railside teachers remained active contributors for CPM.

Additional partnerships supported us in thinking about assessment, including the Balanced Assessment Project (www.mathshell.org/ba_mars.htm), centered at the University of California, Berkeley, which developed open-ended tasks that were piloted in several Railside classes. The New Standards Portfolio Project provided inspiration and feedback for student work. Railside teachers were already working on curriculum that was based on groupworthy tasks, and bringing student work to Portfolio Project meetings helped illuminate the companion concept of "portfolioworthy student products." As a result, the Math 8 curriculum grew to encompass projects and writing assignments that not only demonstrated competent mathematics but did so in ways that could be complete and convincing to others.

We also began partnering with researchers, which supported us in gathering data around what we were doing pedagogically, and reflecting on our practice together. One key scholar was Joanne Lieberman, then a doctoral student at Stanford, who came to meet with the math department in the early spring of 1994. She studied how we learned from one another, and the internal and external support that enabled meaningful collaboration. Eight years into the reform, Lieberman (1997) found us to be a collaborative department with agreement on strong core principles of equity, the value of heterogeneous groupings, and the belief that learning math includes talking and working together. She shared her dissertation with us when it was available, and in so doing, she gave us the words to talk about the work we had been doing and named us a generative learning community. While these partners were all instrumental in helping us consider new ways of teaching, of organizing curriculum, and of thinking about students and learning, in many ways, the core of our equity pedagogy was Complex Instruction, to which we now turn.

COMPLEX INSTRUCTION

When the Railside High School mathematics department decided to detrack the 8th-grade algebra courses to make learning mathematics more equitable, we had to address many questions: How will students who had very different previous preparation and achievement in mathematics learn together in the same classroom? What curriculum will we use? How will we teach differently? How will we know that we have achieved our goal? In particular, as teachers, we struggled to support the kind of student conversation that we envisioned. It was at this point that Ruth Tsu, then chair, and Ruth Cossey, then a mathematics educator at the Lawrence Hall of Science, embarked on a common journey. As she started her doctoral studies at Stanford University, Ruth Cossey introduced Complex Instruction to the teachers at Railside. In this chapter, we describe how the principles of Complex Instruction were used and elaborated upon in the service of teaching and learning mathematics at Railside.

Complex Instruction, developed at Stanford University, is a pedagogical approach designed to create and support equitable classrooms. Complex Instruction emphasizes equal-status interactions among students and specifies the conditions under which teachers can establish and support such interactions. Teachers build equitable classrooms by crafting intellectually challenging learning tasks, organizing the classroom for productive collaboration, developing the students' facility with the discourse of the discipline, providing feedback to groups and individuals, assessing their work, and, most importantly, addressing status problems that lead to predictable gaps in participation and consequently in achievement.

Complex Instruction was introduced to Railside High School through deep collegial conversations, frequent faculty workshops, and a course for 8th-graders co-taught by Ruth Tsu and Ruth Cossey. Combining Complex Instruction and mathematics presented special challenges. It required a break from the traditional view of mathematics as a hierarchical collection of procedures best learned quickly by someone with a good mathematical mind. The belief that mathematical understanding can be best demonstrated through narrowly constructed examinations and test items is incompatible with building an equitable Complex Instruction mathematics classroom. Thus, Complex Instruction supported both new ways of thinking about mathematics learning as well as new ways of thinking about equity in the classroom. Below we examine several critical tenets of Complex Instruction.

Creating Equitable Mathematics Classrooms

In equitable mathematics classrooms, students make sense of mathematical problems and concepts that arise in everyday life, analyze patterns and relationships to draw conclusions, and communicate effectively. They reason abstractly and use concrete tools (pencil and paper, manipulatives, calculators, statistical packages, sketch pads) strategically and with precision. They participate actively and interact in balanced, equal-status fashion with their peers.

In equitable classrooms, teachers and students recognize that different intellectual abilities are needed to complete mathematical learning tasks. Students are recognized as "smart" when they think deeply and demonstrate their intellectual competence in different ways.

Research in Complex Instruction classrooms documents a strong positive relationship between the overall level of peer interaction in small groups (as measured by the proportion of students talking and working together) and the average learning gains for a classroom on a variety of pre- and posttest measures, such as standardized tests, end-of-unit multiple-choice items, final essays, and ability tests (Cohen & Lotan, 1997). In mathematics classrooms, Cossey (1997) found that in addition to the overall proportion of peer talk, the quality of this talk benefited all members of the group. In other words, all members of a group who were present when high-level mathematical conversations were occurring demonstrated higher levels of mathematical communication skills. Thus, to raise the average academic achievement, teachers use the pedagogical practices of Complex Instruction to create an environment where the quantity and the quality of interaction are enhanced.

Recognizing and Treating Status Problems

Because participation is an indicator of engagement and thus a predictor of achievement, teachers are intensely concerned when some students participate more and some students participate less. Elizabeth Cohen (1994a) defined such unequal participation of students in small groups as a status problem and argued that they could be ameliorated through interventions called status treatments. According to Expectation States Theory (Berger, Rosenholtz, & Zelditch, 1980), these variable rates of participation in small, face-to-face groups are the consequence of members' variable expectations for perceived intellectual competence by others and by self. When members interact in task-related groups, those who are perceived as more competent, that is, "smart," are given more opportunities to speak and to influence the group's decisions than those who are perceived as less competent.

Expectations of competence are often formed to correspond to so-called status characteristics, which are socially accepted rankings based on visible or inferred background characteristics such as race, ethnicity, linguistic variations on mainstream discourse, socioeconomic status, or achievement in a particular field (even if unrelated to the task at hand). Those who are seen as high status are expected to and perceived to be more competent, and therefore dominate the interaction. Those who are perceived as low status and therefore less competent participate less, and their contributions are often dismissed. Thus, an academic and social hierarchy is established in diverse classrooms based on perceived differences in intellectual ability and competence. Those who are perceived as "smart" participate more; those who are perceived by others and by themselves as "dumb" participate less. Already high-status academically because of stronger academic achievement, those who participate more, learn more. Without an intervention, the achievement gap widens.

In Complex Instruction classrooms, teachers use two interventions to counteract this inequitable process. First, in a "multiple-ability orientation" teachers convince students that in addition to the traditional academic abilities of reading, writing, and calculating quickly, a myriad of different intellectual abilities are needed to complete math tasks successfully. Philip Tucher, a Railside mathematics teacher, explained to his students that doing math included the following alphabetically organized list:

Analyzing	Halving	Organizing	Uncovering
Building	Investigating	Proving	Visualizing
Classifying	Justifying	Questioning	Wondering
Designing	Knowing	Representing	eXplaining
Estimating	Listing	Substituting	asking whY
Formulating	Modeling	Testing	Zipping through mental calculations
Generalizing	Numbering		

While no one person has all these intellectual strengths, everybody has some. By stating that different students will make different intellectual contributions, the teacher creates a mixed set of expectations and thus fosters more equal participation.

Second, by closely observing students who previously exhibit low-status behavior, the teacher can notice successful contributions to the group effort and to the successful completion of the task by those students. In an intervention called "assigning competence," the teacher describes specifically and publicly how the low-status student's contribution becomes relevant to the success of the group. (For video examples of this intervention see Watanabe, 2011.) Research has successfully documented the impact of these treatments on increasing rates of participation and thus academic achievement of students who were previously perceived as low-status by their peers (Cohen & Lotan, 1997). Assigning competence is a powerful intervention not only on behalf of low-status students but also to expand the classroom definition of what it means to be smart. For instance, teachers might assign competence to high-status students for a clear justification, for taking the risk of trying a new method, or for asking an important clarifying question. These are all ways of being smart that are not always named as such but that can be taken on by both low- and high-status students.

To make possible the use of these status treatments and to use them effectively, teachers craft learning tasks that support group interaction and equal-status participation. They redefine both the teacher and student role and prepare the students for new classroom norms and behaviors. They model and monitor the use of academic discourse and continuously assess and provide feedback to groups and individuals.

Crafting Groupworthy Tasks

A key component of the Complex Instruction approach is utilizing groupworthy tasks. Groupworthy tasks incorporate design features that require varied and multiple intellectual contributions and provide opportunities for teachers to use status treatments. Detailed definitions of groupworthy tasks appear elsewhere in this volume (e.g., Chapters 2, 3, and 9; see also Lotan, 2003), so we will just briefly discuss a few of their characteristics here. Importantly, groupworthy tasks need to use different media (text, photos, videos, diagrams, graphs, audio recordings) and resources (books, websites, manipulatives) to provide different entry points for students to understand what they need to do and what is expected of them. In completing the task, students need to have multiple and varied opportunities to demonstrate what they know and can do. Second, open-ended, complex tasks promote problem-solving conversations and conceptual discussions and increase interaction, a precursor of achievement. Third, groupworthy tasks are organized around intellectually compelling big ideas, essential questions, and central concepts of the discipline.

Fourth, a requirement for a group product increases group interdependence, and a requirement for an individual report increases individual accountability. Fifth, "task cards," or a written version of instructions that also include evaluation criteria, are vital so students can assess themselves and understand the teacher's feedback about the quality of their performance. Finally, and especially in multilingual classrooms, incorporating academic discourse of the discipline and providing students with opportunities to produce both oral and written language are essential.

Organizing the Classroom for Productive Groupwork

When students work in small groups on tasks that require an extensive problem-solving process and involve many resources and materials, the teacher will have a difficult time supervising, monitoring, and auditing all groups simultaneously. Studies have shown that when the teacher delegates authority to the groups to manage themselves, interaction increases. To support students in learning how to work together productively, students learn specific skills through a series of skill-builders. Cossey (1997) describes mathematical communication norms necessary for mathematics classrooms: how to gather and share information, look for and describe patterns, and make conjectures and present reasoning, among others. Roles such as facilitator, reporter, resource manager, recorder, and timekeeper are instrumental in making the groups run smoothly. Each student takes on a role, and roles rotate among members of the group. They hold each other and themselves accountable through constant interaction and role performance. Reports from the groups at the conclusion of groupwork are viewed and assessed by the class and by the teacher. (For a detailed description of norms and roles for mathematics classrooms, see Featherstone et al., 2011.)

In addition to the ways teachers organize the classroom for productive groupwork, they also attend to the language students are using, supporting the development of academic discourse. In multilingual and multicultural Complex Instruction classrooms, teachers provide students multiple opportunities to produce oral and written language using different text types, genres, and linguistic repertoires. Interacting with native or near-native speakers of the language of instruction increases opportunities for students to learn and solidify their use of the language.

And finally, as a part of how the classroom space is organized, in a Complex Instruction model, teachers attend closely to issues of assessment. Assessment is built into the structures of practices and the classroom. When teachers delegate authority to the groups and groups successfully manage themselves, teachers are free to observe the performances of the individual students closely. Teachers can then provide feedback on the ways students collaborate, carry out their roles, discuss their ideas, and work toward completing the task. Most importantly, teachers collect evidence for demonstrating and convincing students that many different intellectual abilities are being used to complete the task successfully and that all students are indeed contributing in significant ways. Because evaluation criteria are included in the instruction to the task, students can assess the quality of their own and their peers' group products during the group reports. Completing individual reports is essential for individual accountability and for making sure all students have opportunities to summarize their experiences and thinking in their own words.

These tenets of Complex Instruction became key in the curriculum and pedagogy developed at Railside. The math department worked closely with Ruth Cossey to enact these practices in our classrooms, and the language and assumptions of Complex Instruction infused our practice at every level.

CONCLUSION

Why did this math department embark on the difficult work that resulted in the transformation of teaching and learning at Railside? We know that some schools that received similar evaluation reports from the visiting accreditation committee responded by defending their practice. Perhaps the Railside math teachers were receptive to the report because we already knew that too many of our students were not successful and that the accommodations we had made were not leading to more success. As we started to make changes in our practice, it was exciting to see many students become engaged who had not previously done so, and that was encouraging. For instance, by the end of the first year of the heterogeneous Math 8, many more students were prepared to study algebra. When these same students were seniors, we had enough students ready to offer an AP Calculus class. Soon, having 30% of the senior class in calculus became the norm.

As the core structures and principles became an established part of the department's practice, the Railside math department continued its collegial work to improve practice. How the principles that took shape in the first 8 years of work continued to guide work over time is described in Chapter 12. The groupworthy task of changing curriculum, assessment, and instructional practices to support student learning in heterogeneous classrooms continued to evolve. Work among adults shifted from creating a professional community of learning to sustaining and growing that community as its membership changed.

Questions to Consider

In talking and working together, several important questions emerged for Railside teachers that might be useful for other teacher leaders and departments considering reform. While any category of question could serve as an entry point to reform work, questions from each category are important to consider. Table 8.1 lists some of these questions.

Table 8.1. Category Questions Detailing Approaches to Departmental Reform

In the area of instructional practice:	In the area of assessment:
• What changes do we need to make in our instructional practices so students are more involved/engaged in their learning?	• How do we more clearly communicate the high expectations we have for all students?
• What can we do to create environments (both in classrooms and among ourselves) that encourage and support learning?	• Do we provide sufficient opportunities for students to revise their work to bring it to a high standard?
• What more can we do to help students recognize and value their group discussions as a primary vehicle for learning?	• Do we ask students to reflect on their learning and the progress they are making?
• How can we incorporate the use of manipulatives and technology into our classes to increase student access to learning?	• What do we need to do to provide students a variety of ways to demonstrate their learning?
	• How can we write clearer prompts and how can we more effectively communicate our expectations for the products that we want students to produce?
	• How do we assess students' group skills and the work that they do as a group as well as their individual learning?

In the area of curriculum:	In the area of supporting student learning:
• What do we need to do differently when we have heterogeneous classes?	• What does a successful mathematics learner look like and sound like?
• Can we find curriculum that is more relevant and meaningful and that is sufficiently rich that	• How can we help students understand that major concepts are learned over time and that they will learn if they persevere?

In the area of curriculum:	In the area of supporting student learning:
students need to talk and work together? • Does our curriculum provide opportunities for students to construct meaning and understanding?	• When students are working in groups, do we notice if some students are ignored or if some dominate? If we notice, what do we do about it? • How can we make tutoring more available/accessible on a regular basis? • In classes that precede algebra, what does a student need to experience and learn in order to continue on and be successful in algebra? • How can we better support our students so they develop the habits that will increase their prospects of future success?

Chapter 9

Teachers' Learning on the Job

Ilana Seidel Horn

I first encountered Railside at the end of a months-long search for interesting research sites for a study looking at mathematics teacher communities.[1] The project sought to understand how collegial environments can support teachers' professional learning. I was interested in teacher professional community because of a growing consensus that equitable educational outcomes were not the consequence of a single teacher but rather the product of teams of teachers (Bryk, Sebring, Allensworth, Luppescu, & Easton, 2010; R. Gutiérrez, 1996; Lee & Smith, 1996). Something about collaboration—a certain *kind* of collaboration—supported ongoing improvement and gave teachers a sense of collective responsibility for students that made a big difference in student learning.

What was it, I wondered, that teachers could accomplish together that was so different than what they did on their own? Movies like *Stand and Deliver* and *Freedom Writers* emphasize the hero teacher "saving" students, but research was telling a different story. Coming to academia from my own experiences as an urban high school mathematics teacher, I wanted to understand how teachers working together could better serve historically disenfranchised groups of students.

Like many others, I reasoned that the improvement in practice and student outcomes was a consequence of teachers learning through their engagement in work groups (McLaughlin & Talbert, 2001). As teachers made sense of their work, they did a better job reaching more students mathematically. On this basis, I framed my study around the question: How do high school mathematics teachers engaged in school reform learn about subject matter, student learning, and pedagogy through the contexts of their work?

Our project team[2] had already found an interesting place in a school we came to call South High. There, the schoolwide professional community worked together to focus on student learning in creative ways using frameworks from the Coalition of Essential Schools (Sizer, 1992). Students were put into

Houses, provided with meaningful nontraditional learning opportunities, and had their learning assessed through a variety of rich performances. South was interesting to me as a mathematics educator because, despite this progressive schoolwide culture, the mathematics department remained a bastion of traditionalism. How was it that amidst so much progressive, student-centered innovation, this group of mathematics teachers maintained so many aspects of conventional instruction?

When I entered the school that our team called East High School (which later became known as "Railside"), the differences between the schools were striking. At Railside, instructional innovation *came from* the mathematics department. A promising set of contrasts could emerge through a comparison of the top-down, schoolwide reform at South and the grassroots, departmental reform at Railside.

DATA COLLECTION, RESEARCHER ROLE, AND ANALYTIC APPROACH

I met the Railside teachers during one of their regular after-school meetings. It was a Friday afternoon at the end of the 1998–1999 school year. Everyone was tired. Nonetheless, the teachers had a strikingly thoughtful and supportive conversation about how to wrap up their year of teaching. What topics were most critical to cover? How should they balance coverage and student understanding? What should they do to keep the students' mathematical interest going when everybody was wearing out? Their careful deliberations differed markedly from those at the other schools I had visited as a part of the site selection process.

After the teachers agreed to allow me to observe their work together, an opportunity arose to teach a section of algebra alongside them. I seized it. Since I was interested in the phenomenon of teacher learning, what better way to understand than by learning alongside the teachers myself? As I worked with the Railside mathematics teachers for one term during the 1999–2000 academic year, I participated in the collaborative team conversations, shared a classroom with one of the Railside teachers, and participated in the other collegial activities.

At the same time, I was collecting data at South High School. Their department met less frequently, so I managed to attend and record their meetings during that same school year. Although I had designed this as a comparative case study, my data sets were clearly asymmetrical. This was in part due to my different roles at the two schools, but more importantly, it reflected the differences in the frequency of collaborative activity.

In classroom observations at the two schools, the contrasts in mathematics teaching were immediately obvious. Students' seating arrangements alone reflected something of the teachers' orientations: While teachers at South had students seated individually (whether in rows or in a horseshoe), all of Railside's algebra teachers seated their students in groups. In addition, South's math classrooms reflected traditional mathematics teaching in their emphasis on the mastery of algorithms, while Railside's emphasized conceptual understanding through the use of collaborative investigations of complex problems.

Regarding students' long-term success in mathematics at the two schools, looking at state-level data made it clear that Railside's approach was the more effective of the two. Although more of Railside's students came from groups with historically low participation rates in higher mathematics, 30% of their seniors enrolled in calculus, while only 12% of South's seniors did. Additionally, Railside's advanced math enrollment rate was 61%, compared to 49% at South and a state average of 55%.[3] The ways in which the teachers were changing their practices had an impact on student persistence in the mathematics curriculum.

I drew on a variety of data sources to ascertain differences in teachers' learning opportunities. Primarily, I recorded (via transcribed audiotapes, videotapes, and fieldnotes) teachers' collaborative conversations. I then analyzed these documents to make sense of how teachers' talk might contribute to teachers' learning and support or hinder instructional innovation. In addition, I interviewed teachers, observed other kinds of school activities in which the teachers participated, and spent time in mathematics classrooms.

To build this analysis, I combed through the transcripts, looking for learning opportunities in conversations by identifying the moments when teachers explicitly reasoned about teaching decisions. Something as brief as "I'm not using that worksheet because it bores the kids" gave me a sense of the rationales for teaching decisions. The more interesting moments came when teachers deliberated over a problem together. This might be initiated by a comment like, "I have a handful of kids who are not successful. How is this going to impact our classes next semester?" By looking at the naturally occurring, public reasoning within the teachers' conversations, I could compare the ways that teachers collectively made sense of their work and the resources they used for doing so.

TEACHERS TALKING AND LEARNING TOGETHER

In this section, I report the three major findings of my study and provide examples from each department. In general, South's reform program disposed teachers to view problems of schooling through a lens that highlighted the importance of the student-teacher relationship, independent of subject considerations, while Railside's math reform framed them in a way that called into question the various relationships among students, teachers, and subject matter.

The three resources for collegial learning in teacher talk that I identified were:

1. *Reform artifacts* support teachers' understandings and help them make sense of their practice.
2. *Conversational classification systems* model teachers' work and communicate conceptions of students, mathematics, and teaching.
3. *Representations of the classroom* recount events that have happened or anticipate ones that will happen. These stories reveal values, attitudes, and beliefs about what is important in teaching.

Both groups of teachers were learning through their practice in an ongoing way and engaging similar resources. Nonetheless, the kinds of activities the Railside High teachers engaged in provided a means of *transformative learning*—learning that challenged existing assumptions and had the ability to change classroom practices more fundamentally—so the differences in how these learning resources manifested themselves in the group is of particular note. In this section, I describe learning processes common to both teacher groups, while highlighting the ways they looked different at the two schools.

Reform Artifacts Support Teachers' Understandings and Help Them Make Sense of Their Practice

Both groups of teachers shared with their colleagues some reform-based artifacts, be they curricular materials, assessment instruments, or reform slogans. Most of the teachers oriented toward these in some way and changed their practices according to their understandings of them. However, because of the differences in their opportunities to make sense of these together, reform artifacts varied in the extent to which they guided the transformation of teaching practice. To illustrate, I compare the local meanings of two reform slogans from the groups: "less is more" at South and "groupworthy" at Railside.

"Less Is More" at South High

The meaning of the slogan "less is more," adopted from the Coalition of Essential Schools, varied significantly among South's math teachers. In the text of the Coalition's Ten Common Principles, "less is more" is summarized as follows:

Curricular decisions should be guided by the aim of thorough student mastery and achievement rather than by an effort to merely cover content.

At South High, the math teachers did not get much time to discuss the implications of the whole-school reform for their subject matter. Although they participated in teacher research groups, faculty retreats, and weekly faculty meetings, their monthly mathematics meetings were taken over by bureaucratic demands of the state, school district, and their various funders, limiting opportunities to examine mathematics teaching and learning. As South's senior math teacher remarked, math is often the place where whole-school reform "doesn't work": It becomes the special case in an otherwise changing school. This "everywhere but math" phenomenon was certainly manifest at South High. South had recultured as a school, yet these changes did not trickle down into the mathematics classrooms.

The multiple meanings of "less is more" highlighted this gap between the whole school and the department. Dan Marcus, the teacher who had been in South's math department the longest, explained to me how he applied "less is more" to math: "What I decided 'less is more' meant is that I'm going to teach math in terms of *characteristics* rather than in terms of *problem sets*." He illustrated this with the example of getting students to notice that

$$x + 3x = 4x,$$
$$3x4 + 4x4 = 7x4,$$
$$\text{and}$$
$$(34)(4)n + 3 + (5)(34)(4)n+3 = (6)(34)(4)n + 3$$

are essentially the same problem; they all involve the idea of combining like terms. He felt that by getting students to focus on characteristics of mathematical objects, he could help them make connections across seemingly disparate problems. Barbara Moore, the department chair and a 25-year teaching veteran, invoked the phrase "less is more" in meetings to justify eliminating topics in the overfull traditional curriculum. At the same time, Noah Banes, a 2nd-year teacher, told me in an interview that the Coalition Principles did not come into his thinking about teaching. Dan reported to me that as a department, they had "not had a great deal of time to go deeply" into how each teacher defined the school themes such as "less is more." Impulses to innovate often died out, as when Noah tried to incorporate cooperative learning in his classroom. Ultimately, he resigned himself to Barbara's assessment that this teaching approach worked best with "the cream"—the top students in a school.

"Groupworthy Problems" at Railside High

The Railside math teachers also had guiding concepts in their work, which at the time of the study focused on detracking algebra. They wanted to construct a curriculum driven by what they called "groupworthy problems." Groupworthy problems were a leitmotif in the teachers' conversations. They consistently invoked groupworthiness as the gold standard by which classroom activities were evaluated. In addition, the teachers revisited its meaning in their meetings and retreats. These explicit conversations, grounded in subject, curriculum, and classroom examples, helped to refine the notion for the veterans in the department while initiating the newcomers into the group's vision of mathematics teaching and learning.

According to a conversation the teachers had during their summer Algebra Week,[4] groupworthy problems have four distinctive properties. They:

- illustrate important mathematical concepts,
- include multiple tasks that draw effectively on the collective resources of a [student] group,
- allow for multiple representations, and
- have several possible solution paths.

In this definition, "groupworthy" is an adjective that modifies "problems," which suggests at first that groupworthiness is simply a way of describing curriculum. Embedded in the criteria for groupworthiness, however, are notions of teaching, student participation and learning, and mathematics itself. The view of mathematics encapsulated in this term counters traditional notions of a highly sequential subject organized around the mastery of algorithms (Stodolsky & Grossman, 2000), as it foregrounds concepts and their multiple interpretations and representations.

Indeed, Railside's math classrooms reflected the collective values and goals represented by the term "groupworthy." As mentioned earlier, classroom observations showed that groupwork was the prevailing participation structure for math activities at Railside, often driven by a single complex problem. In interviews, the algebra teachers as a whole exhibited a flexible view of subject matter, as was evidenced by their (uncommon) view that students could successfully learn algebra before they have, for example, mastered fractions. Guillermo Reyes, the department co-chair, once described their approach to curriculum as going "from the outside in": starting from big mathematical ideas, helping students see the connections among them, and then working toward the details. This view lies in stark contrast to the atomic subdividing and sequencing that dominates traditional classrooms.

As will be seen in the next sections, teachers' informal conversations focused on strategies for supporting effective groupwork in the classroom, and they undertook training in Complex Instruction (Cohen, 1994a; Horn, 2012) to integrate this into their classroom practice. Railside teachers also frequently referred to wanting to "help students feel smart." Multiple representations provided different points of entry into a problem. A student who does not have any intuition about an equation, for example, might quickly see a pattern in the empirical situation that the equation represents. The teachers regularly used a variety of manipulatives, including Algebra Lab Gear™ (similar to algebra tiles), geoboards, and graphing calculators, to provide additional representations and worked together to find appropriate places for them in their curriculum.

Artifacts at South and Railside

Slogans and other artifacts highlight the perceived learning demands of a given reform. When teachers orient to them and integrate their meaning into practice, they are learning. Dan and Barbara garnered different understandings of "less is more," and both changed their teaching practices accordingly: Dan focused on characteristics, and Barbara eliminated what she deemed to be superfluous topics from her teaching. Nonetheless, these changes did not fundamentally transform the mathematics teaching in their classrooms, and a new teacher like Noah was not compelled to make sense of the values and goals encapsulated in "less is more." The Railside math teachers also learned as they worked to make a "groupworthy" curriculum, yet individual and collective practice changed fundamentally as they brought complex problems into their classrooms and worked together to effectively use multiple representations and understand student thinking. In the end, they broadened their understandings of what mathematics is, who can do it, and how it can be done.

Although the two slogans were located at different levels of curriculum (the overall course vs. specific activities), neither reform slogan was inherently more meaningful. One could imagine, for example, shallow or varied interpretations of "groupworthiness," as well as conceptually deep and subject-sensitive interpretations of "less is more." The way teachers make sense of slogans, both through their own accounting and in their teaching practice, provides a sense of a reform's reach. While the math teachers at South had opportunities to talk about reform at the whole-school level, they had little time to make sense of its meanings in their classrooms. In an otherwise changing school, the teaching of mathematics at South remained fundamentally untouched. In contrast, Railside math teachers' notion of "groupworthiness" grew out of their own investigation of equitable teaching practices. As shall be seen in the next two findings, they revisited the concept in their ongoing and collective work. In doing so, they pushed one another to connect the values and goals encapsulated by the slogan to their classrooms.

Conversational Classification Systems Model Teachers' Work and Communicate Conceptions of Students, Mathematics, and Teaching

When people work together, they often develop language that highlights the specific concerns of their jobs. For instance, medical people often race against the clock to save lives, using the word *stat* to emphasize the need to work quickly (as in, "Get me the defibrillator, stat!"). American teachers have their own language as well, generally sharing jargon about classes (freshmen, honors classes), colleagues (emergency credentialed, long-term sub, veteran), and curricula (shop class, AP). However, a closer analysis of the teachers' talk in my study revealed distinctive, site-specific language. This language matters, because it is often through language that people model and solve problems of their work (Bowker & Star, 1999).

The uniqueness of the Railside teachers' talk came out most clearly during discussions about curriculum and its relationship to students. The talk about students and mathematics revealed assumptions about teaching, while also shaping teachers' understandings of their work.

Slowing the Curriculum at South High

An analysis of teachers' talk illuminated differences between the two departments during conversations about connecting students and curriculum. Specifically, the teachers' talk highlighted teachers' notions of ability and motivation and the consequences of these understandings for reorganizing course content and student placement. At South High, this talk was presented with virtually no public challenge, whereas at Railside, there was an inclination to interrogate conventional ways of talking about students.[5]

During the conversation analyzed below, the South High math teachers were given a paid workday to plan for the elimination of remedial courses from their curriculum, per a district mandate. In response, they created an alternative to their existing remedial courses with a 2-year algebra option. Since the district had also mandated that students take 4 years of math in order to graduate, they were left puzzling over where to place students who had completed the 2-year algebra sequence. At the start of the following excerpt, Dan expressed his doubt that students can be streamed into the college preparatory geometry class that followed the traditional 1-year algebra course:

> Dan says, "I don't think we can fly geometry."
> Barbara agrees. "You brought it up, and you're telling the truth that our kids cannot get through our geometry as we teach it now. . . . What they won't be able to handle is the logic in the two-column proofs. Our regular kids can't handle that. One of the problems with the kids we're putting in the two-year algebra course is that they don't have the logic component."

As this conversation unfolded, the teachers worked to eliminate remedial courses from their curriculum while figuring out an alternative to their geometry course. In the end, they replaced both algebra and geometry with a sequence of slowed-down college preparatory classes: a 2-year algebra sequence followed by a 2-year geometry sequence—a sequence that would not qualify students for 4-year college, effectively undermining a goal of the district mandate.

The teachers' talk about students tied into how they conceptualized mathematics as a subject and related this to possibilities for the mathematics curriculum. The categories for students invoked during their discussion ("regular," "not quick," "lazy," "college-bound") lay on the two dimensions of *ability* and *motivation*. These categories stayed fairly static and closed as the conversation went along.

The teachers' discussion reveals two critical things about their understandings of relationships among students, mathematics, and teaching. First, on the whole, the South teachers valued formalisms over other ways of understanding and made these available to certain "types" of students. Two-column proofs, for example, were considered an important part of a college preparatory geometry curriculum appropriate for college-bound students, while hands-on geometry was more suitable for the "regular kids" who "don't have the logic component" that such proofs require.

Second, the value of mathematical formalisms trumped student advancement through the curriculum. Students' entry into the college preparatory curriculum required success in the college preparatory math courses, even if it meant redundant content. For example, the teachers decided that in order to change from the slowed-down curriculum to the college preparatory curriculum, a student successful in the first slowed-down algebra class would need to complete the entire 1-year college preparatory algebra class in order to be streamed into that track, even though the entire first half of that course would feature material the student had already covered.

Related to this last point, the commitment to formalisms, as represented by kinds of courses designed, took precedence over sensible pathways for learning. Research shows that students often master mathematical formalisms with little understanding (Boaler, 2002a; Schoenfeld, 1985). Although some students might have a better understanding of, for example, the Isosceles Triangle Theorem through a hands-on investigation than by working on a two-column proof, that understanding was not deemed sufficient by the course hierarchy the teachers developed. In order to move forward, students had to succeed in the designated college preparatory geometry course. Perhaps not coincidentally, this vision of mathematics was in good keeping with the external accountability pressures linked to high-stakes assessments that reified this same perspective.

Although teaching practices were never talked about explicitly in the course of the meeting, the teachers' conversation conveyed a sense of what their collective role was in bringing students and subject together. The curriculum provided the bins. Their work was first to make sure that the right kinds of bins were in place and then sort the students accordingly.

Teaching "Fast Kids" at Railside

By contrast, Railside teachers had developed a set of routines for interrogating conventional classification schemes. In the following excerpt, Tina, who was an intern in Railside's math department, brought up a problem during the weekly Algebra meeting:

> My students . . . they're doing so well. . . . But the thing about my students
> is that there's kids that know a lot and then there's kids that, you know, feel
> like they're slow learners. And I'm trying to find groupworthy activities
> where the kids who are fast learners and the kids who are slow learners, that
> it can close the gap.

In the conversation that ensued, the teachers discussed Tina's problem of the gap between fast and slow kids in her classroom. She described her attempt to solve her problem by finding "groupworthy activities," invoking one of the Railside teachers' guiding principles for their detracking project.

Tina's problem was taken up by the others through a collective examination of issues of students, subject matter, and teaching practices. Carrie and Guillermo responded to her by working to reframe her problem, challenging her initial categories of "fast" and "slow" learners. Carrie speculated:

> I wonder if it's not just the activities you're doing but also just status. . . . I
> mean, even if you did give them a groupworthy task, those kids who feel
> like they have low status will just continue to play that role.

Guillermo was more direct in his challenge to her categories. He said:

> Even if you have great activities, if the perception in the class is, "I'm fast,
> I'm not as fast," it's not going to help with the status issues, I don't think.
> . . . Think of the ones that you think of as fast learners and figure out what
> they're slow at.

Ability and motivation do not sufficiently explain student success for Carrie and Guillermo. Their contributions and challenges constructed a more complex vision of students than the one exhibited at South. Carrie brought up notions of status, complicating Tina's ability-centered categories. Guillermo muddied the waters further by disallowing "fast" as an encompassing category: Even fast learners have things they are slow at.

Tina's initial framing of her problem resembled the model of teaching exhibited in the South conversation, with fixed categories of students and curriculum that needed to be matched to them. Instead of creating different courses to sort students into, however, she sought groupworthy problems that could include them all. Carrie and Guillermo's reframing legitimated Tina's impulse to find better curriculum and activities. At the same time, they also encouraged her to take action in her classroom to address student status issues, problematize simplistic categories, and set "learning agendas" for all individuals—even those who appear "fast."

While the South teachers' conversation valued mathematical formalisms above everything, the Railside teachers focused closely and carefully on students' learning. Elsewhere in the discussion, Guillermo questioned the notion that "fast kids" were necessarily better at math ("they're not stopping to think about what they're doing, what there is to learn from this activity"). The understandings he conveyed represented mathematics not as a subject where only the quickest survive (Boaler, 1997b), but rather one in which students might bring a variety of abilities to be drawn upon. In addition, both he and Carrie extended Tina's portrayal of her work as teacher. Tina characterized her work as one of seeking the right curriculum ("I've been going to the bookstore looking for . . . all kinds of activities, but it's really hard"). Carrie pointed out the ways in which students' status issues could undo her best efforts toward curriculum matching. Guillermo extended Carrie's point about status, turning Tina's whole framing of the problem on its head by pointing out the difficulties that the fast kids often have and the kinds of interventions Tina could do as a teacher ("help . . . kids that are not stopping to set their own learning agenda"). Teachers had a complex role in the classroom in this conversation. Teachers' role in the classroom was more simplified at South—or at least was more opaque, as authority was yielded to the most experienced teachers.

Although Guillermo and Carrie pushed on Tina's framing of her problem by expanding Tina's role as teacher, Tina was not left alone to sort out their suggestions and change her practice. In addition to modeling a possible learning agenda for one of Tina's students, the group offered its support through peer observation and "following" an experienced teacher through the curriculum by staying a day behind, observing, and recontextualizing lessons in her own classroom. In particular, Carrie invited Tina to observe her work on an extensive open-ended problem in her own classroom so that Tina could then try it out with her classes. These structures would provide additional learning resources for Tina to support changes in her practice. Their existence made it easier for the group to challenge one another's ideas, as there were means for follow-up support.

Categories at South and Railside

In both departments, teachers communicated their assumptions about students, subject matter, and teaching through the kinds of categories they invoked in conversation and the ways that they deployed these categories to model and solve their problems. At South, notions of students' abilities and mathematics were fairly stable. Students could be classified along the dimensions of ability and motivation and then sorted into the curriculum accordingly. At Railside, the teachers' detracking effort was premised on assumptions that such sorting cannot succeed, as notions of ability are too often conflated with academic status and schooling know-how. Students' abilities were seen as various and diverse, and mathematics itself was rendered more complex, making such a two-dimensional classification scheme untenable. As Railside teachers became more adept at using these categories to make sense of their practices, they learned the common assumptions behind them.

Representations of the Classroom Recount Events That Have Happened or Anticipate Ones That Will Happen

These stories reveal values, attitudes, and beliefs about what is important in teaching. Both groups often told stories using forms of talk I call teaching replays and teaching rehearsals. Teaching replays and rehearsals render classroom events in teacher-to-teacher conversations. In teaching replays, teachers provide blow-by-blow accounts of classroom events, often acting out both the teacher's and students' roles. In teaching rehearsals, teachers also act out classroom interaction, only they do so in an anticipatory fashion. These participation structures actually lie on a continuum. When teaching replays become more general, reporting on a routine interaction with a broad category of students ("they"), those replays take on the anticipatory nature of rehearsals.[6]

At South High, these replays and rehearsals were less frequent in the math teachers' talk, but the greater contrast was in the content of the replays and rehearsals at South and Railside: At South, they seldom included examples of students' mathematical thinking. For instance, in one rehearsal, a teacher shared a mode of exposition with colleagues by going up to the board and running through a sample presentation ("Here's how I get them to understand percents . . . "). Likewise, a replay provided the teachers with an outlet for a collective chuckle at a student's antics. Enactments of replays and rehearsals define what aspects of classroom life are acceptable to share and discuss with colleagues. These examples value the sharing of effective exposition and the emotional support and bonding that come from storytelling. At the same time, when taken together, they define what is "shareable" about classroom practice. At South, these tales gave a limited window on the classroom and served to reinstate the local norms of privacy in the group's conversations.

Replays and rehearsals occurred more frequently in teachers' talk in the Railside math department. They differed in their form and purpose as well. Most notably, the Railside math teachers' replays and rehearsals extensively included students' voices in interaction with teachers, along with displays of student thinking.

For the Railside teachers, the replays and rehearsals formed the basis for consultations, providing evidence through which to reason about practice. Often the boundaries between replay and rehearsal blurred, as in the following example. Here, while speaking to a 1st-year math teacher, Jill Larimer uses replays and rehearsals to model a response to a common anxiety among students:

> They're really upset about multiplying fractions, "No one ever taught me this stuff!" Just like the conversation we had this morning, "I've never learned this before." So I said "Okay, I'll teach it to you. Here we go. If you want to learn it, no problem."

The sentence "just like the conversation we had this morning" links the first student quote to the second, creating a general class of students' anxious protests rooted in the insufficiency of their prior mathematical learning. In this sense, Jill's reported response ("Okay, I'll teach it to you") applies to the situation at hand as well as the situation in general in language that is directly importable to the classroom.

Because the replays and rehearsals were so much more visible and nuanced at Railside than at South, I devote the remainder of this section to excerpts from a consultation about groupwork at Railside High that distinctively used both modes of talk. In the following conversation, Belinda Watson, a student teacher, consulted with Guillermo Reyes, a co-chair of the department, during a weekly mentoring meeting. Also present at this after-school meeting was Belinda's co-teacher, Gita Richards.

Segment 1: Question and teaching replay

1. *Belinda*: So that was part of this question. (*Reading.*) Do they know how to answer each other in their groups when they ask each other questions in their groups? 'Cause like I was watching Alma ask Daniel a question. And Daniel kind of tossed an answer, he's like, "You do it this way." And it clearly didn't satisfy her, but she didn't come back with another question. And he didn't register that she hadn't processed, understood
2. *Guillermo*: Mm. Right.
3. *Belinda*: What he said.
4. *Guillermo*: Right.
5. *Belinda*: So
6. *Guillermo*: Did you intervene? Did you (*Trails off.*)
7. *Belinda*: It was um during the warm-up.
8. *Guillermo*: Oh, when you said you weren't gonna, oh. That's too bad.
9. *Belinda*: And I saw her thinking and I wasn't quite sure if she was going to go with it. So. . . .

Belinda brought a question to Guillermo that she prepared for her mentoring meeting. She followed the question with a descriptive account of an interaction she observed between two students, Daniel and Alma. In Belinda's replay, Alma asked a question, Daniel provided an unsatisfactory answer, and Alma did not push for further information. Belinda's account stayed mainly at the level of description, although her question provides a preliminary analysis, suggesting that students might not know how to answer one another in their groups when they ask one another questions. Because Guillermo's mentoring routine involved a close observation of Belinda's teaching, the conversation became specific quickly. Guillermo asked Belinda if she intervened (turn 6), indicating that, although he was in the classroom at the time of this event, he had not witnessed this interaction. This suggests that Belinda was retelling an exchange not central to the class but one that took place in the peripheral setting of the student group. Belinda provided a partial response (turn 7), which was truncated by Guillermo (turn 8) because of his contextual knowledge of the class.[7]

Segment 2: Evaluation and teaching rehearsal

10. *Guillermo*: 'Cause that, I mean, just the fact that you noticed that is amazing. I mean that's a, that's a complex back-and-forth interaction. And um. And so given that you noticed it, that you have the instincts to notice it, then intervening and saying wait, this is what I just saw.
11. *Belinda*: (Mhm.)
12. *Guillermo*: 'Cause, 'cause there's/ I mean, "Alma, it was great that you asked a question. Daniel, you tried to answer it, but did you see what happened? Um, you gave an answer but you weren't checking to see whether you were really being helpful to Alma." And then. "Alma, was he being helpful? No, then can you think of, so now think of some follow up questions, like if he just gives you an answer, say I don't want just an answer, I want (this that)." (*Voice trails off.*)

In Belinda's replay of the events in the previous segment, she provided only a provisional analysis of the students' interaction—they might not know how to answer one another in their groups. In turn 10, Guillermo cast the story in evaluative terms: Just the fact that Belinda noticed the students' exchange was amazing. His evaluation of her story confirmed her potential as a teacher, as she displayed what he found to be laudable sensitivity to the interactions of her students. He implied that her ability to notice would allow her, in future situations, to intervene.

In turn 12, Guillermo went into a teaching rehearsal, addressing abstracted versions of Alma and Daniel directly. In doing so, he provided Belinda with language directly importable to the classroom ("Alma, it was great that you asked a question. Daniel, you tried to answer it, but did you see what happened?"). He acted out the teacher's end of an entire intervention with the students. In this case, the teaching replays and rehearsals provided a way to reimagine the interaction between Alma and Daniel, casting Belinda in an active role while simultaneously modeling the kinds of language and questions she might use as a part of that role. The reworking of the event in Belinda's classroom clearly portrayed an alternative ending to the scenario she described in frustration.

In the end, Belinda's descriptive-level account of an event in her classroom became a story that showed her promise as a teacher and paved the way for her to develop competency in facilitating groupwork. We could imagine, as a thought experiment, Belinda having the same classroom experience in a different teaching context. Without this opportunity to reflect on her experience, she may have concluded, for example, that students do not know how to do groupwork, or that groupwork only succeeds with certain kinds of students. Indeed, when Noah made a lone venture into groupwork at South High, he reached exactly this last conclusion in making sense of the practice on his own.

Over time, the ways that replays and rehearsals were used at Railside helped signal "typical" classroom events and communicate appropriate responses. They provided opportunities to analyze teaching, reflect on practice, and communicate collective standards for pedagogy.

HOW DO TEACHERS SUPPORT ONE ANOTHER'S LEARNING ON THE JOB?

To summarize the findings, I found three ways in which collegial conversations support mathematics teachers' learning. First, I found that reform artifacts often provide a conceptual guide for teachers' learning. Slogans such as "less is more" and "groupworthy" may press on teachers' understandings. The interactions around these slogans—or any artifact, including curricula or assessment tools—predict the degree to which these understandings become shared across teachers. Teachers' knowledge may be idiosyncratic in a context in which there is little opportunity to discuss the meanings with colleagues. Alternatively, teachers' understandings may be well-coordinated when they have ongoing occasions to reflect on the meanings collectively.

Second, category systems for talking about students provide a window on teachers' understandings of student learning and subject matter and their roles in joining the two. At South High, the reform focused the teachers on the student-teacher relationship, while their understandings of mathematics remained fairly static. Specifically, in the teachers' conversations, mathematics was a series of procedures to be mastered, a task for which students were more or less able and motivated. This view was reflected in teachers' language describing students as "fast," "slow," and "lazy." At Railside High, with the reform focusing on reconceptualizing subject matter, the teachers' categories for students were more nuanced. Teachers complicated more simplistic ability/motivation categories by bringing up such issues as student academic status and the learning challenges faced by "fast kids."

Rehearsals and replays supported two important dimensions of teacher learning, both conveying norms of sharing and privacy and providing a basis for a collective understanding of teaching. First, the rehearsals and replays communicated what was shareable in the context of the teacher groups. As noted earlier, the South teachers' discussion did not include many actual accounts of teaching; what is more, those that did come through usually represented either teacher or student talk. In contrast, the Railside teachers' talk regularly included highly interactive representations of classroom teaching. I view these rehearsals and replays as a way of "seeing" into the classroom through conversations. The Railside teachers' discussions provided a clearer, more specific, and often messier portrait of that work, indicating a strong norm of sharing. Second, the stories accrued and became organized around particular ideas, and teachers built categories of teaching events. Teaching replays and teaching rehearsals directly imported classroom interactions into teachers' conversations, providing the basis for stories that analyzed practice and specified appropriate pedagogical responses.

During an interview, one of Railside High's math department co-chairs described the intensive learning that goes on in her department: "I think what happens in our department, what happens in our school is so incredibly spectacular . . . It's professional development that takes place with us but it also takes place with our students, and so it's this constant interactive professional development." But what is the nature of these interactions? How are they distinct from the ones found in more typical teacher communities, like the one at South?

Put another way, how do teachers who talk together learn together? In this study, I looked at teacher work groups that had different frameworks and goals and investigated similarities in the ways that their conversations might support learning. By identifying commonalities of dissimilar groups, we can begin to leverage these for more effective forms of professional development that builds off of what teachers "naturally" do together. Because the Railside teachers' frameworks and goals were more aligned with the goals of current mathematics change efforts, it is useful to understand better the nature of their learning.[8]

Drawing on the idea of transformative learning (Mezirow, 1997), I find that the Railside teachers had developed practices that supported a continual shifting of their collective framework for mathematics teaching and learning—a kind of learning that supports transformation as opposed to reinforcing the status quo. Frameworks are constituted by habits of mind and points of view, both important to how teachers make sense of their work. The Railside math teachers developed ways of interaction that supported new habits of mind for teaching and provided ways for them to reflect on their points of view. By coordinating their understanding of their reform slogans, questioning the assumptions underlying their categories for students, and rendering classroom practice visible in their conversations, the Railside math teachers made many aspects of teaching and learning available for collective reflection and inquiry.

South's reform program sought to transform teachers as well, but it appeared to be less successful at fundamentally changing teachers' points of view about mathematics teaching and learning. This could be, in part, because of the distance between the reform activities (interdisciplinary research groups, whole-staff retreats) and the mathematics classroom. The teachers reported few opportunities to make sense of their reform in a subject-specific way; indeed, one of their whole-school reform sponsors did not have any subject-specific professional development available on its list of approved providers. There were no resources within the reform program to support questioning assumptions about students and math learning or opening up windows on classroom practice. While there may be some important benefits to the cross-disciplinary consultations and discussions they regularly engaged in, the mystique of mathematics seemed to make it harder for nonspecialists to question math teachers' classroom practice: Outsiders want to avoid looking "dumb" to their colleagues, despite reporting to our research team some misgivings about the alignment of the math department's teaching with the school's broader mission. Effectively, the math teachers were granted a partial exemption from the whole-school reform. The impetus and ownership for the reform came from the outside and could be deflected by cultural assumptions about and intimidation by mathematics. The Railside math teachers' reform project, on the other hand, came from within. The differences between the way these teacher learning processes worked at the two schools are thus revealing, as they delineate the kinds of changes that would need to happen in order to support meaningful and substantive change in teachers' everyday learning.

The kinds of resources found within the Railside teacher community help us better understand what teachers need to implement reform programs in a serious way. Most reform programs and professional development efforts produce a plethora of artifacts. As was discussed earlier, the reform artifacts used at Railside were not more inherently meaningful than those used at South. While artifacts may provide conceptual resources for teachers' pedagogical reasoning, the ways they are put to use is more significant.

That is where the other learning resources become important. First, the classification systems in use at Railside differed from those in use at South. Since conversational categories are used to model problems of practice, the conceptual entailments of those categories often get built into the solutions to these problems. It is notable that while the Railside teachers had some alternative language to model the curriculum-student mismatch problem Tina presented (e.g., "status"), even Guillermo's ultimate challenge to Tina used traditional ability-centered categories ("Think of the ones that you think of as fast learners and figure out what they're slow at"). This study suggests that researchers and professional developers can contribute to more effective pedagogical reasoning by providing more nuanced category systems for teachers to use in discussing problems of practice. We would greatly assist teachers by helping them to develop more careful technical language through which to model their work.

Second, the Railside teachers' rendering of classroom events in conversations through teaching replays and rehearsals provided a figurative realm for applying and examining general values and principles. These conversations seemed to be a critical supplement to the numerous formal professional development activities in which Railside teachers engaged. For example, during the course of the study, teachers underwent training in Complex Instruction (Cohen, 1994a; Horn, 2012), participated in weeklong summer workshops about graphing calculators in the algebra classroom, and attended and presented at professional conferences. Despite this intensive participation in formal professional development activity, their collegial conversations seemed to serve the important purpose of providing discursive and interactional tools for actually implementing some of these ideas in their classrooms with their students. The specificity of the reported or imagined student-teacher dialogue represented in the replays and rehearsals operationalized reform activities in the teachers' conversations.

Our field would be well served to further specify the resources and mechanisms for teachers' everyday learning. Not only would such work contribute to our theoretical understanding of the nature of learning, but such research would allow us to create more authentic and ecologically valid learning experiences for teachers.

Chapter 10

Learning from Teaching, Together

Ilana Seidel Horn and Judith Warren Little

I started the geoboards today and it—it felt like mayhem. Like, it felt like
no one kind of understood. I just had a vision of what it—I *thought* it
should look like and it didn't look anything like that.
          —Alice March, 9th-grade algebra teacher

Alice's account of mayhem opened the weekly meeting of the Algebra Group,
nine teachers at Railside High School who succeeded, through their collective
activity, in fostering a higher-than-predicted level of student participation and
achievement in mathematics.[1] Alice's words may strike many as typical of those
spoken by beginning teachers, or perhaps by more experienced teachers attempting something new. What is *not* typical is the way the conversation subsequently
unfolded as she and her colleagues worked to understand what happened in
Alice's classroom that day and what it might have meant for their teaching. That
exchange, one of many recorded in this group, provided the starting point for a
generative, analytic conversation among teaching colleagues.

This chapter is motivated by a practical dilemma: Deep, sustained conversations among teachers about matters of teaching and learning remain uncommon,
even among groups that might reasonably be seen as professional communities
committed to instructional improvement (McLaughlin & Talbert, 2001). With
that in mind, we pay close attention to the details of dialogue as teachers talk
with one another about teaching and learning mathematics. In the larger project
that these data come from, we examined recorded talk among teachers in small
working groups within two different schools to suggest how and under what conditions such dialogue might generate professional learning, bolster professional
community, and strengthen classroom practice. Each of the four teacher working groups—some organized within subject departments, others at the grade or
school level—embraced a collective identity (like the "Algebra Group" in which

Alice participated), and each saw itself as engaged in improvement-oriented professional work.

Although the teachers' interactions arose in ordinary workplace contexts, our broader aim is to contribute to a general framework characterizing professional learning opportunity as an avenue for both individual learning and collective capacity. That is, we see this analysis as part of a larger program of research that permits us to understand the possibilities for school change residing in professional communities and other contexts with the potential to stimulate and support teachers' learning.

LOCATING PROBLEMS OF PRACTICE IN THE FLOW OF TEACHER TALK

Teachers talk together in different ways, and different kinds of teacher talk can be viewed as productive in some way. In this analysis, we focus specifically on conversational moments that capture classroom experiences and signal puzzles of teaching practice. We treat the frequency and nature of such moments as indicators of talk that may support professional learning and professional community. We ask questions like, What part do such problems of teaching and learning play in this group of teachers' recorded talk? How often do they arise, with regard to what aspects of teaching, and with what degree of specificity and transparency? What kind of traction do these problems find within these conversations?

When we look for conversations conducive to professional learning, we seek evidence that the dialogue does more than simply report on or point to problems of practice. Instead, we look for interactions that supply specific means for identifying, elaborating, and reconceptualizing the problems that teachers encounter and for exposing or generating principles of practice. In our data corpus, we find that the groups differ with regard to both the incidence of problems of practice — how densely they populate the conversation in any given group — and the ways in which they are taken up or not.

For this chapter, we explore one extended episode of talk — the "Alice's Mayhem" episode — to show how specific discourse practices characterize a teacher group in which professional learning opportunities abound. Specifically, we posit that the way that teachers enact and build on routine ways of normalizing and investigating problems of practice opens up opportunities for learning in, from, and for practice. In 17 meetings of the Algebra Group recorded over a 4-month span, we found a high proportion of sustained talk about problems of practice and thus see this group as a useful case in working toward a conceptual model of generative dialogue. By comparison, in meetings among other collaborative groups spanning the same period, we located substantially fewer such episodes and fewer instances in which expressed problems of practice were taken up at any length.

NORMALIZING PROBLEMS OF PRACTICE

In all of the teacher work groups we studied, we repeatedly saw exchanges in which teachers' expressed problems were met with *normalizing* responses—that is, moves that define a problem as normal, an expected part of classroom work and teacher experience. Normalizing moves supply reassurance ("you'll be fine, don't worry") and establish solidarity ("it happens to all of us"). Yet systematic, patterned differences emerged in the way such practices functioned in interaction across the groups.

Specifically, differences in teachers' moves to normalize a problem resulted in turning a conversation either *away from the teaching* or *toward the teaching* as an object of collective attention. In the former case, teachers conveyed reassurance, sometimes adding specific bits of advice or familiar aphorisms, before turning away from the problem and moving on to other instrumental tasks. In the latter case, teachers treated the shared and expected (normal) character of a problem as the starting point for detailed discussion of specific classroom instances and to help anchor emergent advice to problems in general and larger principles of teaching.

Teachers have much to accomplish in their work together, and the time devoted to unpacking problems of practice varies in relationship to the priorities at hand. In part, the urgency of planning stems from the organization of teachers' work. Teachers do not violate professional norms by not sorting out a student's puzzling contribution, and school leaders would seldom reprimand them for failing to do so. Yet in many schools it would be abhorrent to arrive to school without lesson plans; in fact, teachers are often asked to provide these to administrators on a regular basis.

At the same time, we argue that the foundation for individual professional learning and collective capacity for improvement is more surely supplied where problems of practice stimulate in-depth discussions of the sort outlined in the second scenario. To illuminate the nature of such discussions, we examine the normalizing practices made visible in the Alice's Mayhem episode and the way they function to open up opportunities for learning.

NORMALIZING THE PROBLEM OF "MAYHEM" AND OPENING OPPORTUNITIES FOR LEARNING

The episode we call "Alice's Mayhem" took place on a Tuesday afternoon early in the school year, at the beginning of the weekly meeting of the Algebra Group. Alice, a new teacher, arrived to the meeting drying her tears, accompanied by Jill, the co-chair (head) of the department. The other teachers delayed the start of the meeting, awaiting their arrival and encouraging Alice to share her account of what had happened ("put it out there"). Alice and her colleagues then devoted about 15 minutes to elaborating and probing the rather daunting image of mayhem, successively posing and evaluating three possible explanations for the troubles in Alice's classroom. Over the course of the conversation, "mayhem" was made accessible to reflection and remedy. The talk exposed interpretive resources by which these teachers routinely made sense of their experience, along with strategies for anticipating and curtailing the inevitable instances of mayhem when they occur.

In the following excerpt, Alice's colleagues responded to her account of mayhem. They began by first assuring her that the disconnect between vision and reality is an enduring dilemma in teaching for both novice and experienced teachers.[2]

1. *Alice*: Uh, well my frustration, I think, was just, I started the geoboards today and it—it felt like mayhem. Like, it felt like no one kind of understood. I just had a vision of what it—I *thought* it should look like and it didn't look anything like that and then . . . I was trying to
5. keep students together in their groups, but they, they weren't staying together. And then . . . What was happening? So then I wanted to communicate the whole putting the rectangle around the triangle but it's like, if I do it in front of class, no one's paying attention but if I go around to groups, I felt like I wasn't
10. communicating it to all the students. So I think that—and after processing it with Jill, I think they were getting stuff done. It's just that I have a vision of what groupwork should look like, and it's not looking anything like that. And I just feel like they're getting more and more unfocused in class.
15. *Guillermo*: That would be my fourth block [class].
    [*laughter*]
    Female: And mine!
    Jill: But a reality, right?
    Guillermo: Yeah.
20. *Jill*: Reality check is that we all know what it *can* look like, we all know what we're *striving* for. But my God—we're just like this *all* the time. After 10 years, after 2 years, after 5 years, every day is like that because we don't know what's walking into our classroom. On a daily basis.
25. *Howard*: I'll tell you, Alice, I mean I've been here a long time. <unclear> This was the first time I ever used geoboards with an Algebra One class because I was so afraid of how easily they would just go off and play. And the only reason that I attempted it *this* time was this was our time to do it. And as much as it wasn't
30. meeting like a vision I was putting out, that might have just been low expectations

Alice: Yes.

Howard: I mean, you put something like that in their hands for the first time and there's a certain level of, play with it, <unclear> but
35. whether they're focusing on <unclear>.

As in other groups we observed, the algebra teachers quickly normalized Alice's story through reassurances about her problem: Her class gets likened to other unruly classes (lines 15 & 17); the experience was portrayed as endemic to the work of teaching, no matter what the teacher's level of experience (lines 21–25), and may have been a consequence of using a potentially distracting manipulative (lines 26–28), something that could even happen to teachers who have been here "a long time."

One might imagine the conversation stopping here, with someone saying, "So, really, don't let it upset you," or "It's just a matter of experience—it will get better." Indeed, placation without investigation is one of two main patterns in the other groups, the second being to conclude that the problem was outside the control of the teacher.[3] However, normalizing practices in the Algebra Group did not merely preface a pat explanation ("it's just classroom culture") or quick aphorism ("don't smile until Christmas"). Rather, the normalizing moves were joined to questions that provided a starting place for a deeper discussion by explicitly eliciting more detail and inviting analysis (Horn, 2010). In other words, normalization often activated a crucial transition to focused reflection on a problem of practice. In this instance, after Guillermo, Jill, and Howard rushed to assure Alice that her problem was normal ("reality check"), Guillermo asked:

Alice, can you identify the source of the squirreliness? Like <unclear> they, they wanted to play with the geoboards but didn't have time to do it?

The ensuing discussion was complex and extensive, lasting 11 more minutes and including statements by 8 of the 10 teachers present. Two experienced teachers, orienting to the problem of "starting geoboards," speculated that the squirreliness arose from a familiar kind of teaching challenge: introducing 9th-graders to math manipulatives (geoboards), which naturally lend themselves to playing. But as Alice considered Guillermo's question, she recalled that the trouble did not originate with the geoboard activity. Over the next 3 minutes, she reframed the problem twice. First, she posited that students' understanding of area (or more precisely, lack of it) was at the root of the mayhem problem.

Yeah. I'm not sure, I think it even—it felt like it kind of even started with the warm-up, like they weren't—I don't know. Maybe it was a sense of—it's like, they don't really have a concept of area *at all*. So maybe it was a sense, maybe they're afraid of the—of not being able to do these ideas. No, it was like they were just counting the squares the whole time. I kept saying, "Okay, well, is there a rectangle there?" and it was like—that was going *beyond* for them. Um. So maybe it's just that the concepts are challenging for them. I don't know. (36–44)

This reformulation had a provisional sense to it. A couple of pauses, several unfinished sentences, expressions of uncertainty ("I don't know"), and explicit revisions ("No, it was . . .") all indicated that this was an emerging version of what happened in the classroom and had not yet been carefully reflected upon. Alice's new account considered the students' mathematical understanding: They had just been counting the squares to figure out area, and she wanted them to find rectangles to calculate the areas more efficiently.

Alice then proposed a second revision by introducing an element that had also been missing in the original formulation—her own anger with the students:

Yeah. I guess there was that sense that by the end? I was like—it was like the first time that I just felt *angry* with them like . . . because it felt so—like I wasn't in control? that I started to get angry. And part of that is my control issues. And so, I didn't even know—like by the end I was like, "I want you guys to stay after." And I didn't know if I felt *good* about having them stay after or if that was a good way to handle it, but it was like—I just wanted them to know I mean *business* and we needed to get *work* done and—you know? (*2-second pause.*) So.

Again, a colleague's question ("Were they receptive to that?") invited further elaboration. Accompanied by much laughter, Alice replayed the classroom scene (Horn, 2005) and the students' response:

Alice: Yeah, I mean, they were like (*exhales indignantly*), "This is not fair!"
Jill: (*laughs*)
Alice: I'm like (*2-second pause*)
Jill, Guillermo: (*laughing*)
Alice: I mean like.
Guillermo: Perfect.
Alice: So they stayed after two minutes, you know. And I mean that was. It was fine.
Jill: Snorting, *like holding back a laugh.*
Guillermo: Yeah, but they're like *dying* for those two minutes, right? Like two minutes =
Alice: Yeah I mean, it's like, "Two minutes? Come on!"
Charlie and others: (*laughing*)
Alice: So.

Alice's admission of anger and her humorous replay of the students' response prompted another set of normalizing moves. These focused on the pervasively emotional nature of teaching experience. Guillermo linked her experience to his own of becoming angry in his fourth-period class:

> You really are describing my fourth block. Minus the staying after for two minutes. (*Alice, others laugh.*) Because at some point I'm angry enough that I don't want to SEE them for two more minutes! (*others laughing*). (90–94)

As he expressed his empathy for and identification with her experience, he pointed in passing to a lesson from experience ("I also don't want to try to enforce two minutes of silence or whatever"), then went on to talk through what he had realized through his struggles with his own class:

> So I got angry, too, at what they wouldn't do. I think a large part of that is inevitable first-time-through things. For me, it's first-time-through like fall Math 2, given what they had last semester for Math 1 and some of those frustrations and um—I just don't know what's reasonable for them in terms of expectations. (130–136)

Here, he invoked a teaching principle that had been suggested by earlier comments: The first time through something (be it a curriculum, an activity, or, in his case, a class with a particular history), it is difficult to know what is reasonable to expect of and from students—and anger interferes with one's ability to gauge realistic expectations.

Of course, broad statements of principle do not provide much leverage for changing practice; they do not map out obvious actions to be taken by the teacher in any small or large sense. However, Guillermo's next conversational move applied this principle back to Alice's experience of mayhem. In doing so, he provided a substantively different interpretation of what went on that day. In her emergent account of the mayhem, Alice had bemoaned that students were counting squares to calculate area. She cast this as evidence that the students did not "have a concept" of what was going on mathematically. Having helped develop the curriculum these students encountered in the prior year, Guillermo explicated what might be reasonable to expect, saying:

> So I would have thought that given the unit that they do in 8th grade, that a sense of area would not be an issue. But some of them think that area's length times width. So in some sense, their counting squares is the *right* thing. (136–142)

Applying his own principle about what was reasonable to expect, Guillermo countered Alice's earlier explanation: Their counting squares is the right thing because it was more conceptually on target with the idea of area than the formulaic length times width version that many students have. We cannot say from this single interaction whether this bit of pedagogical content knowledge was incorporated into Alice's understanding of the mayhem, but it certainly was made available to her and others at the table. This instance of turning toward problems of teaching provided this work group with a professional learning opportunity linking student learning, classroom activity, and the teaching practices.

Guillermo's identification with Alice's mayhem went beyond simply normalizing it to assure her. It deepened their affiliation with each other and the group, reinstating them as engaged in similar goals in their teaching. Others' contributions also displayed this pattern of likening Alice's problem of mayhem to their own experience, which served to build both professional knowledge and identities. As the conversation went on, different teachers articulated more principles about teaching and the gradual, uneven process of learning to teach. For example, Jill recognized a similar situation in her own teaching, recounting the "chaos" that ensued the first two times she used a particular activity to introduce area: "And I remember thinking, 'What did I not get the first time around?' You know?" Likewise, Carrie picked up Jill's example, having taught the same activity, and used it to state a more general principle for interpreting and responding to "mayhem" or "chaos":

> *Carrie*: When, when they get upset and they seem to be off task and acting goofy, it usually is motivated by "I'm so confused and the *last* thing I want to do is *admit* I'm confused
> *Alice*: Mhm.
> *Carrie*: so I'm—instead I'm going to find a way to distract myself or distract others so that I don't have to *face* the *fact* that
> *Alice*: Mhm.
> *Carrie*: I don't know how to do something. Um. So I always try to sympathize. Like, I'll feel, feel myself being *mad*, like, "You guys aren't working! What are you doing?" And then I like try to take a step back and say, "Okay. *What* are they afraid of?"
> *Alice*: Mhm.
> *Carrie*: How can I make them feel comfortable with that fear?
> *Alice*: Mhm.
> *Carrie*: "What can I say to them or what can I do for them to make them feel, like, this is a safe place." And that usually takes me somewhere where—it never is *fully* successful, but I see some successes and then that translates into other days that become more successful. (186–203)

Carrie's contribution illustrates characteristic features of the "principled" talk in this group: Principles for teaching are cast not as tips and tricks but as ways of interpreting students' responses. This principled or generalized talk gains specification through what Horn (2005, 2010) has termed "rehearsals" and "replays," or narrations that enact the principle in anticipated or past practice. In this instance, Carrie narrated her own thinking as she helped assuage her students' fears about failing in a mathematics task, which she saw as underlying their rowdy behavior. Over the 15 minutes of talk, the teachers overtly identified with Alice's problem, reinstating their affiliation, and built at least three such principles for interpreting the case of mayhem by attending closely to what students do and say:

> *Interpretive principle 1 (Guillermo, Jill, Charlie):* When teaching any activity, content, or group the first time, you can't anticipate what students will do, but whatever you learn from paying attention to students will help you in the future.
>
> *Interpretive principle 2 (Howard):* When kids act out in this context, it may be because you've underestimated the novelty of the task or materials—e.g., kids want to play with manipulatives at first.
>
> *Interpretive principle 3 (Carrie):* When kids act out in this context, it may be because they're confused or fearful about the content you're teaching and trying to hide their confusion or fear.

Through affiliation, the teachers explicitly relieved one another from *blame* but not from *responsibility* for problems of practice, conveying the expectation that they would all consistently learn in and from their teaching practice. Thus, Jill ended her account of "chaos" by saying, "And so you, you *can't* blame yourself for something that there's *no* way you could know. And you'll take that knowledge and you'll do something with it the *next* time around."

NORMALIZING, SPECIFYING, AND GENERALIZING IN TALK ABOUT PROBLEMS OF PRACTICE

As the conversation develops, certain dynamics emerged that we posit are, in combination, importantly constitutive of professional learning opportunity within a robust professional community. First and most central, teachers in the Algebra Group, like many other work groups, normalized problems of practice. What distinguished their conversations were the ways that they legitimated such problems as deserving of sustained attention. By identifying with a problem and then routinely asking questions to elicit additional information, they communicated the inherent complexity and ambiguity of teaching while supplying themselves with the specifics needed to introduce and evaluate multiple explanations for the problems that surface. That is, normalizing practices functioned here not as a means for merely providing reassurance and moving on to other tasks, but as a means for digging into problems of practice.

Second, the teachers' conversation moved constantly between specific accounts of classroom practice and general lessons from experience. Identification and affiliation could have happened without the deeper learning opportunities. If only tales of woe had been shared with Alice, the conversation might have proved rich in detail, comforting, or even cathartic, but not necessarily generative for the teachers' sense-making. On the other hand, if only general principles of teaching had been shared, unattached to specific examples, the work of applying these principles to actual practice would have remained opaque, left to the individual teachers to imagine. The work of recontextualizing such generic teaching principles or unspecified images of classroom practice is a central challenge of teacher learning. The linking work that happens in this conversation helped the group collectively construct a class of instances and narrated responses clustered around defining and explaining a common teaching problem and a set of principles for responding to it.

GENERATIVE DIALOGUE AS ROUTINE PRACTICE

Analysis of the full array of Algebra Group meetings convinces us that the "Alice's Mayhem" episode is typical in two respects. First, it typified the way that the group spent its time together, structuring talk and activity to make classroom practice visible and available for consideration. There was little or no talk of mundane administrative business in any meeting we observed. A weekly "check-in" routine balanced the need for coordination (what mathematics topics and tasks each teacher is working on this week) with the opportunity to take up problems or pursue new ideas. At the end of the "Alice's Mayhem" episode, Jill asked, "Does anyone else want to check in?" thus confirming the status of the "Alice's Mayhem" exchange as within the expected bounds of the weekly check-in routine.

Across the meetings we recorded, the teachers also worked on the mathematics that they taught, doing problems together to unpack the nature of the cognitive (and social) demands on students or predict what would be difficult to learn. They worked on designing or revising mathematics tasks so that they built students' conceptual understanding and confidence, or talked about using groups effectively so that students contributed to one another's success. And throughout, the group took a stance of learning in and from the classroom practice of its members. References to "struggles" appear repeatedly in our records of the group's meetings, individual interviews, and email messages. *Struggle,* as employed in this group, signaled intellectual and emotional engagement in learning, whether by students or teachers.

Our highlighted episode typified the group's conversational practices as they took up expressed problems of classroom practice. Although problems of practice surfaced in every collaborative group we studied, and although teachers in every group responded by "normalizing" those problems in some fashion, this group consistently employed normalizing moves in ways that highlighted the complex, ambiguous nature of teaching and opened up problems for analysis and reflection. Problems expressed by experienced teachers elicited fewer overt reassurances than novice teacher Alice received, but they otherwise prompted the same kinds of questions and reflection evident in the "Alice's Mayhem" episode. Through the interplay of normalizing, specifying, and generalizing, often seamlessly interwoven in specific utterances, teachers made their pedagogical reasoning transparent. By embracing problems of practice within the scope of the group's shared purposes and tasks, and by cultivating conversational practices that opened up and sustained attention to problems of practice when they surface, the Algebra Group went some considerable distance toward creating opportunity for professional learning and the collective pursuit of ambitious teaching and learning.

CONCLUSION

Energetic, competent, thoughtful teachers who took responsibility for students' success populated each of the groups we investigated. In this respect, they met an accepted threshold of professional learning community. Yet the groups demonstrated quite different orientations toward problems of practice and commanded quite different resources for engaging these problems when they arose. In part, they differed in the conversational room they make for problems of practice in the first place, itself a function of the purposes and tasks that bring them together. But given the disclosure of problems of practice, they also differed in the familiar practice of rendering problems as normal and expected in teaching—and thus shifting the generative potential of their talk together.

One might reasonably ask what enabled the Algebra Group to locate professional learning at the center of workplace professional community in a way that other committed, energetic groups do not. What supported the generative dialogue so consistently and routinely in evidence? In this analysis, we focused on specific conversational practices, but it is *through* those practices that the members of the group marshal other intellectual, social, and material resources.

Central to these resources are those focused on knowledge of mathematics and on shared commitments to expanding students' access to this subject. The Algebra Group teachers took steps to deepen their expertise in mathematics teaching through collective participation in high-quality professional development and through strong network ties with individuals and groups invested in mathematics teaching reform. References to ideas and practices derived from those individuals and groups occurred frequently in meetings and interviews, and outside colleagues periodically attended the group's weekly meetings or the more intensive "Algebra Week" event in the summer. By contrast, the other collaborative groups we studied were more dependent on their own internal resources and more tenuously connected to external sources of expertise or encouragement, especially in the subject domains in which they taught (see also Little, 2003).

In addition, the Algebra Group teachers consistently made use of an extensive, shared set of curricular resources (the "Algebra Binder," together with a bookshelf of related texts, notebooks, and folders) that they located, selected, revised, or designed in their efforts to make mathematics more accessible to all their students. As Ball and Cohen (1996) anticipated, these materials constituted important "terrain for teachers' learning" (p. 8). By contrast, other collaborative groups had fewer shared curricular resources on which they could draw, either because they were in an early stage of collaborative curriculum development, because they did not conceive of curriculum as a public resource for their own learning—or both.

Finally, demonstrated patterns of initiative and leadership sustained the group's attention to problems of practice. Building on the record of a former chair who was described as "remarkable at building community," the co-chairs at the time of our study saw themselves as responsible for maintaining the group's ethos of professional learning. They took a visible role in posing questions, eliciting accounts of classroom practice, preserving a focus on mathematics, teaching, and learning—and encouraging initiative of these sorts by others. Such leadership practice proved less visible, ambitious, or consistent in other groups we studied.

We contend that talk within teacher communities is likely to be generative of professional learning and instructional improvement to the extent that it invites disclosure of and reflection on problems of practice. In the analysis developed here, we identify one commonplace conversational practice—"normalizing" problems of classroom practice—that routinely serves as an identifiable turning point as teachers either open up or close off generative dialogue. When linked closely to questions that invite disclosure and reflection, the practice of "normalizing problems of practice" functioned as a bridge to a more probing investigation of teaching and learning. Variation in this practice may serve as one crucial indicator of the generative potential of teacher talk, but certainly not the only one. By paying close attention to this and other details of dialogue, we propose to make headway on a conceptual model of professional learning opportunity, one that specifies the nature of robust, public pedagogical reasoning, together with the cognitive, social, material, organizational, and normative resources that enable it.

Chapter 11

Building and Sustaining Professional Community for Teacher Learning

*Carlos Cabana, Barbara Shreve,
and Estelle Woodbury*

Creating new and meaningful learning experiences for students at Railside required teacher roles and experiences different from those in a typical school environment. Railside math teachers took a learning stance toward teaching and empowered one another as professionals to reflect on their practice and to make decisions about curriculum and instruction to support student learning. While part of this was an individual response to student understanding, the department also worked as a community to learn from each of its members and to build shared practices. Fostering an environment that supported honest examination of challenges and working together to grow required careful attention to building community and to setting norms for collaboration. While the previous two chapters have discussed the nature of the conversations among department members about teaching and learning, this chapter describes some of the department practices that developed to support collaboration and learning, as well as the more informal ways of working together that sustained the efforts. We highlight four key practices: (1) doing math together, (2) working on "groupworthy" department goals together, (3) distributing leadership, and (4) attending to hiring and new teacher induction.

DOING MATH TOGETHER

Railside math teachers put into place regular activities that allowed the department to work together to make sense of teaching and learning. One way they did this was by doing math together in meetings. By sharing their own solution processes and analyzing the experience of doing the math, teachers were able to see different ways of thinking, reasoning, making sense, and finding solutions, which facilitated the group redefining what it meant to learn math in high school.

Working on math together was a key element of the Algebra Collaboration Week (as mentioned in Chapters 8 and 10) that the department organized each August to prepare for the upcoming school year.[1] Although the week initially focused on Algebra I, teachers participated regardless of which courses they were teaching. During the week different members of the department shared new problems that they were interested in incorporating into the curriculum and presented them to the group as they would to a class of students. Teachers then engaged in "doing the math," working through and presenting solutions as students would in the classroom. After discussing the mathematics, the group would also reflect on and analyze the lesson structure and presentation of the problem. They examined how new problems were scaffolded, and whether those scaffolds supported group interactions or changed the demands of the mathematics and the different learning opportunities the activity afforded. This kind of discussion set the tone and expectation for how members would discuss math and curriculum together throughout the year.

Doing math together served multiple functions in developing a culture of learning and collaboration in the department. It allowed teachers to learn about one another as learners, and to see more strategies for solving problems and for organizing solutions than they were able to see on their own. This directly supported work in classrooms. In class, the teaching style the department developed required teachers to make sense of students' thinking and ideas in the moment, and to help students understand one another's thinking and form those ideas into coherent, specific statements about the mathematics. To do this, teachers needed to be confident in their own understanding of the content as well as comfortable being seen as a learner alongside students, working to understand one another's thinking. Experiencing this first when working on math with colleagues broadened the perspectives and deepened the understanding that teachers brought to problems, and supported their ability to see different solution paths when students shared them in class. Teachers also built familiarity and comfort with responding to strategies they did not initially completely understand. In addition, teachers could practice asking questions and publicly making sense of a new strategy without invalidating it. This public way in which teachers worked to develop their craft also set the expectation that adults would work collaboratively to improve.

Over time, the practice of doing math problems together also allowed the space to reflect as a team on how tasks were presented to students. As different teachers presented their ways of introducing and processing tasks by modeling them with the adults, department members learned from one another's pedagogical decisions. Teachers were able to analyze the kinds of questions that were asked, the different scaffolds that were in place (or omitted) in the activities, the way the written handouts were structured or phrased, and the ways groupwork was supported in the lesson design. These conversations were used to identify opportunities and trade-offs connected with teacher choices. By situating doing math together as part of its collaborative practice, the department was able to deepen individual and collective understanding of the art of teaching mathematics. This helped to build a common set of pedagogical moves that provided coherent learning opportunities for students across courses.

Railside department members created opportunities to do math together beyond formal meeting contexts; teachers would steal 5 minutes in the copy room to share ideas, stop by a colleague's classroom to visit, work together to create lessons after and before school, share student work, and grade together. Through this regular practice of sharing problems and ideas came a collection of common curriculum resources each teacher organized in a personal set of binders.

This collection of resources — drawn from different texts, supplemental resources, workshops and conferences teachers attended, and activities observed in other classrooms — became the foundation of the curriculum used in the department. Teachers' initial work of doing math problems together extended to integrating those problems into their classes, and ultimately to developing a Railside curriculum. Rather than relying on a specific text, course teams together defined objectives and a sequence for major units, and turned to their binders to build the lessons that would comprise those units. After trying activities in their classes, teachers shared their struggles and successes implementing the lessons and what students learned from them with their colleagues, allowing the department to refine curriculum over time.

WORKING ON "GROUPWORTHY" DEPARTMENT GOALS TOGETHER

In the same way Railside students experienced learning mathematics through making sense of groupworthy tasks, the math department grew and evolved over years of taking on challenges, building on contributions from many different members. In that time, a culture in the professional community developed so that teachers were able to tackle difficult issues together and a "Railside Way" of teaching and learning math developed. Looking back at the process of learning and change in the department, at each stage in its development the department was addressing a challenge that could be characterized as a groupworthy task (see Chapters 2, 8, and 9 for a description of groupworthy tasks). Those tasks included:

- detracking 8th-grade math
- creating a reform-based curriculum that supported Complex Instruction pedagogy
- embracing Algebra for All (detracking Algebra I)

- reducing rates of D/F grades
- understanding the needs and experiences of African American students
- responding to the challenge of standardized tests

Each challenge listed above was taken on as a shared task by the Railside math department and was similar to the groupworthy tasks that helped to set the tone and define community in math classrooms. The shared work consistently required the input and participation of all members in order for progress to be made, it illustrated important dilemmas in the learning and teaching of mathematics, it allowed for multiple ways to conceptualize the issue, and it lent itself to multiple paths to arrive at a solution. These groupworthy tasks played a critical role in shaping the professional learning community of the department.

The department's major pieces of work fostered two important principles that became hallmarks of the professional community in the department: teachers as learners and distributed leadership. In each challenge that the department took on as a collective task, there was no individual who could be seen as an expert. Instead, each person had a role to play as a learner in contributing to a successful outcome. For example, as the department took on learning about Complex Instruction, the most experienced members of the department were engaged in training alongside new teachers. As teachers tried things in their classrooms, they were expected to share back with their colleagues in department meetings or course teams, get feedback and more ideas, and then continue to try new things in their classes. Similarly, people who attended summer workshops or professional development during the school year were encouraged and expected to share back what they had learned.

When the department decided to detrack Algebra I, the work was launched by ensuring that nearly all teachers (including two new colleagues) would be teaching the course, which created a common experience that teachers could discuss. The first Algebra Week was held, and the agenda for the week was crafted to emphasize the need to explore and learn together. Coming out of this week, algebra teachers decided to begin meeting after school on a weekly basis to further learn and to plan.

Although the work evolved over time, the department was never without a large question that drove its collective efforts. After several years of making sense of detracking math classes, the department recognized that outcomes for African American and Latino males were not improving as it wanted them to. Together, department members analyzed results and worked to change those outcomes. When the achievement patterns persisted, the department sought outside support to better understand the issues and to advance its understanding of the learning experience of African American males. The department invited university researchers in to help understand and describe the group's math experiences at Railside, and to give the department new lenses through which to view and work on the dilemma.

As standardized testing became the only externally valued method of evaluating student achievement, the Railside department was confronted with another challenge: taking on the task of improving the number of students testing at Advanced and Proficient on the California Standards Test (CST). The department was already successful in supporting student achievement on the California High School Exit Exam; in any given year all but three or fewer seniors[2] passed. The department did this by including proportional relationship ideas in the Algebra I curriculum and creating a California High School Exit Examination (CAHSEE) course for seniors who had not yet passed the test. However, the CST presented another challenge; the curriculum implications were more pervasive and threatened the "Railside Way" of doing math. The requirement that the assessment window be at least 4 weeks before the last day of school meant that Railside students were taking a test that included material they had not yet learned. In response to the mandate, the department worked to make sense of each standardized assessment (Algebra I, Geometry, Algebra II, Summative Math) in course teams and developed curriculum that would directly impact the amount of content reached in time for the assessment window, resulting in an increase in the number of students testing at Advanced and Proficient.

Because the department's learning agenda was always so ambitious, it was also important for each teacher to take leadership in advancing the group's knowledge. Individual teachers were expected to use their strengths to contribute to the work on the department's groupworthy tasks.

DISTRIBUTED LEADERSHIP

Railside math teachers attribute much of their growth as educators to their time together because there was space to tackle big, important dilemmas about students and learning. The work was substantial enough that each person needed to take leadership in one area or another in order for the group as a whole to make progress. This stance of sharing responsibility among its members for the learning and functioning of the department reflected one of the core principles of Complex Instruction: distributed leadership. In a classroom, distributing leadership means that the teacher creates conditions that support students in taking responsibility for their own and their team's learning not by relying on experts (including the teacher), but rather by relying on one another. By using this principle as a framework for organization of adults in the department, individual teachers were able to work from their strengths, see one another as learners, and redefine what it meant to be a teacher and what it meant to be a department member.

Teachers were constantly sorting out what it meant to be a part of a department with distributed roles and responsibilities beyond the classroom. While in traditional school structures opportunities for teacher leadership can be limited to serving as the head of the department, Railside teachers had many avenues for taking leadership roles beyond the classroom. Those opportunities included working with student teachers, supporting new teachers, facilitating Algebra team meetings, leading a course team, writing curriculum to share with other teachers, and attending conferences to learn on behalf of the larger group. Teachers often stepped into the roles they saw themselves as successful in or wanting to grow in, which made it possible for individuals to grow professionally by working from their strengths while making space for individuals to explore their vulnerabilities.

The Railside department chair's most important responsibility was holding space for students and learning at the heart of the department's time together. In order to make this possible the chair was often trying to answer the question, *What is worth our time together?* In grappling with this question, department chairs actively made decisions about what issues were meaty—groupworthy—tasks that were important for the department to take on as a collective. Learning to "filter" so that the department could focus on its most important work was a key role of the department chair, allowing colleagues to be aware of but not distracted by administrative tasks or faddish external pressures. By rotating the department chair role, and usually having co-chairs, more of the department had an awareness of the task of keeping the space safe for substantive conversations. This also built broader understanding of the larger school and district context in which the department was working.

As teachers took on new roles, there were opportunities to see one another as learners because each person had to make sense of the responsibilities and tasks of the new role. For example, when teachers became course team leaders, they could affect how the team made decisions about curriculum by structuring collaboration in particular ways. Some course team leaders chose to incorporate opportunities to look at student work when the team was together in order to focus on particular experiences or results. When planning course team meetings, leaders had to figure out how to make the conversation groupworthy. One way to do this was by creating a big question that the team worked to answer such as, *What do we know about students' understanding when we look at their projects? How much scaffolding does this task require? How do we set up the task in class?*

With distributed leadership as a frame for organizing the department, it became the responsibility of the group to carry out the various tasks required of the math department. Organizing work so that each individual contributed to the strength of the collective group was closely connected to how new staff were brought into the department.

HIRING PRACTICES AND NEW TEACHER INDUCTION

For years, Railside hosted visitors from a wide variety of schools wanting to see reform in action: How did teachers adapt to 90-minute blocks? What did it look like to implement a reform curriculum? Were Complex Instruction and groupwork really effective? How did teachers meet the needs of working-class students, students of color, and English language learners? How were teachers preparing students for standardized tests while maintaining their pedagogical approach? The classrooms people visited conveyed vivid evidence of a high degree of teacher collaboration; classrooms had a similar look and feel, with similar messages on walls and similar pedagogical strategies in use. Inevitably, visitors asked questions about staffing. How did the team get skeptical teachers to participate fully? How did it support teachers who consistently struggled to be effective? The short answer was: the department did not. The department's structures for recruiting, hiring, and supporting teachers put it in a position to sidestep common obstacles when acclimating new department members, despite frequent turnover.

HIRING TOWARD A VISION

Well-qualified math teachers are such a scarce commodity that many schools are happy if they can fill vacancies with teachers with strong content knowledge and reasonable classroom management. At Railside, the department needed more: Department members wanted colleagues who shared their passion, beliefs, and ideals so that they could continue improving their work. Specifically, the group sought colleagues who shared its

- absolute conviction (not just belief) that all students can learn,
- commitment to groupwork as the primary mode of instruction, and
- strong preference to do the work of teaching in a highly collaborative way.

To find potential colleagues who shared this vision, Railside teachers developed strong relationships with Mills College and Stanford University, both of which were local and home to schools of education whose programs fit closely with the Railside math department's work. At different points in time 12 Railside teachers worked as cooperating teachers for student teachers from those schools of education, and 3 teachers taught as lecturers at one of those schools.

In addition to being rewarding and valuable professional development for Railside teachers, working with student teachers gave the department a significant advantage in recruiting new colleagues. Over time, the department developed a process for selecting and supporting student teachers that would benefit Railside students and also help to identify prospective new hires. Department leaders worked closely with schools of education to identify student teachers who would be a good fit for the school. Cooperating teachers asked that student teachers be assigned in pairs that would team-teach for the fall semester. Team teaching allowed for strong support for students and intense conversation and collaboration for student teachers, and it had the effect of preselecting student teachers who valued collaboration. Working with student teachers was so important to the department that it was an explicit design factor in the department teaching schedule. Each cooperating teacher's schedule allowed student teachers to observe their cooperating teacher one day and then implement the same lesson the following day. In nearly all cases, the department avoided having student teachers work in upper-level math courses, because teachers felt this would be inadequate training in setting up and supporting groupwork, classroom culture, and student support.

This attention to student teacher placement meant that, in effect, the department was beginning its process of identifying and screening candidates over a year in advance of when it might know of a job vacancy. Once an opening was firm, the department used a hiring process that was itself a recruiting tool: hiring by consensus. When there was a position to fill, all math teachers worked to agree on a single candidate to bring to the principal for consideration. This let the department say to prospective new hires that each and every department member wanted them to join the team, and it also made explicit the department members' individual and collective commitment to welcoming and supporting those new colleagues. New colleagues would not be left to sink or swim, pay their dues, shuttle among various classrooms, or work alone to begin their careers. They would be joining a professional community that would care about them as much as the teachers in it cared about their students.

To prepare to hire by consensus, the entire department worked to identify what it was looking for in new colleagues, and what questions to ask that would spark revealing conversations with potential candidates. Any department member could bring a candidate to the entire group for consideration. Teachers would go observe the candidate working with students, and the candidate would be invited to spend at least a day observing at Railside. Each candidate would then be asked to come join the entire department for an hour-long conversation. While it often felt intimidating to a prospective new hire to sit in a big circle with a dozen teachers, this was an important opportunity for everyone, including the new hire, to gauge how it felt to talk and work together. While the department had some predetermined questions, the group strove to move beyond these to a more informal conversation. The department wanted the candidate to see how individuals related to one another as well as for department members to develop a feel for what it might be like to have this teacher join the group. All these interactions formed the basis for a consensus decision on which teacher to take to the principal for a hiring decision. The department was fortunate to work with three principals who trusted the department enough to always support the department's process and consensus choice.

INDUCTION

While tremendous time and energy went into hiring teachers who would be a good fit for students and colleagues, this was only the beginning of the induction process. Whenever the department hired a new teacher, department chairs would construct the master schedule to ensure that the new teacher received full support. They made sure new teachers had only one or two courses to prepare for (usually Algebra I, which almost all teachers taught, and an upper-level course), and that they could observe a veteran during their free period. Like student teachers, new teachers watched a lesson one day and then implemented it the following day. This allowed the department to share with new colleagues a complete set of pedagogical practices rather than just a lesson plan or a worksheet. New teachers saw how more experienced colleagues built classroom culture, what questions they asked, how they helped students become powerful group workers, how classroom norms were developed, and how management challenges were handled. This practice provided new teachers with a natural partner for daily conversation and support, and veterans benefited from the opportunity to be explicit about instructional decisions and to have a colleague with whom to debrief a lesson. While this observation expectation was conceived initially as a support structure for new colleagues, it also became an effective recruiting tool because it helped to identify candidates who saw daily observations as an extraordinary opportunity and who eagerly welcomed the collaboration.

Despite this support opportunity, Railside teachers recognized that the 1st year of teaching was usually very difficult no matter how strong the new teacher was. Every department member, especially department leaders, emphasized to new colleagues that they took seriously the commitment to support them. This meant helping new teachers set up and stock their classrooms; checking in routinely to see how things were going, problem solve, and discuss dilemmas; and organizing opportunities to spend both social and professional time together. If new teachers were experiencing extraordinary struggles with a particular class, veteran teachers offered to observe and help, and they often took a demanding student into their class in order to lighten a new teacher's load. Department chairs made it a point to drop by a new teacher's classroom frequently, both to establish that these casual visits were the norm for the department—and did not imply judgment—and also to be able to gather perceptions on new colleagues' strengths.

The professional community at Railside was built over many years, through a process of teachers talking and working together on mathematics and issues of teacher practice. The community was strengthened and sustained over time because principles of distributed leadership and seeing teachers as learners shaped the structures that were created and the ways that colleagues interacted. Creating common experiences for teachers to discuss, whether doing math together or teaching the same course, opened spaces for rich conversations focused on student learning and pedagogical decisions. Hiring practices further supported building a community in which teachers collaborated, and the challenges of the work opened opportunities for teachers to build on their strengths to grow as leaders and teaching professionals.

Part IV

MOVING ON AND LOOKING FORWARD

The fourth and final section of this volume operates as an epilogue of sorts. Ironically, despite the documented success of the teaching practices and approaches at Railside, the department described in these chapters no longer exists today. Many of the teachers have left Railside due to external pressures that made it increasingly difficult to enact their equity pedagogy with integrity. However, former Railside teachers are working in important and productive ways to draw on what they learned and developed together at Railside to positively impact mathematics teaching in other urban districts, both in California and nationally.

In Chapter 12, Na'ilah Suad Nasir and Nicole Louie detail the forces that impinged upon the Railside mathematics department that made it impossible for them to continue their work. This included key changes at the state and district level, but also changes locally that very quickly left the teachers feeling ineffective and impotent to continue their practice.

Chapter 13 takes a more positive turn. Lisa M. Jilk and Karen O'Connell describe the professional development program that they have developed, drawing on the experiences as teachers at Railside and implemented in other states and districts. The chapter depicts in detail the six sites for learning that they have created for the teachers they work with, and how they engage these teachers in learning experiences across these six sites in ways that support their abilities to transform their approach to teaching mathematics.

In Chapter 14, we return to the key practices that defined Railside mathematics classrooms and the teachers' professional community, and to the foundational principles underlying these practices, and consider these practices and principles in relation to one another. Our hope is that this concluding discussion is useful for teachers, math department chairs, district math coordinators, and site administrators as they consider designing and implementing mathematics instruction for equity.

As has been illustrated across the chapters, there is much to learn from the close examination of the Railside mathematics department that we have undertaken in this volume.

Chapter 12

Derailed at Railside

Nicole Louie and Na'ilah Suad Nasir

At a recent conference presentation about Railside's achievements, a 1st-year mathematics teacher turned to a colleague and said that she wanted to know where Railside was so she could visit and experience firsthand what teaching and learning there looked, sounded, and felt like. She may have known that Railside was a pseudonym. What she didn't realize was that it was the very school where she herself was teaching. Railside is no longer recognizable.

In the 2009–2010 school year, both the signature pedagogy and the professional community at Railside collapsed. At the end of that year, several teachers—including three veteran department leaders—left the school. Since then, a traditional, "back-to-basics" textbook has officially replaced the inquiry-based, conceptually oriented curriculum that the department worked to develop. Student desks have been moved out of groups and into rows. More teachers have considered leaving.

This chapter addresses the question, How have teachers interpreted and understood the reasons for these shifts away from what were considered successful teaching practices? We draw on interviews, surveys with the Railside teachers who comprised the department in 2009–2010, and focus groups with three teachers to examine teachers' accounts of the factors that led to the dissolution of their department and their way of teaching. In these accounts, teachers highlight what they experienced as the negative—and often unintended—consequences of local policy changes that appeared to target accountability, standardization, and equity in the face of a serious budget crisis. In documenting the perspectives of these teachers, we advance understandings of the sustainability of equity pedagogy and mathematics reform in the context of the current complex economic and policy climate.

MATHEMATICS REFORM IN A CLIMATE OF
STANDARDIZATION AND ACCOUNTABILITY

Under the right conditions, "reform" approaches to mathematics education—encapsulated by the National Council of Teachers of Mathematics' (2000) *Principles and Standards for School Mathematics*—have been linked to a range of positive learning outcomes, including deeper and more flexible student understanding of mathematical concepts (Schoenfeld, 2002; Silver & Stein, 1996; Tarr et al., 2008) and greater enjoyment of and identification with mathematics (Boaler & Greeno, 2000; Boaler & Staples, 2008; Cobb, Gresalfi, & Hodge, 2009).

However, the availability of reform-oriented teaching for students is not simply a matter of what happens in individual classrooms. For example, several studies have found that high-stakes accountability systems discourage reform-oriented instruction, especially at schools serving students from marginalized backgrounds (McNeil, 2000; Pedulla et al., 2003; Rustique-Forrester, 2005). For example, in her multiyear ethnographic study of the impact of Texas accountability policies on magnet schools with unique academic programs and track records of success, McNeil (2000) found "a new kind of discrimination" whereby resources for poor and minority students were funneled into test preparation programs so that these students could learn "the basics," neglecting reasoning, critical thinking, real-world applications, and other facets of learning that are emphasized in mathematics reform.

At the same time, recent research has examined how various factors at the school and district level can mediate state and federal policies in ways that support (or fail to support) teachers to undertake ambitious reform (Cobb & McClain, 2006; Cobb, McClain, Lamberg, & Dean, 2003; Coburn & Russell, 2008; Spillane, 2000). For example, Coburn's research (2001; Coburn & Russell, 2008) demonstrates that teachers' opportunities to make sense of reforms are substantially shaped by school and district leaders—for example, through the nature and quality of support for teacher networks. Cobb and McClain (2006) have similarly shown that school- and district-level leaders can play critical roles in mediating state and federal high-stakes accountability policies in ways that make space for ongoing mathematics reform—for example, by supporting teacher collaboration and learning, and by engaging teachers in "the discourse of educational reform rather than of high-stakes testing" (p. 226).

Critical to framing the current study, prior research also suggests that classroom enactment of ambitious, reform-oriented teaching depends on teachers' interpretations of both their policy contexts and the meaning of reform itself, together with the material resources available to them. As Spillane (1999) has put it, teachers are "the final policy brokers" (p. 144; see also Coburn, 2001; Tyack & Cuban, 1995). This suggests that understanding processes of policy interpretation and negotiation from the perspective of teachers themselves might be particularly fruitful. Although a small but significant body of research addresses this perspective (e.g., Coburn, 2001; Little, 1996), almost no research addresses how exemplary teachers—much less exemplary mathematics teacher communities—engage in this work.

This chapter focuses on the perspectives of mathematics teachers at Railside as their district navigated a budget crisis and state and federal pressures for accountability and standardization. This case is of particular interest because of the focal teachers' long-term commitment to equity-oriented reform pedagogy, which might indicate that their practices should be especially robust in the face of external changes. Additionally, a wealth of prior research documents and analyzes their efforts—and their significant successes—to innovate around and implement major tenets of mathematics reform, and in doing so, to improve the educational outcomes of low-income students of color (e.g., Boaler & Staples, 2008; Jilk, 2009; Little & Horn, 2007). Thus, the department was productively working toward many of the same results that local and national policies targeted, another reason why their practices might reasonably have been expected to endure external changes. But in fact, the teachers report that they have been unable to sustain their ambitious equity pedagogy in mathematics. In this chapter, we explore the way that teachers made sense of the relationship between the national policy context, as well as the district and school context, and their ability to sustain their equity pedagogy. This case represents a rare opportunity to examine changes over time in teacher sense-making in a reform-oriented and historically successful high school mathematics department.

Policy Changes

In 2007,[1] Railside's district was in its third year of Program Improvement,[2] the designation under No Child Left Behind for districts that fail to make "adequate yearly progress" to raise students' test scores. Under Program Improvement, a new superintendent was hired. The new hire had a corporate background, and he had never been a classroom teacher. He had been trained by the Broad Foundation (2010), a group that advertises its superintendent preparation program with the phrase, "Wanted: The nation's most talented executives to run the business of urban education." As teachers saw it, one of his core goals was to prepare all of the students in the district to be "college-ready," a goal that they shared. However, teachers felt that he took a top-down approach to making decisions about how to reach these goals, and that they were not included in the decision-making process. They were bothered by the way they felt the district office attempted to define their work. They specifically disagreed with the assertion that teachers should be able to do their jobs within a 7-hour work day and the monitoring of classrooms to ensure regular use of the district-adopted textbook, a particular whiteboard configuration, and direct instruction.

In explaining their difficulties in maintaining their "signature pedagogy," teachers identified a number of district policies that they perceived to alter fundamental aspects of Railside's structure going into the 2009–2010 school year (the district's 5th year in Program Improvement). The district mandates that teachers saw as significantly affecting their instruction were (1) district open or "choice" enrollment for incoming freshmen; (2) a traditional bell schedule, replacing Railside's "block" schedule; (3) teacher layoffs; (4) increased tracking in English and mathematics; and (5) increases in class size.

Open Enrollment. Beginning in 2009, Railside's district adopted a policy of open or "choice" enrollment, which made it much easier for students to attend schools outside their neighborhoods through an application process. Under the new policy, Railside lost students. Between the two comprehensive high schools in their district, Railside had traditionally enrolled students from lower-income households, and a larger percentage of them were African American and Latino. Railside had a reputation as the "ghetto"[3] school in the district, and with open enrollment, demographic disparities between schools widened further. The change also meant that any students who came into the district in the middle of the school year were sent to Railside because the other school had already reached capacity, adding more transient families to the Railside community.

Moving Off the Block Schedule/Laying Off Teachers. In 1996, the teachers at Railside pushed for a block schedule and got it. Under the block, periods were 90 minutes long, most year-long courses were covered in a semester, and students took four classes per semester. As mathematics teachers saw it, one of the goals of this schedule was to ensure a rigorous, year-long algebra experience for all students, covering all of the topics traditionally covered in an algebra course without compromising their signature pedagogy. The block schedule was also intended to give students more time to make up gaps in their mathematics learning; if they needed to repeat a course, they could do so and still have enough time to get to calculus by their senior year. The department prided itself on both the size and the diversity of its calculus classes; at the time of Boaler's (2008) study, 41% of Railside seniors were taking calculus, compared to 27% at the other two schools in the study.

In the spring of 2009, Railside's district announced that the school would return to a traditional bell schedule, arguing that the block schedule was too costly. Under the block, teachers spent 75% of their contracted day with students (three periods out of four). By moving to a traditional schedule in the fall of 2009, with six 60-minute periods per day, the district was able to increase that number to 83% (five periods out of six). This schedule cost less by requiring fewer teachers to staff each department. The math department itself shrank by almost 25%, from 13 teachers to 10.

Increased Tracking. Besides saving money, the switch away from the block schedule made time in the school day for the district to place more students in support classes for English and mathematics. Incoming 9th-graders were especially targeted for these classes. Railside already offered "Algebra Success" as a supplement to regular Algebra 1 classes (begun in 2006 as a response to the district's probationary status). However, the district changed the character of Algebra Success classes substantially in 2009, perhaps as a reaction to a state accountability initiative that listed increased instructional minutes in English and mathematics for "strategic support" (i.e., to raise the test scores) as an "essential program component." Prior to 2009, Algebra Success classes ran in the spring semester only, and students enrolled in it based on interim assessments, grades, and attendance, supplemented with teacher recommendations and conversations between students, families, and teachers. By teachers' reports, these conversations were essential to the function of Algebra Success; through them, teachers were able to clarify that placement was based on a belief in each student's ability to do better with some extra time and attention. Beginning in the fall of 2009, Algebra Success became a year-long class that students were put into based solely on achievement data—low test scores, in particular—from 8th grade. At the school level, this change in placement criteria nearly tripled the number of students taking Algebra Success, expanding it from three sections (about 60 students) to eight (160 students). For individual students assigned to the remedial class, it replaced personal conversations with familiar teachers with an anonymous bureaucratic process. The year-long class also prevented many students from taking any electives.

The district also applied pressure on middle schools to increase the number of 8th-graders taking algebra, perhaps responding to equity-oriented calls nationwide for "algebra for all." However, the 8th-grade Algebra classes did not cover the same material in the same depth as the 9th-grade classes, and as a result, many of the students who took Algebra in 8th grade were not prepared to participate fully in Railside Geometry and Algebra 2. Additionally, the push of 9th-graders into Geometry created three tracks for incoming freshmen: Algebra 1, Algebra 1 plus Algebra Success, and Geometry. This contrasted sharply with the Railside math department's philosophy, pursuing heterogeneous, detracked freshman classes to promote equity in accordance with mathematics and school reform principles.

Increased Class Sizes. Another money-saving change made by the district was to increase class sizes, especially in Algebra 1. It had been a department priority to keep Algebra classes small, but in 2009, first-semester Algebra went from a student-teacher ratio of 20:1 up to the contractual maximum of 36:1. Second-semester Algebra went from 25:1 up to 36:1. Geometry classes went from 32:1 to as high as 40:1 at the beginning of the year (though the district was obligated to lower it to 36:1 by the end of September). One consequence, at the structural level, was that it was harder to move students whose initial placement was inap-propriate (for example, in Geometry when they should have been in Algebra), since all of the classes were so full.

EFFECTS ON TEACHING

Teachers perceived that three aspects of their work changed in response to the new policy context: (1) their classroom culture, (2) their instruction, and (3) their levels of emotional engagement with their work. Teachers reported that their style of teaching—emphasizing collaboration, intellectual risk-taking, student exploration, and deep mathematical connections—was extremely difficult to maintain under the circumstances created by changes in district policies. We detail each of these three perceived effects below.

Effects on Classroom Culture

According to previous research, the social and academic culture at Railside was typified by "relational equity"; students had meaningful appreciation for the diversity of backgrounds and perspectives in their school, and they respected one another and one another's ideas (Boaler, 2006a, 2008). The sense that they were losing this special student community was prevalent in teacher interviews. Al-though the interview protocol did not specifically ask teachers about changes to their classroom culture, every teacher without exception reported that it had become more difficult to achieve the kind of classroom environment that he or she found most equitable and most conducive to learning.

The causes for this change were widely agreed upon: less individualized attention for students, increased tracking, and a changing student popula-tion (largely due to "choice" enrollment). Teachers perceived that students' social and emotional needs were now greater on average than the needs of Railside's typical student body, prior to 2009. These needs seemed to teachers to be heightened further by increased tracking, as a large proportion of incom-ing students were placed in remedial classes, sending them the message that they were not smart or capable. The negative impact of these issues on student learning was further compounded by a diminished capacity on teachers' part to build strong relationships with students, for a number of reasons but most obvi-ously because of increases in class size and the schedule change, shortening class periods from 90 to 60 minutes. Together, these changes resulted in more problems with classroom management and an atmosphere in which student-to-student collaboration was harder to achieve. We briefly discuss each of these causes below.

Changes in Population. Railside has traditionally been considered the "ghetto" high school in its district—but as a neighborhood school, with enrollment determined by residential boundaries, it still enrolled many motivated, talented, and well-supported students. When the district implemented open enrollment, however, families who were more active in their children's education were freer to choose to send their students elsewhere. The most direct impact of the change in student population, as reported by teachers, was that it created behavior issues in the classroom. Six of the seven teachers (86%) said that open enrollment had affected their teaching by giving them "rougher," "needier" students who presented classroom management problems on a scale that they found challenging to deal with despite their years of experience. Many used the phrase "critical mass," saying that their classrooms were less heterogeneous than they had been. They were used to seeing students with "bad academic habits" who were not invested in school, and they had been successful in the past in turning many of those students around. With additional resources, they might have continued to be successful. However, given larger classes, more periods of teaching each day, and a smaller department, teachers reported finding themselves ill-equipped to manage the relatively homogenous classrooms full of high-need students that open enrollment, combined with more tracking, produced at their school.

Increased Tracking. Changes in tracking policies for mathematics courses compounded the effects on classroom culture of greater stratification between the high schools. The number of students placed in Algebra Success almost tripled in 2009–2010, meaning that a large proportion of the 9th-grade class—roughly two-thirds of it—entered the school in a low-status course with no explanation of why they were there. Guillermo summarized the message as, "Welcome to [Railside], we think you're mathematically stupid." He was the only teacher to perceive almost no effect from going to open enrollment; he reported that in his mind, any effects of "choice" were simply overshadowed by the tracking within the school via the expansion of the Algebra Success class. By all the teachers' accounts, this change was devastating to the Railside culture. Teachers reported that tracking influenced the classroom environment in two closely related ways: (1) It became much harder to get students to listen to one another, work together, and believe that their peers could make meaningful contributions to their learning; and (2) it became more difficult to convince students that they themselves were smart, capable of thinking and learning, and safe enough to take intellectual risks. Julian described the latter phenomenon this way:

[It was as if we were telling students], you've never gotten math, so therefore you're here [in Algebra Success]. It just felt more global and in some ways more out of their control. It was like a character flaw instead of like, "You didn't do homework for a semester, so we're going to figure out how to do that and then we'll be back on track." It made it harder to change that narrative in kids' heads.

Teachers argued that students internalized the stigma of being placed in the remedial track, and the fact of that placement undermined teachers' efforts to show students that there was an alternative to the failure they had experienced in prior mathematics classes. Five of the seven (71%) teachers interviewed echoed Julian's sentiments, stating that it had become more difficult to cultivate confidence and respect as a result of tracking.

Weaker Student Support. On top of tracking and a more difficult student population, teachers saw structural changes as making it harder for them to cultivate trusting relationships with students, especially important in the context of Railside's high-need student body and the school's increased tracking. Four teachers (57%) mentioned that larger classes and shorter class periods decreased the amount of individual attention that they were able to provide students. Deborah described what was lost, capturing both the academic and interpersonal aspects of attending to individual students:

> With 90 minutes and 20 kids, if I could get the groups working well, I could give the kids that attention that they needed to remediate. Or if kids had behavioral issues, I could give them the personal attention to let them know that (a) I'm watching, (b) I care, (c) I'm going to follow through.

The cumulative quantitative effect of larger class sizes on teacher contact with students was to more than double the number of students each teacher saw in a given day, raising it from 80 under the block schedule to 180. Several teachers connected their difficulties giving students individual attention to lower student achievement and weaker student investment in their own mathematics learning.

Effects on Instruction

Structural changes like increases in class size and a smaller faculty created two kinds of instructional challenges for teachers: increases in their administrative workload and additional intellectual challenges as teachers struggled to make sense of how to fit their pedagogy to new and unsupportive conditions. On the administrative end, the changes increased the volume of teachers' work: Bigger classes and fewer colleagues meant more students, more grading, and a wider variety of courses to plan and prepare for. Many teachers (5/7, 71%) felt that increased class size and shorter periods made it more difficult for them to implement the practices they had developed with equity in mind, namely portfolio assessment, extended warm-ups to launch student discussions, and groupworthy problems.

In several of the comments that teachers made, it was apparent that these practices meant more to them than isolated, replaceable strategies in a "bag of tricks" for teaching. Rather, they defined a coherent style and a philosophical commitment to student collaboration and inquiry around a brand of mathematics involving multiple perspectives, multiple representations, and deep connections. Increased class size was the most salient change for Deborah (though it was not the only one that she noticed). It was harder for her to manage "interactive, discovery-type activities" with larger classes, and portfolio projects also fell by the wayside; she explained, "I simply cannot read 200 of them. . . . Just keeping up with the daily homework is a struggle. Keeping track of the classwork is a struggle. It's just logistically impossible to do well."

Guillermo emphasized the disruption to his teaching style caused by the move off of the block schedule. He described the severity of the shift from 90- to 60-minute periods, explaining how for him adapting to the change was not a simple matter of moving 30 minutes of activity from one day to the next, but rather one of rethinking the fundamental structure of his lessons:

> It's not just what fits but what our lesson plan *is*. Because we got, I think we got really good at a block-schedule lesson plan that had an extended warm-up that . . . was around student voice and that generated a feel that launched the class with a certain kind of tone that allowed us to do a big, a group-work thing and now I can't figure it out. I can't, I can't do a daily extended warm-up because an hour's too long for it and then another day of groupwork—that's too interrupted, and I can't do two small versions of the same because that doesn't work. I don't get it.

Thus, Guillermo and his colleagues did not feel able to adjust to a 60-minute period simply by asking students to finish classwork at home, or by pushing the end of one day's discussion to the beginning of the next; the whole flow of their instruction needed to change. Wrapping their heads around how to use 60-minute periods required reworking significant portions of their curriculum, but with each teacher teaching more students and many teaching a wider variety of classes (since the department shrank), and shorter prep periods as well, there was very little time to either write curriculum or think carefully about instructional decisions. Furthermore, with heightened demands on their time, teachers described losing a valuable resource for making sense of their work and designing instruction: collaboration with one another (as we describe in more detail below).

In addition to the general challenges to their pedagogy that teachers felt, they reported making four specific modifications to their instruction as a result of the structural changes and shifts in classroom climate described above. These modifications were less use of extended warm-ups, less use of groupwork and groupworthy problems, and more use of test preparation materials and the district-adopted textbook. Teachers saw these changes as connected to noticeable declines in student achievement.

Extended Warm-ups. Teachers viewed extended warm-ups as important tools in mathematics instruction at Railside. In addition to laying groundwork for a lesson's mathematical content, they contributed to productive classroom culture in ways that shorter warm-ups did not, in teachers' opinion. The extended warm-ups used at Railside also set the tone for mathematical discussions, giving students a model for conducting their small-group discussions. In addition, they gave teachers important opportunities to "assign competence," publicly recognizing the mathematical insights and contributions of individual students, particularly those with lower status in the class. Three teachers—Guillermo, Julian, and Alicia—commented on their inability to use extended warm-ups in the 2009–2010 school year, noting that the absence of these warm-ups in their instruction seemed to have a negative impact on their classroom culture, making it harder to use groupworthy problems and other pieces of their signature pedagogy.

Groupworthy Problems. As has been noted in prior chapters, one particular piece of their pedagogy that teachers had used to enculturate students was the groupworthy problem (GWP). Railside teachers had crafted and refined these problems to engage students while drawing on an array of mathematical competencies so that each student had something mathematically valuable to contribute, giving traditionally "low" students confidence and "high" students "the chance to see others as smart also," as William said on his survey. Charlotte also pointed to the benefits for all students of working on GWPs, focusing on how collaboration allows students to tackle challenging ideas:

> A groupworthy problem is often an open-ended exploration with multiple
> entry points to engage all students in the group, reinforcing group roles
> and community. Although groupworthy tasks are sometimes very difficult,
> a nicely designed one can keep students working/struggling without giving
> up and helps them remember the benefits of truly collaborating.

Descriptions of GWPs as tools to shape students' perceptions of themselves and one another while engaging them with challenging mathematics content were common across all ten surveys, and the consistency of teachers' language indicates a high degree of collaboration around these problems.

Even more than their use of warm-ups, the frequency with which Railside teachers use groupworthy problems is a vital sign of their instruction, given the significance of these problems in the history of the math department's work around equity and reform (Boaler, 2008; Horn, 2005). On the survey, seven out of ten teachers reported using GWPs less in 2009–2010 than they had the previous year, and one teacher who reported no change on her survey described significant changes in her interview (Deborah). Teachers reported collaborating with colleagues around the use of GWPs on a weekly basis in 2000–2005, but only once or twice per semester in 2009–2010. Similarly, teachers reported using GWPs in their classrooms almost daily in 2000–2005, but only about once a week in 2009–2010.

Teachers described a destructive cycle between instruction and classroom culture. They felt that more negative classroom culture made it harder to use tools like extended warm-ups and groupworthy problems, while decreased use of instructional tools like groupworthy problems kept classroom culture from improving. For Alicia, the connection between students' beliefs about one another and her ability to use Complex Instruction was clear. She found that "group tasks were not going to happen" in her Algebra Success class because "the students in there . . . didn't believe that each other could learn. They didn't believe each other had anything to contribute." Like others in the department, Alicia described how her efforts to earn students' trust and shift their beliefs about themselves seemed foiled by students' knowledge that they were in the remedial track. In teachers' eyes, the negativity that resulted was incompatible with the attitude of mutual respect required to work well in a group or participate in peer presentations, and it spawned classroom management issues that made it harder to use the groupworthy problems and extended warm-ups that could have shown students their own and their peers' intelligence.

Textbooks and Test Preparation. Teachers reported that explicit pressure from the district to change their teaching methods to include more use of the textbook, more preparation for standardized tests, and more direct instruction had a negative effect on them—though the impact seems to have been primarily on their sense of professionalism and emotional engagement with their work (documented below) and less on their actual instruction.[4]

Effects on Student Achievement

Each of the five teachers who raised the issue of student achievement said that students learned less in 2009–2010 than they had in the past. Teachers attributed this change in part to changing demographics but even more to instruction that they felt was less rich and less conceptual. Julian highlighted the role of the groupworthy problems, saying, "It really struck me this year when I felt like we had fewer of them in geometry, fewer of the big groupworthy activities, that I didn't see kids consolidating their knowledge in the same way and knowing how to apply it." William depicted the changes to his pedagogy and its effects on student learning even more dramatically:

> All these lessons were just bombing, bombing, bombing. They weren't coming away with the ideas we needed to get across. . . . Because we weren't able to build that trust in each other as a class, those team conversations weren't happening. . . . It killed me, but it was either, keep throwing stuff against the wall and having none of it stick, or just saying, you know what, forget the way we'd been teaching, I need to just get the idea to them somehow and just lecture it out, or just put it on the board. It didn't feel like teaching to me, and it came through in the results. They did not learn.

William described the achievement of his algebra classes as "frightening" and said that even his Calculus students did not learn as much as the students the previous year. In addition to this kind of qualitative data, a number of teachers reported that more students were getting failing grades. For example, Guillermo described the number of D's and F's across the school's 12 Algebra classes as "shockingly" and "horrifically" high.

Effects on Teachers' Professional Community

With all of the changes detailed above, teachers found that they had less time to devote to collaboration. The average frequency of collaboration around groupworthy problems fell from over once per week in 2000–2005 to once or twice per semester in 2009–2010, with four out of ten teachers reporting that they *never* collaborated to design, use, or refine GWPs in the latter period.

The drop in collaboration around GWPs reflects a more general decrease in collaboration in the math department. Several teachers mentioned that the Algebra Group, which met weekly for some 10 years, had essentially dissolved. The change was so noticeable that Jasmine, a student teacher, remarked on it:

> At the beginning of the year, we used to have meetings. We used to meet once every Wednesday, or every other Wednesday, to talk about goals for the future, where teachers are and where teachers need to be, and how [Algebra] Success classes can support that. . . . Then that changed to, once a month. And then people were like, "Let's just email each other," and now I don't get any more emails from anyone. . . . A lot of teachers feel overwhelmed and overworked, I guess.

The cessation of meetings and even email updates was quite consequential for the Railside math department. Sustaining the kind of teaching in which they were engaged—even in the absence of external challenges—requires teamwork

(Franke, Carpenter, Levi, & Fennema, 2001; Little, 2002; McLaughlin & Talbert, 2001). As Railside teachers described, they were constantly innovating and problem solving, often covering new and unfamiliar territory that required teachers' collective resources. Even Guillermo, one of the most senior members of the department, said that the drop in collaboration took away the "resources for sense-making and alternative ideas" that he had relied on colleagues to provide in years past.

Teachers experienced this as a significant disruption of their department's work toward equity. Instead of working with their colleagues to figure out how to support failing students, teachers described getting caught up in bureaucracy and a whirlwind of acronyms (CST, AYP, API, APS, EPC). Alicia spoke about her plans to organize department discussions about how to better serve African American students—plans that she perceived as "derailed" by demands that the department attend to the district's interpretations of accountability and test-based equity in place of their own.

EMOTIONAL IMPACT ON TEACHERS

Feelings of frustration and loss—and on some level, failure—were ever-present in the interviews we conducted. Toward the end of most interviews, we explicitly asked teachers about the emotional layers of their work over the last school year, but even without this prompt, all but one of the teachers clearly communicated the rawness of the year's emotional toll on them. This came across in the tone of their voices, with several teachers verging on tears at one point or another during our interviews. It also came through in the content of their statements, especially in three areas: (1) their assessments of their work with students in the last year, (2) their concerns over the weakening and dissolution of the professional community within the math department that had nourished and supported them for many years, and (3) their descriptions of their administration's respect for them as professionals—or, more often, the lack thereof. This section describes these emotional impacts on teachers.

Work with Students

If particular practices defined the Railside style, they also seem to have defined the teachers themselves. Feeling unable to fit their practices to changing circumstances was a blow to professional identity that almost every teacher conveyed. Deborah opened her interview by saying, "I feel like a new teacher. . . . It's a little bit better now, late in the year, but the first half of the year, I was in complete survival mode." All seven mentioned being unable to do some significant part of their job, from giving students the individual attention that they needed to delivering a mathematically rich curriculum. As mentioned above, Deborah felt that it was "logistically impossible" to do many of the things she valued as a teacher, and Guillermo didn't "get" how to adapt core elements of his practice to 60-minute periods.

The struggle to make sense of their work with students in the new context affected five of the teachers in a deeply personal way. Teachers continued to take responsibility for student achievement despite feeling that much was out of their control, and here, too, failure was quite emotional. The supportive, inclusive environment that had existed before (Horn, 2005, 2007) disappeared as teachers lost track of achievements that they could build on, as William described:

> It just seemed like every time we met and talked about the experiences we were having, it was just failure after failure after failure after failure. Before, we could point to successes with this, and then here's what we would like help with or advice on. This was just like everything is crap. We're five weeks behind in the curriculum, none of my kids know anything, I can't get them to do any work. . . . Looking back I'm not surprised at all at the way we kind of panicked and just stopped talking.

According to teachers, their feelings of failure with their students made them less able to support one another, and their inability to support one another only made it harder for each of them to do their work with students. It appears that teachers' need for support ballooned—just as students' did—at the same time that teachers found themselves least able to give it.

Professional Community

The professional community within the Railside math department changed in three important ways in 2009–2010. First, it shrank from 13 teachers down to 10. The move off the block schedule to 60-minute periods allowed the district to cut three full-time mathematics positions. Saying goodbye to three members of the department was hard for those who were left; Guillermo described the sadness of "losing people because they were pink-slipped, and people we had just welcomed into the community and had worked to support." Having to go on with a department that was almost 25% smaller left the remaining teachers with both the logistical challenges of more students and more courses, and the emotional challenge of feeling that their department was a "skeleton," a "shell" of what it had been.

The second major change was less concrete but equally powerful for the five teachers who mentioned it: a change in the character of the math department. Teachers met less frequently, and when they did meet, they felt less capable of supporting one another. As Julian described, feeling unsuccessful with students was difficult in its own right, but not having support to improve added another, more hopeless layer of distress:

> I felt really unsuccessful for huge portions of this year. . . . [I]n our old schedule, in our old department configuration, I could have a tough class and feel unsuccessful with that group and feel like I could ask a colleague on their prep to come watch me. I can go to them with my dilemma and get some help. And I didn't feel like I could grow in that way [this year], I just didn't feel any source of support, not from a lack of willingness, but from a lack of capacity. I would feel awful going to [Guillermo] and saying, "I know that you have 6th period free, and I know that it's not really free, you've got lots of work to do, [but] I'm struggling, can you come watch me?" I can't do that right now.

This contrasts with the community of teachers as learners that Horn (2005, 2007; Chapter 9, this volume) described—which included many of the same people. Where before teachers had planned together, observed one another routinely, and thought through problems of practice as a group, they now felt unable to ask one another for help, not wanting to add to one another's burdens. Instead of thinking critically about how to translate their vision of equity into mathematics instruction, they spent their meetings "just need[ing] to move through the agenda" (Alicia), which they felt was set by administrators who seemed to teachers to prioritize compliance with the letter of state and federal laws, regardless of the effects on students and student learning.

A third change that stemmed from all the others was a sizeable exodus from the Railside math department at the end of the year. Four of the ten teachers—including three who had chaired or co-chaired the department over the last 20 years—decided to leave the school. For teachers who remained, losing their leadership was a shock. Discussing the state of their professional community brought several teachers to the point of tears. Asked where she thought the department was going in the next 2 to 5 years, Deborah bluntly replied, "To hell." Grace said, "We've been blown to shit. I feel like a shotgun's gone right through my heart."

William explained his decision to leave Railside in highly emotional terms that capture the year's toll on teachers:

> I felt like I was too early in my career to stagnate, and I feel like that's what I did this year. I not only stagnated, I feel like I regressed in my teaching. My energy level, I didn't have that same motivation to get better. That was a very unhappy thought to have with myself as a teacher . . . [but] I needed to believe that making an effort to improve would actually show results in the classroom, and I didn't see that this year.

Teachers reported that as much as anything else, the sense that their efforts did not matter drained their energy and damaged their capacity to engage emotionally with their work. This was apparent in some of their descriptions of their work with students. Teachers were even clearer about their distress in their stories of interactions with district-level administration.

Professionalism and Autonomy

For all but one of the teachers (Audrey), feeling disrespected by their administration was a tremendous source of stress. (In fact, there are more than double the number of instances of this code than any other.) Teachers described feeling "micromanaged," characterizing the district's management style as "insulting" and "offensive." Grace's metaphor of a deli illustrates how dehumanized teachers felt by the district's approach: "I might as well be salami, and you could be mozzarella, and you could be prosciutto. However it slices, I don't feel that they give a goddamn about what it is that I do or who I am. . . . We have no value."

Accompanying the sense of abject anonymity was a loss of voice. Julian felt a "lack of even having any interest in hearing us, or acknowledging that teachers might have a perspective to offer that wasn't just self-serving." To teachers who often worked 12-hour days and who were used to being consulted and valued for their professional expertise, within their district and beyond, this hurt. Several teachers said that the sting felt especially sharp because top decisionmakers had quite limited experience with high school mathematics. The superintendent came from a business background and had never worked in a school, and the Director of Secondary Education had worked as an administrator in elementary and middle schools, but not high schools. Some teachers interpreted the district's failure to listen to them as a tragically lost opportunity; others took it as a cause for outrage.

Julian described what the new district office personnel seemed to him to value as "compliance behavior." He and his colleagues found themselves being evaluated on how often they were using the district-adopted textbook and whether state standards were written on their whiteboards each day. This kind of "checklist" accountability set up an us-versus-them mentality among teachers, and they conveyed a sense of betrayal. Teachers experienced compliance-behavior accountability as fostering a toxic environment, a "spirit of conflict and noncooperation . . . even on little things that don't really matter," as William observed. Teachers also took the shift in management style as an insult to their professional expertise. Deborah summed up the feeling by saying that they had been "spit on."

While some teachers responded with anger, others tried to cooperate with administrators. But these teachers also described becoming frustrated with decisions that felt random and capricious. A number of teachers described their exasperation with trying to meet "moving targets." They also found cooperation with the district office nearly impossible; finding common ground from which to advocate for their ways of working was difficult when, from their perspective, the ground kept shifting and the goals were unclear. In addition, teachers perceived the district as uninterested in collaborating or finding common ground. Julian and Alicia were co-chairs of the math department when the new superintendent took office, and they reported making several attempts to speak with him about their department's work, including pulling him into conversation when he attended a school football game. But according to them, he never agreed to a serious meeting with them; at any rate, they never felt that they had engaged him in dialogue. To Julian, he seemed to say, "If you argue with me, you don't think our kids are capable." Thus, teachers perceived disagreement on any score as off the table—and with it an important element of trusting teacher-administrator relationships.

Feeling that increasingly hands-on administrators did not care either about them as individuals with professional expertise or about the kind of teaching and learning that they valued made it difficult for teachers to maintain mental and emotional engagement with their work. William described losing the will to improve his practice and "stagnating." Julian said, "Why put energy into really brainstorming and getting a creative solution, because we'll probably have it yanked out from under us later." Perceiving that they had been positioned as low-status and not worth hearing, teachers felt that hard work and emotional investment were futile—perhaps running parallel to the experience of students placed in remedial mathematics.

CONCLUSION

Railside High School's mathematics department has been nationally known as a model of equity-oriented mathematics education reform. The teachers were leaders in developing a rigorously conceptual and widely accessible mathematics curriculum, in building instructional practices that supported rich mathematics learning, and in creating a professional community that sustained innovation for over 2 decades. In recent years, these practices have not been sustained. How did teachers experience and explain this fundamental change? In our interviews, we found that teachers attributed their difficulties in maintaining various aspects of their work to shifts in local policies and the local policy climate. They described the difficulty—despite their years of experience and deep commitment to engaging students in learning rich mathematics—of establishing a positive classroom culture, of teaching rigorous mathematics, and of investing themselves mentally and emotionally in their work. According to every teacher with whom we spoke, tracking and school "choice" made classroom culture less supportive and less inclusive, not more so. Many teachers observed that students' perceptions of themselves and their peers as "dumb" had become more entrenched. At the same time, teachers found that the shift away from the block schedule to more standard 60-minute periods, combined with increases in class size, made it more difficult to establish meaningful relationships with students. In teachers' experience, such relationships had played crucial roles in supporting positive student attitudes and identities as doers and learners of mathematics.

Teachers perceived significant changes to their curriculum and instruction as well, noting declines in both the rigor of their teaching and their students' academic achievement. Six of the seven teachers we spoke to experienced difficulty using tools like groupworthy problems, portfolio assessments, and extended warm-up discussions for a variety of reasons, including changes to classroom culture, lack of support for teachers to adapt their instruction to 60-minute periods, and heavier loads with more students and more different courses to teach. Five teachers specifically linked these changes with alarming increases in the number of students failing their classes. With all of the challenges that they faced, teachers felt that they had less time and energy to collaborate with one another. The time that they did spend as a department seemed to them to be absorbed by administrative requirements, filling out forms, and trying to explain their work to district officials instead of planning instruction, developing curriculum, or exchanging ideas about student support.

In addition to changes in classroom culture and instruction, the emotional distress that teachers shared in our interviews cannot be ignored. Teachers felt their lack of success in their work with students in very personal ways, but they reported feeling upset and insulted by their administration's attitudes and behavior toward them with even greater frequency and passion. According to teachers, their professional opinions and expertise were discarded in exchange for "compliance behavior," as officials came into their classrooms with checklists assessing the number of minutes that the class used the textbook and whether state standards were written on the whiteboard. Furthermore, teachers felt that their efforts to communicate their priorities with administrators were shut down. As much as anything else, it appears that the loss of autonomy to work toward their vision of rigorous, equitable mathematics instruction—of the "freedom to dream," as Julian put it—damaged teachers' sense that they could advance or adapt their pedagogy, or even maintain their emotional engagement with their work.

These changes in the work of teachers in this mathematics department are the result of a complex set of changes in both the local and national economic and policy context and cannot be attributed to just one simple root cause. Indeed, many of the effects that teachers reported in this study may not be inevitable consequences of policies targeting standardization and accountability. But it is noteworthy that the teacher reports at Railside align with findings from other research on the effects of high-stakes accountability systems on teaching and teachers, which have found that such systems narrow the curriculum and decrease teacher morale, especially in high-need schools serving poor and minority students (e.g., Lipman, 2004; McNeil, 2000; Mintrop, 2003; Pedulla et al., 2003). Focusing on compliance, diminishing risks by removing autonomy, and striving for efficiency and equality through standardization appear to be a common local interpretation of state and federal policies.

The case of Railside is perhaps a cautionary one for mathematics educators, policymakers, and district officials, and for all those concerned with classroom learning, that it is not enough to simply attend to what we know about classroom teaching practices that provide rich and engaging mathematics instruction for students. If we are going to provide high-quality mathematics instruction in urban districts, we must also attend in deep and sustained ways to how we create and nurture school and district contexts that make such teaching work possible on the part of teachers and mathematics departments. This attention to the contexts and politics of instruction is necessary if we are to make rich and engaging opportunities to teach and learn mathematics available to all.

Chapter 13

Reculturing High School Mathematics Departments for Educational Excellence and Equity

Lisa M. Jilk and Karen O'Connell

Originally, we authors were math teachers at Railside High School. Collectively, we were at Railside for 11 years, and we were there at the same time for 2 of those years. In addition, we were department co-chairs at different points in time. In 2008, we found ourselves living in Seattle, Washington, after pursuing different personal and professional goals outside of Railside. Here, Karen was again teaching math in a public high school, and Lisa was consulting with schools and math departments about Complex Instruction (CI). We seized on the opportunity to work together again, because we were passionate about re-creating the kind of community we had been a part of at Railside, one focused on teaching and learning math with social justice. For the past 5 years, we have been deeply immersed in supporting several public school math departments to reform their classrooms and department communities as they try to increase participation and learning for students in highly diverse classrooms. This chapter is about how we've built from our experiences as members of the Railside math department to create a professional development program that supports these efforts.

Throughout the world, teacher educators and teachers are working together to transform mathematics classrooms to enhance student learning. Over the past 20 years, the Railside High School mathematics department (Boaler & Staples, 2008) has been a site for applying and developing Elizabeth Cohen's sociological perspective on group learning through the implementation of Complex Instruction pedagogies (Cohen, 1994a; see also Chapter 8, this volume). As an academically, racially, and linguistically diverse school, Railside saw great successes in student achievement, learning, pass rates, and retention rates in mathematics and had many students who claimed positive mathematical identities (Boaler & Staples, 2008; Jilk, 2007).

The Railside mathematics department operated quite differently from most high school mathematics departments—and we believe these differences were critical to the department's successes. As part of the work of teachers and the culture of the department, we teachers at Railside developed systems for ongoing renewal, sustainable practices, and enculturating newcomers (Matusov, 1999; see also Chapter 11, this volume). Teachers collaborated to design courses, examine student work, and explore mathematical ideas and concepts. New teachers, and teachers who had not recently taught a particular course, regularly observed in other teachers' classrooms during their prep periods (Horn, 2005). Teachers also made hiring decisions and advocated for school-wide structures and systems to support student success in mathematics. This success with students and teachers has drawn the attention of both researchers and practitioners around the country and created opportunities for Railside teachers to support other schools in achieving positive outcomes for their students (Boaler, 2008; Boaler & Staples, 2008; Hand, 2003; Horn, 2005, 2008a; Jilk, 2007, 2010).

As both classroom teachers and department chairs at Railside High, we have used our experiences to transport the Railside vision and practices for teaching and learning mathematics to other departments. This work requires a nuanced understanding of Complex Instruction pedagogies, deep and connected content knowledge, an orientation toward equity and social justice, the ability to notice inequity in a variety of forms, and a committed community of colleagues. We are learning more each day about what is necessary to successfully support such reform in other schools without the benefit of an existing model in which to apprentice teachers.

Training decisions for our work are not motivated by literature about effective professional development, although we do have sufficient evidence to suggest that our program addresses many of the challenges and concerns presented in both professional development research and practice. Rather than starting with research, we created a professional development network that is modeled on the unique learning culture and opportunities for learning that we had at Railside. In this network, we focus on the mathematics department, rather than individual teachers, as the unit of change and source of intellectual support and sustainability. We have found that reform focused on individual teachers transforming individual classrooms is not a sustainable model for successfully implementing Complex Instruction. The tenets of Complex Instruction are grounded in beliefs about collective sense-making and mutual support rather than individual acquisition and competition. CI classrooms build from strengths rather than fixing weaknesses. They require a community of students and teachers who recognize brilliance in each of its members and feel a sense of responsibility for one another's learning. This kind of social system is so different from traditional classroom models that to effectively create and sustain this unique culture requires changing the multiple contexts in which teachers' work and the ways they function in each. We have learned that to affect students' learning in mathematics, teacher learning must be taken up in the context of the department, where teachers collectively construct what it means to teach and learn mathematics and how to participate in and operate differently from typical math classrooms. To reform individual teacher practice, then, and ultimately impact student learning, it is necessary to reculture the departmental community in which teachers are situated.

We facilitate six different learning spaces with the common goal of developing the skills, knowledge, dispositions, and beliefs to effectively implement Complex Instruction within all math classes. We bring the same strong beliefs and practices we have as math teachers working with young people to our work with adults. We deeply believe that all teachers are smart and capable of learning. We find and build from teachers' strengths and position ourselves as members of learning communities rather than outside experts by embedding ourselves within the departments and in their day-to-day work.

We have learned that this approach to instructional reform takes a lot of time. It is definitely not a quick fix or a one-size-fits-all model. We ask teachers to take on intellectual work that they were never hired to do as they deprivatize their practice and collaboratively engage in never-ending cycles of inquiry. However, amidst the many challenges, we have also witnessed great success. The people with whom we have worked have become teams of highly committed practitioners whose purpose is to collaboratively take up the challenge of creating coherent secondary math programs that are active, rich, rigorous, and inviting, that provide each of their students with opportunities to engage with and learn important mathematics. This is the work of teaching.

In the following chapter we first provide background information about our project. Then we present our current model for professional development and describe the six spaces in which teachers participate and the learning made available in each. We also explain how these learning spaces are connected to create a coherent network focused on reculturing departments for excellence and equity.

PROFESSIONAL DEVELOPMENT USING THE RAILSIDE APPROACH

Beginning in the early 2000s, several of us math teachers from Railside began teaching a course about secondary mathematics and Complex Instruction around the country. This course was designed by a core group of Railside teachers based on their extensive knowledge about CI and experiences with its implementation at Railside. The goals of this course were to introduce math teachers to the theoretical underpinnings of CI, immerse teachers in learning experiences that use tasks and instructional strategies that are specific to Complex Instruction, and challenge teachers to consider their beliefs about teaching and learning mathematics.

Success with the uptake of Complex Instruction following this course varied across sites, and similar to many other professional development designs, this isolated, short-term approach to supporting individual teachers' learning and instructional change was rarely sufficient. Teachers with whom we worked have been challenged by several issues. These include (1) the "theory-practice gap," making it difficult to take what was learned during the course and make it work with students in classrooms, (2) district and school structures that are often incongruent with the philosophies of CI pedagogies and unintentionally undermine its implementation, such as tracking students into particular classes or assigning all of the algebra classes to the new teacher, (3) teachers' beliefs both about *what it means* to teach and learn mathematics along with *who* can successfully learn math can conflict with the philosophies that undergird Complex Instruction, and (4) the absence of a collaborative professional community in which teachers tackle the problems of their practice and continue learning.

To address these concerns, some of us teachers from Railside have had the opportunity to work with several districts and schools that wanted additional and ongoing support. Some of these sites included large urban districts in the Midwest and on the West Coast as well as smaller suburban and rural districts in California, Oregon, and Washington. This work has taken a variety of forms. For us, supporting math teachers to implement Complex Instruction has evolved from periodically coaching individual teachers to long-term, embedded coaching and program development with grade-level teams and entire departments. We developed our most current model of support over the past 5 years with opportunities to work with and build from a project facilitated by Horn (2008b) and make connections to our experiences as teachers and department chairs at Railside. The end result is a network of middle and high school mathematics departments that participate in six long-term professional development spaces for the purpose of implementing Complex Instruction and reculturing their department communities. These professional communities continually negotiate how to use Complex Instruction to create rigorous and coherent mathematics programs that are internally sustained and engage *all* students in learning more mathematics.

PROFESSIONAL DEVELOPMENT MODEL

In the following section, we provide a brief overview of our project and describe each of the six learning spaces in which teachers participate to reculture their professional learning teams and individual classrooms. Then we highlight the learning that is targeted in each of the six spaces as a way of showing the breadth of learning that is available as well as the connections between them.

Project Goals

Reculturing departments means changing participation in department communities. This program focuses on supporting teachers to gain the skills, knowledge, and dispositions to be teachers in recultured mathematics departments who effectively implement Complex Instruction. More specifically, the goals for this professional development network include: (1) restructuring what it means to be a mathematics teacher and learner in secondary math classrooms for the purpose of increasing students' engagement and math learning, (2) training secondary mathematics teachers to create classroom systems steeped in Complex Instruction beliefs and pedagogies, and (3) building and sustaining site-based teacher learning communities that take up problems of practice and effectively advocate for and maintain CI classrooms.

Mutually Informed Learning Spaces

We have learned that effective implementation of Complex Instruction requires significant reculturing of mathematics classrooms, departmental interactions, and dispositions toward the work of teaching and the activity of learning. To accomplish this, we must provide math teachers and department communities with access to varied, ongoing, and coherent learning opportunities that are situated both inside and outside of their classrooms. To that end, we provide six interconnected and mutually informed learning spaces and begin with the mathematics department as the unit of change. These learning spaces include an introductory course called Designing Effective Groupwork, In-Classroom Support, Common Planning Team meetings, Peer Reciprocal Observations, Video Club, and the development of Teacher Facilitators (TFACs) (see Figure 13.1).

Each of the learning spaces in this network is modeled on an activity that we participated in at Railside to grow our teaching practices and sustain this collective enterprise. Each space has a particular focus, along with affordances, limitations, and overlaps. We create, adapt, and facilitate each. Our integral participation informs our decisions about process and content and allows us to help teachers connect with and adapt ideas from each space to their particular department and classrooms. The result is that teachers are engaged in professional learning that is coherent, connected, and collaborative.

All of the teachers with whom we work participate in each of the learning spaces with members of their departments or course teams for 3 consecutive years. The structure of the team largely depends on the level of funding that a district is able to commit and the readiness of a particular site. Sometimes entire departments are positioned with prior knowledge and beliefs that make them prime candidates for joining as an entire department, and sometimes a smaller subgroup of a department begins this reculturing process with the goal of expanding to include successive course teams in each of the following years. When a

Figure 13.1. Mutually Informed Learning Spaces

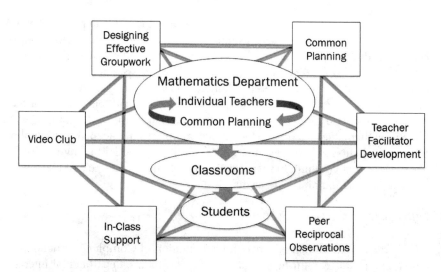

team joins the network, they join a handful of teams from other schools who gather monthly for Video Club and TFAC sessions and receive weekly or bimonthly support at their school sites from us facilitators. In-Classroom Support, Common Planning Team meetings, and Peer Reciprocal Observations are all imbedded in their daily work of teaching, as we restructure how teachers spend their time during the school day. Finally, this model for professional learning relies heavily on our membership in the 1st year. Our goal is to gradually remove ourselves from the process as teams develop internal and distributed expertise and leadership to grow and sustain these new practices.

INTRODUCTORY COURSE: DESIGNING EFFECTIVE GROUPWORK

We launch teams into our professional development network in the introductory course, Designing Effective Groupwork. This 30-hour class was designed to introduce teachers to the theory and practices of Complex Instruction and immerse participants in multi-ability, groupworthy tasks in which they engage as learners.[1] The class is most often made up of middle and high school mathematics teachers and administrators from several different school districts.

One of our goals with this course is to help teachers feel what it is like to be learners in a space where mathematical strengths are valued and built on, learners depend on one another as intellectual resources, and everyone is considered mathematically competent and expected to be successful. To achieve these outcomes, we teach this class with and constantly model the principles and structures of Complex Instruction. Immersion in this community culture with colleagues from the same site, even for only 1 week, has proven valuable for teachers as they continue this work during the school year.

Complex Instruction pedagogies foreground issues of social and academic status and aim to prevent and intervene with these issues to keep them from negatively affecting students' relationships with one another and their engagement with learning math. From our understanding, there is no other program of cooperative learning that considers this social phenomenon, thereby making it a critical component of this course. Participants learn about academic and social status and how it can undermine equitable learning opportunities for students, consider different methods for addressing status issues, observe status issues in action through video cases, experience status treatments and observe us modeling them throughout the course, and raise questions and insights about status relative to their own experiences.

As teachers learn about Complex Instruction in this course, they simultaneously craft multi-ability, groupworthy tasks with a small group of peers that use CI structures. Then they teach this task to the class and receive feedback from their colleagues. Teachers often report that collaboratively constructing these activities, especially with members of their own departments, is one of the most useful components of the course. The experience of task creation within a CI framework provides an opportunity to make connections between new ideas and practices and a chance to see their plans in action. In our experiences with this course, we have learned that developing groupworthy tasks is the one thing most participants focus on immediately upon starting a new school year as they begin their journeys with Complex Instruction.

Challenges with the "Designing Effective Groupwork" Course

There are two big challenges we face when facilitating this course. The first is about beliefs. People come to us with their own life experiences as people and as teachers from which they have constructed beliefs about teaching, learning, mathematics, and students. If teachers' orientation toward teaching and learning coincide with the principles and beliefs that undergird Complex Instruction, then this course tends to be an affirming and exciting experience. If, on the other hand, teachers enter the class with a set of beliefs that are in stark contrast to CI pedagogies, it can be a pretty tough week for everyone. After many years of managing this challenge, we have created a component of the course that addresses this concern by asking participants to first consider the beliefs about math, teaching, and learning that are promoted by both traditional and reform-oriented practices and then revisiting this conversation throughout the week. We are not in the business of changing belief systems; however, we do want to be transparent about the fact that beliefs drive practice, and it is extremely difficult—if not impossible—to successfully implement and sustain a classroom community steeped in Complex Instruction if one does not believe in its underlying tenets.

Teaching with Complex Instruction is about attending to inequitable participation, which often has roots in systems of inequity that have been normalized and perpetuated within our larger society. Becoming aware of and addressing these systems in our classrooms is what makes Complex Instruction an equity pedagogy. Its very purpose is to deal with the fact that people assume intellectual competence, or lack thereof, based on certain characteristics that are valued in society, and that these assumptions can influence how people interact in social situations.

The demographics of our course participants mirror those of the U.S. teaching force. They are mostly White, middle-class, native English speakers who have been privileged by systems of race and class and are often unaware of the many ways in which our education system has worked in their favor. We run into a second big challenge when we begin taking up issues of inequity to better understand how students are often marginalized by the very same systems from which most of our teachers have benefited. Effectively implementing Complex Instruction requires a political and social awareness of how classroom structures can perpetuate the status quo, and some people become very uncomfortable at this point in the course. Teachers work tremendously hard to help students, and they take pride in being part of a solution. This can be difficult to reconcile with ways we may have inadvertently subjugated our students to less than high-quality learning opportunities or blamed students for not "getting it" instead of recognizing the many underlying issues that contribute to the challenges of learning math. Our challenge then is to figure out how to talk about inequities in ways that are authentic and meaningful and foster change rather than cause resistance.

Successes with Designing Effective Groupwork

Teachers are often aching to take on issues in their classrooms that they know need serious attention, but rarely do they have many solution strategies that seem realistic and manageable. Concerns about racism, gender stereotypes, bullying, and inequality in general abound in schools and classrooms, and it is often thrilling for teachers to realize that there are tools available to help them manage these issues that are related to learning mathematics. Teachers who come to us with a belief that each of their students can be successful or that working together really does support more learning but have not yet been able to actualize these beliefs are often very excited to have found a pedagogical "home" that resonates for them.

Another important outcome of this course is that it launches professional learning communities that are oriented toward the beliefs and practices of Complex Instruction and committed to working together during the school year. Since math departments or course teams participate in the class together, they have common experiences from which to build and connect as they begin planning and adapting this work in their own contexts. All too often, one or two people from a department are sent to a professional development workshop only to return to school with a report or set of materials to distribute to colleagues. In the design of this course, however, we recognize that leadership and expertise for reculturing departments and math classrooms must be distributed across team members in order to shift and sustain beliefs and practices about teaching and learning. We hope that this common course experience provides each teacher with access to the theories and practices of CI and opportunities for the entire team to collectively construct meaning and make connections to their own students and classrooms.

IN-CLASSROOM SUPPORT

Supporting teachers to effectively implement Complex Instruction in their own classrooms has been an essential follow-up to the Designing Effective Group-work course. As often happens with much professional development, teachers struggle when they try to connect what they have learned in our course with their particular students and classroom contexts. In fact, it is quite common for teachers to leave our class excited and eager to try out their new ideas but feel completely discouraged and declare CI impossible only weeks later.

The theories and practices of CI might be easily understood in isolation; however, putting them into action is much more complicated. The challenge of enactment (Kennedy, 1999) is exacerbated by the fact that teachers must simultaneously manage new ideas and practices that are not scripted. To effectively reculture mathematics classrooms with an orientation toward collaborative, equitable participation and learning, teachers must "rethink key ideas, practices, and even values in order to change what they are doing" (Hammerness et al., 2005). Complex Instruction teachers must constantly act in relationship to students as students act in relationship to mathematics (Lampert, 2001). This relationship is key. No longer are teachers delivering content through lecture and note-giving while managing students' behaviors such as talking out of turn or falling asleep in class. In Complex Instruction classrooms, students are most often actively engaged in mathematical sense-making, and the teacher's role is "to foster and optimize this interaction" (Cohen & Lotan, 1997, p. 33) during class time so that more learning happens. Students' learning is not merely a product of a special curriculum, strategies, and cooperative groups. Learning in classrooms that are steeped in Complex Instruction is the result of teachers who effectively navigate and manage mathematics content, student understanding, and a dynamic classroom social system. This is very intellectually demanding work.

We visit classrooms weekly during our 1st year with a math department and bimonthly in years following. We take our role as classroom guests seriously and aim to become members of these communities rather than outside experts. In this way, we are attending to potential issues of status that might disrupt and undermine the social interactions that support our learning about the teachers and students with whom we will work during the school year. We also spend a lot of time building relationships with students. We learn about their likes and dislikes, connect with them about music and sports, ask questions about family, and share information about our lives as well. We genuinely enjoy life in classrooms and have great respect for the work of teaching and learning, and these attitudes undergird the work we do.

We do not have a script for what we do in classrooms. Nor do we implement particular checklists or protocols. Our strong relationships with students and teachers; our scope of Complex Instruction tools and strategies, strong content, and pedagogical content knowledge; and the vision we hold for teaching and learning allow us to move fluidly in classrooms and adapt our support to teachers' needs. We work with teachers in the same way we work with students, by first excavating their strengths and then building from these strengths as they are used during a lesson. We might co-plan a lesson, observe the class in which it's taught, and then debrief with the teacher about what happened and what might be improved. Often we model Complex Instruction strategies during a lesson, help teachers notice issues of status, point out opportunities for assigning competence, and suggest instructional moves they might try. We listen to students' math talk, help teachers construct questions that build from student understanding, manage student engagement, and hold students accountable for participation and learning. Being members of classroom communities affords us opportunities to help teachers reconnect to the theories and ideas they learned about in the Designing Effective Groupwork course and help them figure out how to implement them in real time with their students.

Challenges with Supporting Teachers in Classrooms

Many secondary mathematics teachers have never experienced, and therefore do not have a vision for, the kind of learning environments we are trying to help them create. This is one of the most difficult challenges we face across all aspects of this program and an issue that is most apparent when we work with teachers in their classrooms. As novices at Railside, we were lucky to be apprenticed into a department culture that supported our learning and development as teachers new to Complex Instruction. We were able to discuss ideas with more experienced colleagues and visit classrooms to watch specific kinds of teaching and learning unfold. In these ways, we knew exactly what to aim for in our own practices. Unfortunately, we are not able to provide this same opportunity for the math teachers with whom we work. Instead, we are all challenged to collabora-tively figure out exactly what this classroom vision entails at the same time we are learning how to enact it. The lack of an apprenticeship model means that there is no easy pathway to our collective success. How we become successful math teachers and, in fact, *what* we define as success are in constant negotiation.

Additionally, we face a lot of the typical challenges that arise when any math teacher tries to reform his or her practices. We are continually challenged by shifting the focus of teaching away from delivering content toward working with students' mathematical ideas, and redefining learning from listening and note-taking to active intellectual and social engagement. This challenge is very much about helping teachers redefine what it means to teach and learn mathematics for themselves and for their students.

While we are acting on belief systems, we challenge teachers to simultane-ously attend to students' math learning and participation. This is the crux of Complex Instruction, and it is extremely difficult work. Teachers who are shifting from a teacher-centered model of instruction to one that is student-centered find it difficult to interact with the myriad ways students construct understanding and make sense of new skills and ideas. Research has taught us that working in rela-tion with students while they are "working in relation with the ideas, processes and language they are to learn" (Lampert, 2001, p. 31) is indeed an ongoing problem of practice. Shifting focus to students' ideas by looking and listening to their math talk, asking good questions, pressing for understanding, or formatively assessing in the moment takes much practice and skill. Now, in addition to man-aging students' engagement with mathematics, we ask teachers to manage small-group engagement and simultaneously pay attention to *equitable* interactions to ensure success for all. *Who* is participating, *how* do they participate, *when* do they participate? Do all students have access to the resources? Are all students asking questions, checking in with their peers, sharing ideas, and trying new strategies? Are all students engaged in the kind of messy intellectual work that learning mathematics requires to be successful?

Successes During In-Classroom Support

Our teachers seem to feel most successful when we are engaged in creat-ing CI classrooms together. Our ability to effectively manage both mathematical content and students' participation, given the complex and ever-shifting nature of classrooms, often gives teachers hope that using Complex Instruction is possible. By setting clear objectives and manageable goals, the teachers start developing their own expertise and feel more confident and motivated to continue learning. By the end of the first semester with a math team, it is common for our teachers to admit that although they are working harder than ever before, they are see-ing and hearing *their* students engaged in learning math in ways they had only imagined. When this happens, they begin to shift their perceptions about what it means to learn and who can successfully do it. They raise their expectations for participation and understanding and push students a little harder and a little further than they had before. They start to find more opportunities to ask good questions and build from students' thinking. They come to see school mathematics as rich and connected and relevant to students' lives. Most importantly, teachers who are learning to reculture their classrooms become more aware of the brilliance in each of their students and recognize their own agency with respect to students' mathematical achievement.

Using In-Classroom Support to Foster Peer Reciprocal Observations (PROs)

As part of the support we provide teachers in their classrooms, we have developed the tool of Peer Reciprocal Observations (PROs). At Railside, observing our colleagues' classrooms was a common practice. Time spent in others' classes afforded us many things that we might not have learned otherwise. Through these observations, we developed common language for how to talk with students about their mathematical ideas, we became more aware of opportunities to assign competence, and we learned how to ask good math questions and press students for understanding. We learned new strategies for holding students accountable for their participation, we figured out how to better assess students' ideas in the moment, and we developed distributed expertise and a common vision for how Complex Instruction could be enacted. In addition, the time spent in others' classes provided us with common experiences that we could bring to Common Planning Teams (CPT) for reflection and analysis. Although we often used stories to give context to the dilemmas we shared in CPTs, the experiences we shared during peer observations were often more poignant, because we had multiple perspectives about the same classroom events.

In our current work, we have learned that teachers struggle to realize how Complex Instruction can look and sound when working with students. Theories, stories, examples, and video clips abound from the Designing Effective Groupwork course and Video Club, but again, teachers are challenged to transfer new ideas from these spaces into their own classrooms (Putnam & Borko, 2000). At Railside, many of us learned how to teach with Complex Instruction through apprenticeship into a department that was already practicing CI. We had several examples to watch and reflect on as we tried to enact these practices ourselves. Unfortunately, we do not have this luxury in our professional development network. Outside of Video Club, the teachers with whom we work are trying to reculture their individual practices along with their department communities without any existing models. Reciprocal observations, then, serve as a place for teachers to begin imagining a vision for Complex Instruction in their particular school contexts and use one another as resources for ongoing implementation.

A Peer Reciprocal Observation, as the name suggests, has a minimum of two teachers observing each other's classes. Often, these teachers teach the same course. Alternately, the teachers might teach consecutive courses, such as Algebra and Geometry. In either case, we co-facilitate a preobservation meeting, two classroom observations, and a follow-up conversation for the PRO experience. In the preobservation meeting we discuss each teacher's learning objectives, reasons for using particular participation structures, concerns about status, expectations for students' mathematical understanding, and any challenges or misconceptions they expect students to face. We then observe each teacher teach a class and again co-facilitate a postobservation conversation. We encourage a conversation between teachers rather than following a strict protocol, because our goals include helping teachers see and hear critical moments during the lesson that are opportunities for inquiry into practice and develop teachers' capacities to sustain these professional conversations without our presence.

Teachers' schedules are our biggest challenge for constructing successful PROs. Department teaching schedules are rarely created with the goal of opening up space for teachers with common courses to observe one another, which means that we've had to ask teachers to give up their preparation periods and then advocate for this kind of planning with administration in following years. This scheduling challenge is often exacerbated in smaller schools, because many of the teachers there tend to teach all the sections of a given course and therefore do not have any courses in common with one another. In these cases we've found that teachers are often less interested in doing a reciprocal observation altogether because they assume that there is not much to learn when the lesson content is unfamiliar. At all our schools, big or small, we've had to think very creatively and rely deeply on our network community to get PROs to happen.

COMMON PLANNING TEAMS (CPTs)

As members of the Railside Mathematics Department, we had the opportunity to participate in Common Planning Teams (CPTs) organized around courses. These teams met weekly to reflect on student learning, analyze classroom experiences, and prepare next steps in math instruction. In addition to providing moral support and collegiality, the Common Planning Teams were critical spaces for our everyday learning. It was here that we figured out how to launch a lesson or consider good questions to prompt student thinking. We wrestled with ideas for how to help a student participate more often or whether or not to use roles in the next day's lesson. We did math together, created groupworthy tasks, and analyzed student work. Always we were expected to give and take ideas and perspectives, knowing that each of us would go back to our classrooms as better teachers than if we had to do the job alone.

Our planning teams at Railside were also agents for shifting and sustaining our collective conceptions about school mathematics, participation in math class, and our strong belief that all students were smart and capable of achieving mathematical success (Horn, 2005). In addition, our teamwork gave us opportunities to develop a common and coherent vision for math learning across the entire department. It is an ongoing challenge to create new norms for teaching and learning while trying to sustain them within larger social and political systems that are not always supportive. This work requires both resisting conventional practices and socializing students into new classroom cultures. We found power in these common planning teams, where we created shared knowledge and expertise about our students, our pedagogies, and our learning communities that enabled us to protect and advocate for the kind of teaching and learning we knew to be good for students.

Common Planning Teams are core sites for learning in our professional development network. They afford us opportunities to collectively take up the problems of our practices, align curriculum and pedagogies, and develop shared understandings, beliefs, and a common vision for teaching and learning math. We consider issues that arise in our classes, analyze student work, develop tasks that build on student thinking, and dig deeply into challenges around status and accountability. Time with teams is not about lesson planning. Although we may map out the trajectory of big ideas across a week or a month, we do not go through a textbook and map sections onto days in our lesson planning books. We use this valuable time to reflect on and discuss students' math understanding and our teaching practices.

Our decisions for focus and co-facilitation of CPTs are informed by the other learning spaces in our network. For example, we might borrow an idea for a new teaching strategy from Video Club, agree to try it in each Algebra class, and debrief the experience during the planning meeting. There might be a particular teacher move made during In-classroom Support that we ask a teacher to discuss in CPT so we can highlight a specific CI strategy and deliberate its effectiveness. Very often, especially in the 1st year of working with a Common Planning Team, we help teachers make connections between the theories and strategies from the Designing Effective Groupwork course and what happens in their classrooms. We might point out instances of inequitable participation, reframe behavioral challenges as status issues, make evident opportunities to assign competence, or hold a small group accountable for working together on the same problem. We ask teachers to share classroom events and describe situations that highlight critical learning opportunities. Although In-classroom Support provides similar opportunities to make such connections, bringing them into CPT meetings is a unique and powerful practice. In CPTs, we move these artifacts from the privacy of individual classrooms and make them publicly available to the team for reflection and analysis. Doing this means that this example is no longer one person's problem to be solved, or even a success story to be lauded, but rather an artifact of our collective practice that is now available as a resource for learning.

Success with Common Planning Teams

We have helped to grow several successful common planning teams at different sites over the past 3 years. Since the CPTs are only one part of the larger professional development network, it is difficult to know exactly how much they contribute to teachers' overall feelings about their learning to teach with Complex Instruction. However, we know from interviews and the decisions teachers have made to continue teaching and participating in our network that they believe these on-site communities have significantly impacted their learning and their teaching. Trinh, a 3rd-year member of our program and a self-declared habitual long-term substitute job-hopper prior to joining our team, explained how his participation in his Common Planning Team aided his transformation as a math teacher. Trinh's response is an excellent summary of the reactions to CPTs that we've had from other teachers in our network.

> So I think the reason why I transformed is because now I feel valued by my team, by my coaches, by my students. I feel like I have a purpose, as opposed to just teaching kids math. It's just . . . I don't know! I guess I just feel like the job that I'm doing I guess is useful. You know? I think everybody needs a purpose, and I think if you feel needed, I think that's probably what it really comes down to. I feel like I'm part of a team. You know? I feel like if I'm absent, people would know. It wasn't like that before. So I think that's one of the biggest transformations. And I feel like an adult, I guess, in a sense. Because I used to be really isolated in the sense that I'd get to do whatever I want. And I think most people that I know that work, let's say, in the business world, they get to work with other adults on a consistent basis. And that's nice! To actually bang out ideas. Actually, one big aspect of this [transformation] was intellectual. I was actually intellectually stimulated just like my students. If you feel like you're stimulated and it feels like it's useful, you want to be a part of it, right? Because there's a point when you work in isolation, it becomes . . . well, let's face it, our kids are smart, but they're just not the same as talking to a 30-year-old adult. You know? And I think that's part of the transformation. I get to be stimulated intellectually in a way that I hadn't had before.

Trinh's words remind us of how good it feels to be part of a community that cares about us and values our presence and participation. We all want to feel important and necessary in our departments and schools. It's a great feeling to know that our colleagues are looking out for us and might notice if we were absent for a day. However, Trinh's math department serves a larger purpose than providing him with lunch dates or shared lesson plans. Trinh's team and the other common planning teams provide teachers with the kind of joint intellectual enterprise that defines a "community of practice" (Wenger, McDermott, & Snyder, 2002), because they have ongoing opportunities to collaboratively deepen their knowledge and expertise about teaching and learning mathematics. Trinh, much like most of the teachers in our network, relishes the time together to "bang out ideas," brainstorm structures that might better encourage student participation, or create a group test or assessment rubric. We have found teachers very eager for the kind of collective intellectual work that often accompanies many other professions, and they usually feel more competent as teachers and satisfied as employees as a result of participating in these teams.

Challenges with Common Planning Teams

Building these site-based communities can be difficult for many reasons. The biggest obstacle we face is the amount of time teachers need to invest in this kind of collaboration. Although most teachers eventually find that working as a team is far more interesting and intellectually stimulating than working alone, they often find it difficult to surrender their individual preparation time to collaborate with others—especially since this kind of collaborative work is not what most teachers initially signed on for as part of their jobs. The assumption that it would be quicker and "easier" to work in isolation is hard to disprove, made worse by the incredibly steep learning curve at the beginning of collaboration and the fact that things—curricular units, sharing of tasks, beliefs behind the use of an instructional strategy, common assessments—often get messier before they get better.

Adding to this challenge, CPTs sometimes become frustrated when they learn that we do not provide answers. Unabashedly, we do not attempt to fix problems. We position ourselves as members of these communities with strengths and smartness to offer—but no answers—because our intention is to apprentice people into this meaningful learning practice. Instead of this space being one where problems always get solved, common planning is a space where teachers create a self-sustaining community focused on inquiring into their teaching practice.

Lastly, we are always challenged to find time within a typical school schedule for Common Planning Teams to meet. Traditional scheduling usually affords one preparation period per day, meaning that a teacher has time to plan as an individual or time to plan with a team. Doing both is not an option. Further, CPTs complicate the school's master schedule significantly because they require a common preparation period for anyone who is teaching the same class. This means that the course that teachers are meeting about cannot be offered to students at that particular time during the day.

VIDEO CLUB

The Video Club (VC)[1] we facilitate as one of the six learning spaces was designed to provide a shared, local experience from which a heterogeneous group of teachers could learn to "notice" (Sherin, Jacobs, & Philipp, 2011; van Es & Sherin, 2002) students' mathematical thinking, noteworthy features of CI classrooms, and connections between classroom interactions and the principles of Complex Instruction. Classroom video can be used to facilitate meaningful teacher learning (Ball & Cohen, 1999; Putnam & Borko, 2000; van Es & Sherin, 2002), and Video Club has greatly contributed to teachers' uptake of CI because it accomplishes two goals: It enables teachers to make connections between the ideas and experiences generated in the other learning spaces, and it also affords the opportunity to develop a community with a coherent and common vision for teaching and learning mathematics. We created a model for Video Club based on a version designed by a group of educational researchers from the University of Washington (Horn, 2008b) and expanded their vision for using VC as a means for analyzing and developing knowledge about students' math understandings. Our goals were twofold. First, we wanted to create coherence in focus across the six learning spaces within the professional development network. Second, we wanted to foreground instructional practices that specifically address equitable participation in math classrooms, the primary goal of Complex Instruction.

Video Club meets monthly, for 2 hours, and participants include all of the mathematics teachers who are members of the network along with some administrators and instructional coaches from participating schools and districts. We typically draw 25 participants each month. All of the teachers with whom we work agree to have their classrooms videotaped several times during the school year by an external videographer who is knowledgeable about Complex Instruction. We facilitators view the tapes, discuss the content, and edit a 10-minute clip that is relevant to the goals of Video Club and our learning agenda for teachers. Our ongoing presence in classrooms and common planning meetings gives us access to teachers' ideas about and challenges with Complex Instruction, and we use this information to inform our decisions about the clips we eventually use. In some cases, we may even ask the videographer to capture a particular kind of classroom event or dig into our archives to showcase a particular feature of CI instruction for analysis. Since this network is a social system, we must also consider potential issues of status as we plan for Video Club meetings in our efforts to promote equitable participation and increased learning for all members. Some examples of how we might attend to status include rotating the math course and school from which the video clip is taken, showcasing a clip of a particular teacher who might need a status boost relative to her team or the larger network, and using a video clip to assign competence to a teacher who has developed a new CI structure or whose practice with CI has recently improved.

Once we have selected a video clip, we meet with the teacher in the clip (called the "feature teacher") and the Teacher Facilitators of VC. Teacher Facilitators are members of the professional development network whom we carefully select each month, with attention to potential issues of status within the network. We aim to apprentice teachers into the role of VC facilitators in order to distribute knowledge and expertise across the community so they can eventually sustain this practice without us. We convene as a small group to collaboratively develop the ability to notice important classroom events that impact the successful implementation of Complex Instruction. In addition, this analysis and discussion about the month's feature video ensures that the feature teacher is prepared to hear the range of observations and comments that might surface during Video Club before the event unfolds. We recognize that it is a huge risk for any teacher to offer his or her classroom practice as a public artifact for analysis, and we take much time to prepare the feature teacher for comments that might be interpreted as negative so that Video Club is a positive learning opportunity instead of an experience to be endured. We will discuss how we prepare the feature teacher for Video Club in the section about Teacher Facilitators.

Finally, we have developed a formal, evidence-based protocol to frame the analysis of video and reflection conversations, promote equitable participation among participants, and provide intellectual safety within the large group. This protocol, shown in Figure 13.2, centers around five topics of discussion, interspersed with repeated viewings of the video clip and time for individual reflection. The questions in the protocol are meant to press teachers to consider students' beliefs about math learning alongside teacher moves and how each contributes to or detracts from students' equal participation and mathematical understanding (Day, 2011). The protocol aims to promote safety and intellectual risk-taking during Video Club by focusing attention on what is going well (e.g., what students *do* understand) and prompting participants to ground their statements in concrete, specific evidence from the video. The protocol emphasizes the theoretical anonymity of the feature teacher and students in the clip, thereby helping participants recognize how each video is relevant to their own classrooms, by using sentence starters that begin with "*The* teacher . . ." or "*The* students . . ." as opposed to naming the people in the video. As one teacher stated during an interview, "The Video Club mantra of, 'These are *our* kids. This is all of us as a teacher on any given day,' permits us to see other classrooms as reflections of our own" (C.B., personal communication, June 2010).

Success with Video Club

The group that attends Video Club is heterogeneous in terms of teaching experience in general and with the use of Complex Instruction in particular. This heterogeneity promotes a broad range of "noticings," which we consider a great

Figure 13.2. Video Club Protocol and Focus Questions

1.) Do the math problem that is featured in the video.

2.) Learning Objectives

What will students understand or be able to do as a result of completing this task?

3.) Watch video

4.) Student Understanding

What do students understand?
What is your evidence from the video to support your statement?

I think (name of student) understands **OR** is on the way to understanding (math concept or skill) because I heard/saw (evidence from video).

5.) Watch video

6.) Participation Norms

What are the norms for participation that students are enacting?
What are they saying and doing as math learners that supports their participation and learning?

I think the students understand that being a math learner requires (participation norm), and I think this because (evidence from the video).

7.) Strengths

What did students do or say that was mathematically smart?

I think it was smart when (name of student) did/said (evidence from the video), and I think this because

_____.

Take-aways

What are you taking away from this conversation? (What have you learned? What are you left thinking about, wondering, asking? What might you do differently in your classroom as a result of our discussion?)

success. Even with a protocol and a well-chosen video clip that intends to focus participants' attention on specific Complex Instruction practices, the teachers see and hear very different things. Again, we consider this a positive component of Video Club, because we interpret these results to mean that we are meeting the learning needs of a diverse group of educators and providing for a wide range of opportunities to participate.

Research conducted by Day (2011) analyzed participants' responses collected during 2 years of Video Club meetings. Results from this study indicated that teachers attended to three categories during Video Club conversations. These categories are: (1) classroom norms that supported students' participation with one another as they engaged in learning mathematics, (2) the content of teachers' questions and their effect on students' participation, and (3) the physical space of the classroom and how it was organized and used by the teacher to promote participation. We claim that these categories of noticings are critical for creating equitable classrooms, because teachers' awareness of such practices is directly related to developing their CI expertise.

Video Club often motivates teachers to create or revise groupworthy tasks, try new practices in their classrooms, or develop entirely new goals for themselves relative to their instruction. It is difficult to disregard evidence from the classrooms of colleagues as irrelevant or only something certain teachers and young people can do. More often than not, teachers exhibit collective pride in the video being shown and in the teacher whose classroom is highlighted, and this pride often motivates them to continue the process of reculturing their classrooms and departments. We often hear Common Planning Teams inquiring about a teacher move they witnessed on video or collectively planning to implement a new practice in their classes and report back with results. Congruent with the philosophy of Complex Instruction, we recognize that no one of us in this community is as smart as all of us together (Cohen & Lotan, 1997), and we applaud and encourage the thoughtful ingenuity of teachers to make connections between Video Club and the other learning spaces that push their practices in ways we might have never imagined.

Video Club Challenges

The biggest challenge we face with Video Club is finding a video clip that meets the needs of a diverse group of math teachers. We want people with a range of Complex Instruction experiences to be able to notice something meaningful in the video and engage in a collegial conversation that pushes their thinking and teaching practice. We have learned that teachers who are more new to CI tend to focus on very specific CI structures used in the video, such as a Multiple-Ability Orientation or team roles. In contrast, a seasoned CI teacher is more likely to attend to the subtle decisions that the feature teacher makes. These might include the format of a task, particular questions used to press for student understanding, or the teacher's position when he or she enters a small group. Needless to say, finding a video clip that addresses such a variety of features proves challenging for each Video Club.

A second major challenge has been getting teachers to open their classrooms for videotaping. Most of the teachers with whom we work have rarely had classroom visitors, and if they have, the visitors were usually there for evaluation purposes. This can be a high-stakes and stressful situation for any teacher. Our goals for gathering video data are never for evaluation. Instead, we are eager to collect evidence of teachers and students engaged in regular classroom routines, as these provide for the most interesting learning opportunities. However, it is not always easy to convince teachers that observation without evaluation is possible, and it sometimes takes much concerted effort on our part and several experiences with peer-reciprocated observations and Video Club before a teacher is willing to be taped.

Teacher Facilitators (TFACs)

As the math communities develop at various school sites and the culture among teachers and students starts to cohere, we spend a significant amount of time looking forward—anticipating forces such as district mandates and school structures that could affect or disrupt the developing vision or recent culture changes. We found this position to be quite familiar as former department chairs at Railside who learned how to anticipate, negotiate, and work proactively to protect our department and classroom communities. During the 20 years that Railside developed its interpretation and enactment of CI for teaching high school mathematics, the department had become uncommonly agentive. We math teachers at Railside learned that our ability to teach effectively was directly related to the stability of our environment. As such, the department chair responsibilities extended to include an amount of forecasting. We reacted early to any news from the district and administrators so our department could offer suggestions or solutions that considered our needs. Frequently, our proactive measures prevented outside decisions that might have unintentionally undermined our department stability and the collaborative cultures we were creating in our classrooms.

In our present work, our budding math communities require the same kind of proactive protection led by respected, forward-thinking teachers within each community. Thus, we opened a new learning space in the network and dubbed it Teacher Facilitators, or TFACs. Based on our experiences at Railside, we attempt to help the TFACs develop two distinct ways of "looking" at their departments. First, TFACs need to look outward—by attending to the many people in schools who make decisions that can impact a department community and the effective implementation of Complex Instruction in all classrooms. Second, TFACs need to look inward—toward the department, with an ethic of care and responsibility to its members. Looking both outward and inward requires anticipating and acting in thoughtful, proactive ways to influence any and all decisions that might affect teachers' abilities to effectively manage CI classrooms and positively contribute to the health and growth of the department community. Our goals for the TFACs' learning space, then, are to train present and future department chairpersons to protect their existing CI communities and to enable the growth and sustainability of CI teaching and learning within and beyond their school sites. Our formal interaction with the TFACs happens in three settings: at monthly meetings, through Video Club facilitation and facilitator preparation, and through weekly logs.

Monthly meetings, attended by TFACs from across sites and co-facilitated by us, provide both a learning community for the Teacher Facilitators and an enormous opportunity for us to reculture and mentor. For example, the school contexts in which our teachers work are organized hierarchically. In monthly meetings we help the TFACs consider the unidirectionality of these hierarchies—especially concerning the generation and flow of ideas and directives from the district and site administrators. We share our experiences from Railside and ask the TFACs to reconsider a number of processes and procedures that are typically "received" by the department such as hiring new teachers, creating a department teaching schedule, placing students in appropriate courses, and apprenticing new teachers into the department. Instead of accepting these major decisions and department influences as given, we encourage the TFACs to look outward, for example by collaborating with their administrators and counseling staff and by talking with the supervisors of student teachers so they might inform and influence important outcomes and protect their department's vision for teaching and learning mathematics.

Additionally, we train the TFACs to look inward and develop consciousness about the inner workings of their departments so they can maintain healthy and strong communities. Much in the same way that it is the teacher's responsibility in a CI classroom to help each individual recognize his or her strengths and ways of being smart that contribute to everyone's learning, it is the department leader's—in this case TFAC's—responsibility to help each department member recognize his or her strengths and how he or she contributes to the expertise and success of the department. Looking inward and maintaining an ethic of care for the math department such that everyone can reach their full potential and simultaneously feed the larger community requires leaders who thoughtfully consider teachers' schedules, the development of course team leaders, the placement of student teachers, support for new teachers, and opportunities for individual and department learning. In addition, looking inward requires caring for department members as human beings by celebrating birthdays, checking in on new teachers, and creating opportunities to socialize outside of school. Attending to the ebb and flow of people's lives so that everyone feels valued and connected to the community is vital for the community's health and longevity.

A large component of our TFAC training has been through Video Club facilitation, where we work with the TFACs to become both instructional leaders and skilled Video Club facilitators for their schools or districts. In the first part of this process, we meet with one or two TFACs to preview, analyze, and discuss the selected video clip as a way of helping them to better notice important classroom features and practices. Second, we prepare TFACs to use the Video Club protocol by considering the intended purpose of each question and anticipate teachers' responses. Since they will eventually co-facilitate a Video Club session, we want TFACs to feel confident and competent to manage the structures of VC and effectively respond to questions and concerns that might arise. These meetings provide all involved with opportunities to dig more deeply into the beliefs and practices of Complex Instruction in ways that are similar to but more rich than what we can accomplish during Common Planning Team meetings, because we are fewer people focused on a specific artifact of practice. Several TFACs have claimed that these monthly meetings spurred many new ideas for their own classroom practices and trained them to consider how their colleagues might approach similar dilemmas.

In addition to the monthly meetings and Video Club facilitation, we ask the TFACs to submit weekly logs to support their efforts as department leaders. The log consists of two parts, one quantitative and one open response. The quantitative part of the log includes questions that prompt TFACs to consider how they might use their time to look both outward and inward as they aim to protect and sustain their department's work with Complex Instruction. Some of these prompts include, "How much time this week did you spend working as a collaborative course team?" or "How much time this week did you spend 'making rounds' to interact or socialize with math department members?" Next, the open response section asks TFACs to summarize any perceived effects of their work and envision what they might need to do in the coming week. Our goal as TFAC facilitators is not to evaluate how the teachers spend their time or how much time they spend on each activity, but to provide ideas for how their time can be spent. The open response part of the log reminds teachers that effective leadership requires reflection about what has been done to inform planning for what might come next.

In the end, the weekly log serves three purposes. First and foremost, it provides an opportunity for TFACs to reflect on their leadership work and its potential effects on a regular basis. In addition, the log gives us facilitators with an opportunity to suggest desired leadership activities that the teachers might not otherwise consider. Last, the log informs us about the health of each department community, so we can provide support or intervene as necessary.

Outside evaluation of the TFAC component of our program done by the Noyce Foundation (Lee, Leblang, & Porter, 2012) explains how the TFACs increased their leadership repertoires and infiltrated their departments with new ideas and suggestions for how their math departments might better advocate for and protect the vision for teaching and learning with Complex Instruction. Administrators from the schools in which our TFACs work reported that these teachers have become "models of good math teaching" and "in-house resources" as they influence how their colleagues in other subject areas now talk and work together (p. 29). One principal from a school where we completed a 3-year implementation cycle explains below in data correspondence how the TFACs and the math department became site-based leaders for the entire staff as they advocated for a new vision for teaching and learning throughout the school:

> As the year progressed and the [math] teachers became more and more comfortable with the structures and routines established to create equitable learning opportunities for students, the conversation amongst them shifted from "this is what I did and saw in MY classroom" to "this is what WE did and this is what WE saw in OUR classrooms." The conversations, facilitated by the coaches, set the conditions for these teachers to create leadership opportunities amongst themselves and empowered them to step outside the department and begin to facilitate the same conversations amongst other staff.
>
> We typically have one week before school starts and I had them [math department] do a demonstration for the whole staff, a two-and-a-half hour session that was for the whole staff, special ed., language arts, everybody. It was well received and immediately had an impact on how teachers structured their groups. They [math department] explained how they structured their kids, so everyone started using protocols for groupwork.

This feedback speaks to our goal to help teachers become change agents within their local sites as they advocate for new ways of teaching and learning, and the power of community to maintain and grow new practices. Successful reform requires much more than outsiders coming into an organization to share ideas and expertise. Learning communities that are committed to growth and sustainability must have aligned purposes, perceptions, and commitments (Gamoran et al., 2003, p. 173) and continually modify and adapt their practices, including how they work together, in response to new collaborative inquiry, reflection, and new learning.

CONCLUSION

Our model for transporting the Railside vision for math teaching and learning is coherent and comprehensive, and its various components capitalize on much of what we know about research for teacher learning and professional development in addition to our experiences as math teachers at Railside. Learning opportunities within our network blend broad-based theories and concepts about Complex Instruction along with support for implementation that is situated in classrooms and is flexibly responsive to teachers' needs. In addition to individual teachers, we aim to reform mathematics departments in order to maintain the growth and sustainability of these new practices. We support teachers to reculture their beliefs about what counts as school mathematics, what it means to be mathematically competent, who can be a successful math learner, and the role of the teacher in classrooms and interactions within the larger school community that affects students' learning.

The six sites for learning that make up the professional development network are connected by a common vision and set of practices and a primary focus on issues of social and academic status. Our participation in each activity as facilitators provides us with opportunities to access and build from teachers' ideas, questions, and strengths so we can create learning agendas that meet the needs of individuals and departments. For example, we might use an idea generated from a Video Club session as part of a lesson that gets planned during a Common Planning Team meeting and then implemented and analyzed as part of a Peer Reciprocal Observation. Alternately, we might take up a dilemma of practice posed during common planning that stemmed from a classroom coaching session and then try to capture classroom video that allows for reflection on this particular challenge in the next Video Club. Each of the learning spaces has its unique affordances and limitations. Collectively, they provide multiple perspectives and representations of practice that supports a department to reculture its community toward a specific vision for teaching and learning mathematics.

However, even with so much support, it takes lot of time for a department to reculture itself. Several generations of teachers at Railside had been hard at work for close to 20 years before much of the research about its success started to spread. Current political pressures and financial realities usually limit us to about 3 years before school districts want something bigger and faster. Scaling up our model is a huge concern, and we are currently faced with the question of how to grow to meet the needs of interested parties while being faithful to our vision of our work. To this end, we are beginning to apprentice new facilitators into the network by tapping into the cadre of secondary math teachers who have been successful with their implementation of Complex Instruction with students and their reculturing efforts within their departments.

With a little data under our belts, we can claim several success stories within our program. With the exception of one department that disbanded itself after 3 years of rotating administrators and threats from the district to close the school, we have maintained 100% retention with the teachers with whom we've worked, as they choose to continue teaching secondary mathematics with Complex

Instruction as their primary pedagogy. Teachers claim that they choose to stay engaged in this network for many reasons, including increased job satisfaction, positive membership in a professional community, and opportunities to learn and grow their teaching practices. In addition to staying on the job, our teachers tend to recruit and train like-minded teachers into their departments in order to sustain these new department and classroom cultures they have worked hard to build. Enrollment in the Designing Effective Groupwork course continues to grow each year. In summer 2011 we had 65 participants, including teachers from at least seven different school districts as well as community college professors. Additionally, attendance at monthly Video Clubs continues to hover right around 25. We've recently worked with one district's high school and the middle schools that feeds into it, and another district is 5 years into implementation of our program at the secondary level. We are excited by these opportunities to develop articulation and cross-site coherence in both content and practice.

Finally, interview data suggest that many of our teachers are renewing their beliefs about what it means to teach and learn mathematics and what it means to be a math learner through their participation in the network. For example, one teacher told us that he now understands math as "connected pieces instead of just a bunch of disjointed stuff," and yet another claimed, "Every student can learn and comes in with a lot of math already." Such beliefs about content and students support the vision for CI classrooms and make it more likely that teachers will sustain these powerful new learning cultures.

Chapter 14

Conclusion

Reflections on the Practices and Principles That Supported Equity Math Teaching at Railside

Na'ilah Suad Nasir, Carlos Cabana, Barbara Shreve,
Estelle Woodbury, and Nicole Louie

The chapters in this volume have undertaken to give a detailed window into the practices, beliefs, and effects of the equity pedagogy developed over the course of more than 2 decades of collaborative work among teachers in the mathematics department at Railside High. We have intended this volume to be descriptive rather than overtly prescriptive. Teaching for equity in mathematics is not a paint-by-numbers process; rather, it involves knowing the local context, working within existing constrained systems, building and sustaining complex human relationships, and engaging in a continual cycle of reflection.

In this concluding chapter, we reflect back on the key practices and the overarching core principles of the Railside approach that we have detailed throughout the volume. As we do so, we consider the implications and necessary conditions for implementing the kinds of practices and growing the kind of departmental teaching culture that was created at Railside. As we write this, we are struck by the inherent challenges in such a task. All three of the teachers who are co-editors of this volume have, since leaving Railside, attempted to enact some of the practices that were successful there in new contexts and settings, including other large urban districts as well as small charter schools. These efforts have been an occasion not only to reflect on the robustness of the practices, principles, and structures that supported such successful outcomes at Railside, but also to reconsider how what was developed there cannot be imported wholesale, but rather must be adapted in ways that are congruent with existing local conditions. Thus, what we have presented in this volume, and the points we raise in this concluding chapter, are best taken not as a set of rigid prescriptions, but as a description of a complex setting, network of relationships, and set of processes. As a way to bring together what we have learned across the volume, and to provide a set of ideas for those considering implementing the kind of equity pedagogy that was enacted at Railside, we return in this chapter to the distillations of the important aspects of practice and the guiding principles that underlie those classroom and professional community practices.

FIVE ASPECTS OF EQUITABLE MATHEMATICS INSTRUCTION

In Chapter 3, we articulated five aspects of practice that comprised the instructional approach at Railside. Those aspects of practice are:

1. Structuring lessons to support engagement in *groupworthy tasks*
2. Approaching math concepts through *multiple representations*
3. Organizing curriculum around *big ideas*
4. Using *justification* to push students to articulate their mathematical thinking
5. Making students' thinking public and valued through *presentations at the overhead*

We have described each of these aspects of practice throughout the volume, and we reiterate them here to make them easily accessible to readers, and to make the point that these aspects are intimately connected both to a somewhat parallel set of practices around supporting professional community as well as to the key principles highlighted in the introduction to the volume.

FOUR PRACTICES OF PROFESSIONAL COMMUNITY

In Chapter 11, we identified four important practices of the teacher professional community at Railside. These include:

1. Doing math together,
2. Working on "groupworthy" department goals together,
3. Distributing leadership, and
4. Attending to hiring and induction.

It is striking to notice the ways that these aspects of teacher professional community practice mirror and support the aspects of classroom teaching practice. For instance, in order for teachers to have deep understandings of what it means for students to do math together, teachers themselves engage in doing mathematics together, and in doing so come up against some of the same challenges and successes that students might experience in their classrooms. As another example, a key aspect of the teachers' practice with one another was to work on groupworthy department goals, which mirrors the classroom focus on engaging students in groupworthy mathematical tasks. This focus on engaging both teachers and students in tasks that are important and that demand collaborative work fosters the sense of community between teachers and students, and requires that teachers walk the walk, engaging in the same types of practices in which they are asking students to take part.

KEY OVERARCHING PRINCIPLES

The aspects of teaching practice and professional community at Railside described above were only powerful when connected to important and meaningful overarching principles. We began the volume by articulating the key principles that emerged across the chapters. They are:

- All teachers and students are learners
- Working from strengths while making space for vulnerability
- Redefining "smart"
- Redefining what it means to do math in school
- The importance of relationships

It is not accidental that these five principles are where we began the volume. These underlying principles encapsulate the beliefs and ways of understanding the Railside department's work together that made possible the enactment of the practices that are described across this volume and in the lists above. They show up again and again in the chapters as authors describe the "magic" that happened in Railside classrooms. Without the belief that all teachers and students are learners, for instance, the openness and unconditional support for intellectual engagement that characterized the Railside professional teacher community as well as Railside classrooms would not have flourished. Furthermore, these principles breathe life into and reflect the practices—when both teachers and students engage in doing complex math together, the principle that all students and teachers are learners is reinforced. The overarching principles, in many ways, have to do with the spirit of the work. In other words, they don't all translate into a set of concrete practices; rather, they represent a set of stances or frames or ethical commitments that are necessary to enacting the practices in ways that support learners and learning.

We cannot overstate the importance of the attention and commitment to supporting the intellectual work and the habits of mind that are necessary for students to engage with complex mathematical thinking, as well as to the emotional and psychosocial aspects of teaching and learning. In the equity pedagogy at Railside, these two components worked together to create classrooms where students were held to high academic expectations, but were supported (both emotionally and cognitively) in fulfilling those expectations.

It is important to acknowledge that enacting these practices and principles does require some preconditions that do not sit entirely at the department level, as becomes evident in the analysis of the collapsing of the professional community at the foundation of the equity pedagogy at Railside. For example, to enact the practice of distributed leadership, the department must have the independence and the flexibility for teachers to take up different roles, and the time in which to carry out the responsibilities of those roles. Similarly, to have significant departmental input into hiring and induction practices, the site principal must be willing and able to accept this input from teachers. As the ultimate fate of the Railside mathematics department makes evident, the absence of critical contextual support can make the work itself exceedingly difficult, if not impossible.

Enacting the practices and principles also requires an orientation to students that pushes back on stereotypical racialized notions of which students are smart and which students can be good at math. It is an orientation to equity that requires one to eschew racial stereotypes about intelligence that are still all too common in our society. Throughout this book, we and other authors have said relatively little about race. This is because in the day-to-day practice of teaching at Railside, it was not a concept around which they organized their work. However, their commitment to achieving equitable outcomes, and their commitment to raising the bar for all of their students, was undergirded by the goal to disrupt racialized patterns of achievement in mathematics. And to a large degree, using the strategies and practice described in this book, they achieved that goal.

In conclusion, we hope that this volume can serve as a way to document and preserve the transformative work done at Railside over the decades that the equity pedagogy was in existence there; as a resource for those looking to create pedagogies of equity in their own math departments and schools; and, finally, as a caution that enacting equity pedagogies requires support at multiple levels and, even after years of work, can be fragile in the face of an unsupportive context. Importantly, the case of Railside illustrates that it is possible, with enough will, hard work, and sustained commitment, to create classrooms where students from marginalized groups succeed in learning complex mathematics. We hope that the legacy of Railside will live on through this work.

Notes

Chapter 1

1.   "Railside" is a pseudonym coined by Boaler (2006b) based on the school's location, literally on the wrong side of the railroad tracks that separated the school's attendance zone from the more affluent parts of town.

Chapter 2

1.   This chapter is an adaptation of Boaler, J., and Staples, M. E. (2008). Creating mathematical futures through an equitable teaching approach: The case of Railside School. *Teachers College Record, 110*(3), 608–645. This work is sponsored by a grant from the National Science Foundation (Division of Research, Evaluation and Communication, REC 9985146). The views expressed herein are those of the authors and not those of the funding agency.

2.   All data in this chapter that have been obtained from websites have been rounded to the nearest 10 to preclude identification of the schools, unless otherwise indicated. Consequently, for values related to percentages, not all totals will sum to 100.

3.   Our analyses only include students who gave permission to be in the study, approximately 87% of the eligible students.

4.   This percentage includes all seniors at Greendale and Hilltop, whether they attended the "traditional" or IMP classes. At this time we have been unable to separate the traditional students from IMP, but as they were few in number this will not affect the reported percentage greatly.

5.   Although Table 2.6 indicates that 40% of the Greendale students were at or above basic level, this result is inflated due to rounding of the data prior to adding. When the percentage of students at or above basic level is determined first and then rounded, the result is 30%.

6.   Greendale had one 50-minute and two 110-minute periods per week. Hilltop had three 55-minute and one 100-minute periods per week.

7.   At the time this research was first published, students and schools in California were held accountable to the California Standards Tests, which comprised multiple-choice questions aligned to the California Content Standards. Those standards, adopted in 1997, outlined specific content to be included in each high school course. As this book is being written, California and other states across the nation have adopted the new Common Core State Standards for Mathematics, which reorganize content and include expectations of more conceptual understanding. The CCSS also include Standards for Mathematical Practice. New state tests, scheduled to be introduced in the 2014–2015 school year, will reflect these standards. At the time of this writing, it is

not clear how the new assessments will document and evaluate students' mathematical thinking and reasoning.

Chapter 3

1.   This scene is a reconstruction based on a specific lesson and the authors' recollections of interactions with individual students.

2.   This problem was later published as part of the CPM *Connections* series. It appears here with permission. Copyright CPM Educational Program. All rights reserved.

3.   Lab Gear™ is a manipulative that models algebraic expressions and equations using a geometric representation. The Lab Gear™ and related curriculum were created by Henri Picciotto (1995; see www.MathEducationPage.org). Railside teachers also drew inspiration from "Algebra: Themes, Tools, Concepts" by Anita Wah and Henri Picciotto, also available on the same site.

4. Multiple representations extended to content beyond linear relationships. Examples include using graphs, tables, and equations to examine function families throughout the course sequence; in geometry, examining relationships on similar right triangles using trigonometric functions, similarity relationships, slope ratios, proportions, and Pythagorean Theorem; and in algebra, multiplying and factoring binomials using Algebra Lab Gear™, an area model, and product and sum relationships in number pairs.

Chapter 4

1.   This chapter is an adaptation of Staples, M. (2008). Promoting student collaboration in a detracked, heterogeneous secondary mathematics classroom. *Journal of Mathematics Teacher Education, 11*, 349–371. An earlier version of this paper was presented at the Annual Meeting of the American Educational Research Association, Chicago, 2007, as part of the Tracking and Detracking SIG session *Teaching, Learning, and Other Outcomes in Tracked and Detracked Environments*.

Chapter 5

1.   These projects were all part of the Geometry class at Railside. The Transamerica Building Project required students to develop a strategy for finding the volume of a specific floor of the pyramid-shaped skyscraper, knowing only the side length of the building's base (which is square), the building's height, and the total number of floors. The Barbie Project required students to determine what a Barbie doll would look like if one of her body measurements (height, waist, foot length, bust) were made life-sized and the rest of her body were enlarged proportionally. The Flagpole Project is described below.

Chapter 6

1.   The author wishes to thank the students, Lucia and Santiago, for their stories; the Railside teachers, for their support and collaboration; and her research assistant, Stephanie Barr, for her invaluable contribution to the ideas presented in this paper.

2. STEM is an acronym for the combined fields of science, technology, engineering, and mathematics.

Chapter 7

1. In an attempt to unearth the identities to which the participants assigned the most salience, I used an activity called Diversity Toss (Nieto, 2004). This activity required the women to make decisions about the relative importance of their identities and encouraged a dialogue about the meanings they assigned to each.

2. The capitalization of words within a quote represents emphasis made by the speaker.

Chapter 9

1. An earlier version of this chapter was published as Horn, I. S. (2005). Learning on the job: A situated account of teacher learning in high school mathematics departments. *Cognition & Instruction, 23*(2), 207–236.

2. Judith Warren Little, principal investigator, and Lora Bartlett, research associate.

3. This is calculated by taking the number of students in grades 9–12 enrolled in courses above geometry as a percentage of total enrollment in grades 11–12. This statistic was computed by greatschools.net using data from the California Department of Education.

4. The Algebra Group teachers attended different professional development workshops over the summer and shared key learnings during a weeklong retreat before the start of school. This event came to be known as Algebra Week.

5. For a more detailed analysis of these exchanges, see Horn (2007).

6. For a fuller account of teaching replays and rehearsals and their role in teacher learning, see Horn (2010).

7. This exchange (turns 7 and 8) shows the extent to which the speakers rely on contextual knowledge to make sense of their conversations. Hanks (1996) describes how such telegraphic exchanges signal a degree of intimacy or familiarity among the speakers. For the teachers' purposes, these truncated utterances allow them to get to the heart of the problems quickly, as they are not required to retell the particular circumstances that created Belinda's dilemma. Analytically, I rely heavily on my own intensive participation and ongoing access to the participants to make sense of this exchange.

8. The strengths of South's reform were not highlighted in this analysis but have been explored more fully by the work of Bartlett (2004) and Little, Horn, and Bartlett (2000). The main strengths were the organizational structures and funding resources that allowed teachers' reform work to be both "on the clock" and coordinated across subject areas. The extramural funding they received through whole-school grants allowed them to restructure their work time and pay teachers to meet weekly after school and participate in monthly teacher research groups. Teachers did not need to put in long uncompensated hours outside the workday to meet the demands of reform work (Bartlett, 2004).

Chapter 10

1. An earlier version of this chapter appeared as Little, J. W., & Horn, I. S. (2007). Resources for professional learning in talk about teaching. In Louise Stoll and Karen Seashore Louis (Eds.), *Professional Learning Communities: Divergence, Depth, and Dilemmas*, (p. 204). Berkshire, UK: Open University Press. We thank the editors of this volume, especially Barbara Shreve and Carlos Cabana, for helping us rewrite this piece for a different audience.

2. For purposes of this narrative, we have eliminated or modified most of the detailed transcription conventions that aid a more fine-grained analysis of the data.

3. For examples in which both of these patterns are evident, see Little (2003, pp. 933–935) and Horn and Little (2010, pp. 202–207).

Chapter 11

1. The department held its first "Algebra Week" in 1999 and continued to meet for a week in August annually through 2010. Prior to 1999, the department met in the summer to collaborate on 8th-grade math, but the meetings were not an annual event. As the week extended to include time for teachers to collaborate on other courses, it was referred to as "Algebra Collaboration Week."

2. This does not include seniors not graduating because of the California High School Exit Exam.

Chapter 12

1. Though many of the most dramatic policy changes occurred in 2009, which was also the year our study began, shifts in the district's priorities and management style were gradual. Teachers traced the roots of this to the district's entrance into Program Improvement in 2005, followed by the hiring of a new, business-minded superintendent in 2007, as pressures associated with Program Improvement status grew.

2. In Railside's case, the district initially entered Program Improvement because of its failure to make AYP in reading scores for students in Special Education.

3. Teachers picked up students' use of the word "ghetto" as a descriptor for Railside. The term is associated with urban poverty and dysfunction.

4. While district pressures around textbooks and standardized testing appear to have had only small impacts on instruction as of this writing—at least as compared to the structural changes that the district office has made—there is reason to believe that they will have greater force in the future. Four teachers have left the school, and the new teachers who will be hired to replace them are unlikely to have either the vision and skills, or the security of tenure, to resist pressures from above.

Chapter 13

1. A multi-ability, groupworthy task requires high cognitive demand, deals with important mathematical concepts, is open-ended, requires complex problem solving,

provides students with multiple entry points and opportunities to demonstrate intellectual competence, requires positive interdependence, and includes clear criteria for the evaluation of a final product (Lotan, 2003).

2.   Video Club was not a learning tool used at Railside. We facilitators developed this activity to support teachers to observe each one another's classrooms, which was a routine practice at Railside High.

References

Alper, L., Fendel, D. M., Fraser, S., & Resek, D. (2003). *Interactive Mathematics Program*. Emeryville, CA: Key Curriculum Press.

Alrø, H., & Skovsmose, O. (2002). *Dialogue and learning in mathematics education.* Dordrecht, The Netherlands: Kluwer Academic Publishers.

Ball, D. L., & Cohen, D. K. (1996). Reform by the book: What is — or might be — the role of curriculum materials in teacher learning and instructional reform? *Educational Researcher, 25*(9), 6–8, 14.

Ball, D. L., & Cohen, D. K. (1999). Developing practice, developing practitioners: Toward a practice-based theory of professional education. In L. Darling-Hammond & G. Sykes (Eds.), *Teaching as the learning profession* (pp. 3–32). San Francisco, CA: Jossey-Bass.

Barab, S. A., Cherkes-Julkowski, M., Swenson, R., Garrett, S., Shaw, R. E., & Young, M. (1999). Principles of self-organization: Learning as participation in autocatakinetic systems. *The Journal of the Learning Sciences, 8*(3&4), 349–390.

Bartlett, L. (2004). Expanding teacher work roles: A resource for retention or a recipe for overwork? *Journal of Education Policy, 19*(5), 565–582.

Becker, J., & Jacob, B. (2000). California school mathematics politics: The anti-reform of 1997–1999. *Phi Delta Kappan, 81,* 529–537.

Berger J., Rosenholtz, S. J., & Zelditch, M., Jr. (1980). Status organizing processes. *Annual Review of Sociology, 6,* 479–508.

Bernal, D. D. (1998). Using a Chicana feminist epistemology in educational research. *Harvard Educational Review, 68*(4), 555–582.

Boaler, J. (1997a). *Experiencing school mathematics: Teaching styles, sex and setting.* Buckingham, UK: Open University Press.

Boaler, J. (1997b). Setting, social class, and survival of the quickest. In J. Boaler (Ed.), *Experiencing school mathematics: Teaching styles, sex and setting* (pp. 125–142). Philadelphia, PA: Open University Press.

Boaler, J. (2000). Mathematics from another world: Traditional communities and the alienation of learners. *Journal of Mathematical Behavior, 18*(4), 379–397.

Boaler, J. (2002a). *Experiencing school mathematics: Traditional and reform approaches to teaching and their impact on student learning* (rev. ed.). Mahwah, NJ: Lawrence Erlbaum Associates.

Boaler, J. (2002b). The development of disciplinary relationships: Knowledge, practice and identity in mathematics classrooms. *For the Learning of Mathematics, 22*(1), 42–47.

Boaler, J. (2003). When learning no longer matters — Standardized testing and the creation of inequality. Phi Delta Kappan, *84*(7), 502–506.

Boaler, J. (2004). Promoting equity in mathematics classrooms: Important teaching practices and their impact on student learning. Paper presented at the International Conference for Mathematics Education, Copenhagen.

Boaler, J. (2006a). How a detracked mathematics approach promoted respect, responsibility, and high achievement. *Theory into Practice, 45*(1), 40–46.

Boaler, J. (2006b). Promoting respectful learning. *Educational Leadership, 63*(5), 74–78.

Boaler, J. (2008). Promoting "relational equity" and high mathematics achievement through an innovative mixed ability approach. *British Educational Research Journal, 34*(2), 167–194.

Boaler, J. (2009). *What's math got to do with it? How parents and teachers can help children learn to love their least favorite subject.* New York, NY: Penguin.

Boaler, J., & Brodie, K. (2004). The importance, nature and impact of teacher questions. In D. E. McDougall & J. A. Ross (Eds.), Proceedings of the 26th annual meeting of the North American chapter of the International Group for the Psychology of Mathematics Education (Vol. 2, pp. 773–781). Toronto, Ontario: Ontario Institute of Studies in Education/University of Toronto.

Boaler, J., & Greeno, J. G. (2000). Identity, agency, and knowing in mathematics worlds. In J. Boaler (Ed.), *Multiple perspectives on mathematics teaching and learning: International perspectives on mathematics education* (pp. 171–200). Westport, CT: Ablex Publishing.

Boaler, J., & Staples, M. (2008). Creating mathematical futures through an equitable teaching approach: The case of Railside School. *Teachers College Record, 110*(3), 608–645.

Bowker, G. C., & Star, S. L. (1999). *Sorting things out: Classification and its consequences.* Cambridge, MA: MIT Press.

Broad Foundation. (2010). The Broad Superintendents Academy. Available at www. broadacademy.org/

Bronfenbrenner, U. (1979). *The ecology of human development: Experiment by nature and design.* Cambridge, MA: Harvard University Press.

Brutlag, D. (1994). *Equals investigations.* Berkeley, CA: Lawrence Hall of Science, University of California.

Bryk, A. S., Sebring, P. B., Allensworth, E., Luppescu, S., & Easton, J. Q. (2010). *Organizing schools for improvement: Lessons from Chicago.* Chicago, IL: The University of Chicago Press.

Burris, C. C., Heubert, J., & Levin, H. (2006). Accelerating mathematics achievement using heterogeneous grouping. *American Educational Research Journal, 43*(1), 105–126.

Cammarota, J. (2004). The gendered and racialized pathways of Latina and Latino youth: Different struggles, different resistances in the urban context. *Anthropology & Education Quarterly, 35*(1), 53–74.

Civil, M. (2002). Everyday mathematics, mathematicians' mathematics, and school mathematics: Can we bring them together? *Journal for Research in Mathematics Education* (Monograph Series #11: Everyday and academic mathematics in the classroom), 40–62.

Cobb, P., Gresalfi, M., & Hodge, L. L. (2009). An interpretive scheme for analyzing the identities that students develop in mathematics classrooms. *Journal for Research in Mathematics Education, 40*, 40–68.

Cobb, P., & Hodge, L. (2002). A relational perspective on issues of cultural diversity and equity as they play out in the mathematics classroom. *Mathematical Thinking and Learning, 4*(2&3), 249–284.

Cobb, P., & Hodge, L. (2007). Culture, identity, and equity in the mathematics classroom. In N. S. Nasir & P. Cobb (Eds.), *Improving access to mathematics: Diversity and equity in the classroom* (pp. 159–172). New York, NY: Teachers College Press.

Cobb, P., & McClain, K. (2006). The collective mediation of a high-stakes accountability program: Communities and networks of practice. *Mind, Culture, and Activity, 13*(2), 207–230.

Cobb, P., McClain, K., Lamberg, T., & Dean, C. (2003). Situating teachers' instructional practices in the institutional setting of the school and district. *Educational Researcher, 32*(6), 13–24.

Coburn, C. E. (2001). Collective sensemaking about reading: How teachers mediate reading policy in their professional communities. *Educational Evaluation and Policy Analysis, 23*, 145–170.

Coburn, C. E., & Russell, J. L. (2008). District policy and teachers' social networks. *Educational Evaluation and Policy Analysis, 30*(3), 203–235.

Cohen, E. G. (1994a). *Designing groupwork: Strategies for the heterogeneous classroom.* New York, NY: Teachers College Press.

Cohen, E. G. (1994b). Restructuring the classroom: Conditions for productive small groups. *Review of Educational Research, 64*(1), 1–35.

Cohen, E. G., & Lotan, R. A. (Eds.). (1997). *Working for equity in heterogeneous classrooms: Sociological theory in action.* New York, NY: Teachers College Press.

Cossey, R. (1997). Mathematical communication: Issues of access and equity. Unpublished doctoral dissertation. Stanford University, Stanford, CA.

Darling-Hammond, L. (2010). *The flat world and education: How America's commitment to equity will determine our future.* New York, NY: Teachers College Press.

Davis, B., & Simmt, E. (2003). Understanding learning systems: Mathematics education and complexity science. *Journal for Research in Mathematics Education, 34*(2), 137–167.

Day, W. L. (2011). The role of a Video Club in fostering teachers' noticing of equitable participation in mathematics classrooms. Unpublished master's thesis. University of Washington, Seattle, WA.

de Abreu, G., & Cline, T. (2007). Social valorization of mathematics practices: The implications for learners in multicultural schools. In N. S. Nasir & P. Cobb (Eds.), *Improving access to mathematics: Diversity and equity in the classroom* (pp. 118–131). New York, NY: Teachers College Press.

Dreier, O. (1999). Personal trajectories of participation across contexts of social practice. *Outlines, 4*, 5–31.

Featherstone, H., Crespo, S., Jilk, L. M., Oslund, J. A., Parks, A. N., & Wood, M. B. (2011). *Smarter together! Collaboration and equity in the elementary math classroom.* Reston, VA: National Council of Teachers of Mathematics.

Flores-Gonzalez, N. (2002). *School kids/street kids: Identity development in Latino students.* New York, NY: Teachers College Press.

Forsyth, D. (1999). *Group dynamics.* Boston, MA: Brooks/Cole.

Foucault, M. (1980). *Power/knowledge: Selected interviews and other writings, 1972–1977.* New York, NY: The Harvester Press.

Franke, M., Carpenter, T., Levi, L., & Fennema, E. (2001). Capturing teachers' generative change: A follow-up study of professional development in mathematics. *American Educational Research Journal, 38*(3), 653–689.

Freedman, S. W., Delp, V., & Crawford, S. M. (2005). Teaching English in untracked classrooms. *Research in the Teaching of English, 40*(1), 62–126.

Gamoran, A., Anderson, C. W., Quiroz, P. A., Secada, W. G., Williams, T., & Ashmann, S. (2003). *Transforming teaching in math and science: How schools and districts can support change.* New York, NY: Teachers College Press.

Glaser, B. G., & Strauss, A. L. (1967). *The discovery of grounded theory: Strategies for qualitative research.* London, UK: Weidenfeld & Nicholson.

González, N., Moll, L., & Amanti, C. (2005). *Funds of knowledge: Theorizing practices in households and classrooms.* Mahwah, NJ: Lawrence Erlbaum Associates.

González, N., Moll, L., Floyd-Tenery, M., Rivera, A., Rendon, P., Gonzales, R., & Amanti, C. (1993). *Teacher research on funds of knowledge: Learning from households.* Berkeley, CA: National Center for Research on Cultural Diversity and Second Language Learning.

Goodenough, W. (1970). *"Describing a culture": Description and comparison in cultural anthroplogy.* Cambridge, UK: Cambridge University Press.

Greeno, J. G., & Middle School Mathematics Through Applications Project. (1997). Theories and practices of thinking and learning to think. *American Journal of Education, 106*, 85–126.

Gresalfi, M. (2009). Taking up opportunities to learn: Constructing dispositions in mathematics classrooms. *Journal of the Learning Sciences, 18*(3), 327–369.

Gresalfi, M., Martin, T., Hand, V., & Greeno, J. G. (2008). Constructing competence: An analysis of student participation in the activity systems of mathematics classrooms. *Educational Studies in Mathematics, 70*(1), 49-70.

Gutiérrez, K. (2008). Developing a sociocritical literacy in the third space. *Reading Research Quarterly, 43*(2), 148–164.

Gutiérrez, K., Baquedano-López, P., & Tejada, C. (2000). Rethinking diversity: Hybridity and hybrid language practices in the third space. *Mind, Culture, and Activity, 6*(4), 286–303.

Gutiérrez, K., Rymes, B., & Larson, J. (1995). Script, counterscript, and underlife in the classroom: James Brown versus "Brown v. Board of Education." *Harvard Educational Review, 65*(3), 445–471.

Gutiérrez, R. (1996). Practices, beliefs and cultures of high school mathematics departments: Understanding their influence on student advancement. *Journal of Curriculum Studies, 28*(5), 495–529.

Gutiérrez, R. (2008). Research commentary: A "gap-gazing" fetish in mathematics education: Problematizing research on the achievement gap. *Journal for Research in Mathematics Education, 39*(4), 357–364.

Gutstein, E. (2005). *Reading and writing the world with mathematics: Toward a pedagogy for social justice*. New York, NY: RoutledgeFalmer.

Haberman, M. (1991). The pedagogy of poverty versus good teaching, *Phi Delta Kappan, 73*, 290–294.

Hammerness, K., Darling-Hammond, L., Bransford, J., Berliner, D., Cochran-Smith, M., McDonald, M., & Zeichner, K. (2005). How teachers learn and develop. In L. Darling-Hammond, J. Bransford, P. LePage, K. Hammerness, & H. Duffy (Eds.), *Preparing teachers for a changing world: What teachers should learn and be able to do* (pp. 358–389). San Francisco, CA: Jossey-Bass.

Hand, V. (2003). *Reframing participation: Meaningful mathematical activity in diverse classrooms*. Unpublished doctoral dissertation. Stanford University, Stanford, CA.

Hand, V. (in press). Seeing power and culture in mathematics learning: Teacher noticing for equitable mathematics instruction. *Educational Studies in Mathematics*, Special issue.

Hanks, W. F. (1996). *Language and communicative practices*. Boulder, CO: Westview Press.

Holland, D., Lachiotte, W., Skinner, D., & Cain, C. (1998). *Identity and agency in cultural worlds*. Cambridge, MA: Harvard University Press.

Horn, I. S. (2005). Learning on the job: A situated account of teacher learning in high school mathematics departments. *Cognition & Instruction, 23*(2), 207–236.

Horn, I. S. (2007). Fast kids, slow kids, lazy kids: Framing the mismatch problem in mathematics teachers' conversations. *Journal of the Learning Sciences, 16*(1), 37–79.

Horn, I. S. (2008a). Turnaround students in high school mathematics: Constructing identities of competence through mathematical worlds. *Mathematical Thinking and Learning, 10*(3), 201–239.

Horn, I. S. (2008b). The inherent interdependence of teachers. *Phi Delta Kappan, 89*(10), 751–754.

Horn, I. S. (2010). Teaching replays, teaching rehearsals, and re-visions of practice: Learning from colleagues in a mathematics teacher community. *Teachers College Record, 112*(1), 225–259.

Horn, I. S. (2012). *Strength in numbers: Collaborative learning in secondary mathematics.* Reston, VA: National Council of Teachers of Mathematics.

Horn, I. S., & Little, J. W. (2010). Attending to problems of practice: Routines and resources for professional learning in teachers' workplace interactions. *American Educational Research Journal, 47*(1), 181–217.

Jilk, L. M. (2007). Translated mathematics: Immigrant women's use of salient identities as cultural tools for interpretation and learning. Unpublished doctoral dissertation. Michigan State University, East Lansing, MI.

Jilk, L. M. (2009). Becoming a "liberal" mathematician: Expanding secondary school mathematics to create space for cultural connections and multiple mathematical identities. In *31st annual meeting of the North American Chapter of the International Group for the Psychology of Mathematics Education* (Vol. 5). Atlanta, GA: Georgia State University.

Jilk, L. M. (2010). Becoming a "liberal" math learner: Expanding secondary school mathematics to support cultural connections, multiple mathematical identities, and engagement. In R. S. Kitchen & M. Civil (Eds.), *Transnational and borderland studies in mathematics education* (pp. 69–94). New York, NY: Routledge.

Kennedy, M. (1999). The role of preservice teacher education. In L. Darling-Hammond & G. Sykes (Eds.), *Teaching as the learning profession: Handbook of policy and practice* (pp. 54–85). San Francisco, CA: Jossey-Bass.

Kilpatrick, J., Swafford, J., & Findell, B. (Eds.). (2001). *Adding it up: Helping children learn mathematics.* Washington, DC: National Academy Press.

Kirshner, B. (2007). Youth activism as a context for learning and development. *American Behavioral Scientist, 51*(3), 367–379.

Kysh, J. M. (1995). College preparatory mathematics: Change from within. *Mathematics Teacher, 88*(8), 660–666.

Ladson-Billings, G. (1994). *Dreamkeepers: Successful teachers of African-American children.* San Francisco, CA: Jossey-Bass.

Lampert, M. (2001). *Teaching problems and the problems of teaching.* New Haven, CT: Yale University Press.

Lee, C. (2008). The centrality of culture to the scientific study of learning and development: How an ecological framework in education research facilitates civic responsibility. *Educational Researcher, 37*(5), 267–279.

Lee, S., Leblang, J., & Porter, G. (2012). Park City Mathematics Institute and districts partner to design professional development: Noyce supplement evaluation report, May 2012. Available at www.noycefdn.org/aboutus.php

Lee, V., & Smith, J. B. (1996). Collective responsibility for learning and its effects on gains in achievement for early secondary school students. *American Journal of Education, 104,* 103–147.

Lieberman, J. C. (1997). Enabling professionalism in high school mathematics departments: The role of generative community. Unpublished doctoral dissertation. Stanford University, Stanford, CA.

Lieblich, A., Tuval-Mashiach, R., & Zilber, T. (1998). *Narrative research: Reading, analysis, and interpretation* (Vol. 47). Thousand Oaks, CA: SAGE Publications.

Lipman, P. (2004). *High stakes education: Inequality, globalization, and school reform.* New York, NY: Routledge.

Little, J. W. (1996). The emotional contours and career trajectories of (disappointed) reform enthusiasts. *Cambridge Journal of Education, 26*(3), 345–359.

Little, J. W. (2002). Locating learning in teachers' communities of practice: Opening up problems of analysis in records of everyday work. *Teaching and Teacher Education, 18*(8), 917–946.

Little, J. W. (2003). Inside teacher community: Representations of classroom practice. *Teachers College Record, 105*(6), 913–945.

Little, J. W., & Horn, I. S. (2007). "Normalizing" problems of practice: Converting routine conversation into a resource for learning in professional communities. In L. Stoll & K. S. Louis (Eds.), *Professional learning communities: Divergence, depth and dilemmas* (pp. 179–192). London, UK: Open University Press.

Little, J. W., Horn, I. S., & Bartlett, L. (2000). *Teacher learning, professional community, and accountability in the context of high school reform.* Report to the National Program for Excellence and Accountability in Teaching (NPEAT), Office of Educational Research and Improvement, U.S. Department of Education. Washington, DC.

Lotan, R. A. (2003). Group-worthy tasks. *Educational Leadership, 6*(6), 72–75.

Lou, Y., Abrami, P., Spence, J., Poulsen, C., Chambers, B., & d'Apollonia, S. (1996). Within-class grouping: A meta-analysis. *Review of Educational Research, 66*, 423–458.

Lubienski, S. (2000). Problem solving as a means towards mathematics for all: An exploratory look through the class lens. *Journal for Research in Mathematics Education, 31*, 454–482.

Madison, B. L., & Hart, T. A. (1990). *A challenge of numbers: People in the mathematical sciences.* Washington, DC: National Academy Press.

Martin, D. (2000). *Mathematics success and failure among African American youth.* Mahwah, NJ: Lawrence Erlbaum Associates.

Martin, D. (2007). Beyond missionaries or cannibals: Who should teach mathematics to African American children? *The High School Journal, 91*(1), 16–28.

Martin, D. (2009). *Mathematics teaching, learning, and liberation in the lives of black children.* New York, NY: Routledge.

Martino, A., & Maher, C. (1999). Teacher questioning to promote justification and generalization in mathematics: What research practice has taught us. *Journal of Mathematical Behavior, 18*(1), 52–78.

Matusov, E. (1999). How does a community of learners maintain itself? Ecology of an innovative school. *Anthropology and Education Quarterly, 30*(2), 161–186.

McLaughlin, M., & Talbert, J. (2001). *Professional communities and the work of high school teaching.* Chicago, IL: University of Chicago Press.

McNeil, L. M. (2000). *Contradictions of school reform: Educational costs of standardized testing.* New York, NY: Routledge.

Mezirow, J. (1997). Transformative learning: Theory to practice. *New Directions for Adult and Continuing Education, 74*(Summer), 5–12.

Mintrop, H. (2003). The limits of sanctions in low-performing schools: A study of Maryland and Kentucky schools on probation. *Education Policy Analysis Archives, 11*(3). Available at epaa.asu.edu/epaa/v11n3.html

Moje, E. (2007). Developing socially just subject-matter instruction: A review of the literature on disciplinary literacy teaching. *Review of Research in Education, 31,* 1–44.

Moll, L. C., Amanti, C., Neff, D., & Gonzalez, N. (1992). Funds of knowledge for teaching: A qualitative approach to connect homes and classrooms. *Theory into Practice, 31*(1), 132–141.

Moschkovich, J. N. (2002). An introduction to examining everyday and academic mathematical practices. In M. E. Brenner & J. N. Moschkovich (Eds.), *Everyday and academic mathematics in the classroom* (pp. 1–11). Reston, VA: The National Council of Teachers of Mathematics.

Moses, B., & Cobb, C. (2001). *Radical equations: Math literacy and civil rights.* Boston, MA: Beacon Press.

Nasir, N. S. (2002). Identity, goals and learning: Mathematics in cultural practice. *Mathematical Thinking and Learning, 4*(2 & 3), 213–247.

Nasir, N. S. (2008). Everyday pedagogy: Lessons from track, basketball, and dominoes. *Phi Delta Kappan Magazine, 89*(7), 529–532.

Nasir, N. S., & Hand, V. (2008). From the court to the classroom: Opportunities for engagement, learning and identity in basketball and classroom mathematics. *Journal of the Learning Sciences, 17*(2), 143–180.

National Council of Teachers of Mathematics. (2000). *Principles and standards for school mathematics.* Reston, VA: Author.

Nieto, S. (2004). *Affirming diversity: The sociopolitical context of multicultural education* (4th ed.). White Plains, NY: Longman Publishers.

Oakes, J., Wells, A. S., Jones, M., & Datnow, A. (1997). Detracking: The social construction of ability, cultural politics, and resistance to reform. *Teachers College Record, 98,* 482–510.

Ogbu, J. (1991). Immigrant and involuntary minorities in comparative perspective. In M. A. Gibson & J. U. Ogbu (Eds.), *Minority status and schooling: A comparative study of immigrant and involuntary minorities* (pp. 3–33). New York, NY: Garland Publishing.

Olsen, L. (1997). *Made in America: Immigrant students in our public schools.* New York, NY: The New Press.

Pedulla, J. J., Abrams, L. M., Madaus, G. F., Russell, M. K., Ramos, M. A., & Miao, J. (2003). *Perceived effects of state-mandated testing programs on teaching and learning: Findings from a national survey of teachers.* Chestnut Hill, MA: National Board on Educational Testing and Public Policy.

Picciotto, H. (1995). *Lab Gear activities for algebra 1.* Aslip, IL: Creative Publications.

Polman, J. L., & Miller, D. (2010). Changing stories: Trajectories of identification among African American youth in a science outreach apprenticeship. *American Educational Research Journal, 47*(4), 879–918.

Portales, R., & Portales, M. (2005). *Quality education for Latinos and Latinas: Print and oral skills for all students, K-college.* Austin, TX: University of Texas Press.

Putnam, R. T., & Borko, H. (2000). What do new views of knowledge and thinking have to say about research on teacher learning? *Educational Researcher, 29*(1), 4–15.

RAND. (2002, October). Mathematical proficiency for all students: Toward a strategic research and development program in mathematics education (Dru-2773-OERI). Arlington, VA: RAND Education & Science and Technology Policy Institute.

Rosen, L. (2001). Myth making and moral order in a debate on mathematics education policy. In M. Sutton & B. A. U. Levinson (Eds.), *Policy as practice: Toward a comparative sociocultural analysis of educational policy* (Vol. 1, pp. 295–316). Westport, CT: Ablex Publishing.

Rosenholtz, S. J., & Wilson, B. (1980). The effect of classroom structure on shared perceptions of ability. *American Educational Research Journal, 17,* 175–182.

Rustique-Forrester, E. (2005). Accountability and the pressures to exclude: A cautionary tale from England. *Education Policy Analysis Archives, 13*(26), 1–39.

Sallee, T., Kysh, J., Kasimatis, E., & Hoey, B. (2000). *College preparatory mathematics.* Sacramento, CA: CPM Educational Program.

Schoenfeld, A. H. (1985). *Mathematical problem solving.* Hillsdale, NJ: Lawrence Erlbaum Associates.

Schoenfeld, A. H. (2002). Making mathematics work for all children: Issues of standards, testing, and equity. *Educational Researcher, 31*(1), 13–25.

Schoenfeld, A. H. (2004). The math wars. *Educational Policy, 18*(1), 253–286.

Schoenfeld, A. H. (2008). Problem solving in the United States, 1970–2008: Research and theory, practice and politics. In G. Törner, A. H. Schoenfeld, & K. Reiss (Eds.), *Problem solving around the world—Summing up the state of the art* (Special Issue of the *Zentralblatt für Didaktik der Mathematik*: Issue 1, 2008).

Schroeder, T., & Lester, F. (1989). Developing understanding in mathematics via problem solving. In P. Trafton & A. Shulte (Eds.), *New directions for elementary school mathematics* (pp. 31–42). Reston, VA: National Council of Teachers of Mathematics.

Sherin, M. G., Jacobs, V. R., & Philipp, R. A. (2011). Situating the study of teacher noticing. In M. G. Sherin, V. R. Jacobs, & R. A. Philipp (Eds.), *Mathematics teacher noticing: Seeing through teachers' eyes* (pp. 3–14). New York, NY: Routledge.

Silver, E. A., & Stein, M. K. (1996). The QUASAR Project: The "revolution of the possible" in mathematics instructional reform in urban middle schools. *Urban Education, 30,* 476–521.

Simpson, C. (1981). Classroom structure and the organization of ability. *Sociology of Education, 54,* 120–132.

Siskin, L. S. (1994). *Realms of knowledge: Academic departments in secondary schools.* Washington, DC: Falmer Press.

Sizer, T. (1992). *Horace's school: Redesigning the American high school.* New York, NY: Houghton Mifflin.

Soja, E. W. (1996). *Thirdspace.* Cambridge, MA: Blackwell.

Spillane, J. P. (1999). External reform initiatives and teachers' efforts to reconstruct their practice: The mediating role of teachers' zones of enactment. *Journal of Curriculum Studies, 31,* 143–175.

Spillane, J. P. (2000). Cognition and policy implementation: District policymakers and the reform of mathematics education. *Cognition and Instruction, 18*(2), 141–179.

Staples, M. (2008). Promoting student collaboration in a detracked, heterogeneous secondary mathematics classroom. *Journal of Mathematics Teacher Education, 11*(5), 349–371.

Staples, M., & Colonis, M. (2006). *Sustaining mathematical discussions: A comparative analysis of two secondary mathematics teachers.* Paper presentation at the annual meeting of the American Education Research Association Annual Conference, San Francisco, CA.

Stein, M. K., Smith, M., Henningsen, M., & Silver, E. (2000). *Implementing standards-based mathematics instruction: A case book for professional development.* New York, NY: Teachers College Press.

Stodolsky, S., & Grossman, P. L. (2000). Changing students, changing teaching. *Teachers College Record, 102*(1), 125–172.

Straehle, C. (1993). "Samuel?" "Yes, dear?": Teasing and conversational rapport. In D. Tannen (Ed.), *Framing in discourse* (pp. 210–229). New York, NY: Oxford University Press.

Strauss, A., & Corbin, J. (1998). *Basics of qualitative research: Techniques and procedures for developing grounded theory.* Thousand Oaks, CA: SAGE Publications.

Suárez-Orozco, M. M. (1991). Immigrant adaptation to schooling: A Hispanic case. In M. A. Gibson & J. U. Ogbu (Eds.), *Minority status and schooling: A comparative study of immigrant and involuntary minorities* (pp. 37–62). New York, NY: Garland Publishing.

Suárez-Orozco, M. M. (1997). "Becoming somebody": Central American immigrants in U.S. inner city schools. In M. Seller & L. Weis (Eds.), *Beyond black and white: New faces and voices in U.S. schools* (pp. 115–129). Albany, NY: State University of New York Press.

Talbert, J., & McLaughlin, M. (1996). Teacher professionalism in local school contexts. In I. Goodson & A. Hargreaves (Eds.), *Teachers' professional lives* (pp. 127–153). Washington, DC: Falmer Press.

Tarr, J. E., Reys, R. E., Reys, B. J., Chávez, Ó., Shih, J., & Osterlind, S. J. (2008). The impact of middle-grades mathematics curricula and the classroom learning environment on student achievement. *Journal for Research in Mathematics Education, 39,* 247–280.

Tsu, R. (1998). *Moving toward a professional community: Talking and working together.* Unpublished master's thesis. University of Washington, Tacoma, WA.

Tyack, D., & Cuban, L. (1995). *Tinkering toward utopia.* Cambridge, MA: Harvard University Press.

Valenzuela, A. (1999). *Subtractive schooling: U.S.–Mexican youth and the politics of caring.* Albany, NY: State University of New York Press.

van Es, E. A., & Sherin, M. G. (2002). Learning to notice: Scaffolding new teachers' interpretations of classroom interactions. *Journal of Technology and Teacher Education, 10*(4), 571–596.

Varenne, H., & McDermott, R. (1998). *Successful failure: The school America builds.* Boulder, CO: Westview Press.

Watanabe, M. (2011). *"Heterogenius" classrooms: Detracking math and science—A look at groupwork in action.* New York, NY: Teachers College Press.

Webb, N. (1991). Task-related verbal interaction and mathematics learning in small groups. *Journal of Research in Mathematics Education, 22,* 366–389.

Weiler, J. D. (2000). *Codes and contradictions: Race, gender, identity and schooling.* Albany, NY: State University of New York Press.

Wenger, E. (1998). *Communities of practice: Learning, meaning and identity.* New York: Cambridge University Press.

Wenger, E., McDermott, R., & Snyder, W. M. (2002). *Cultivating communities of practice: A guide to managing knowledge.* Boston, MA: Harvard Business School Press.

Yackel, E., & Cobb, P. (1996). Sociomathematical norms, argumentation, and autonomy in mathematics. *Journal for Research in Mathematics Education, 27*(4), 458–477.

About the Contributors

Na'ilah Suad Nasir is the H. Michael and Jeanne Williams Chair of African American Studies, and she holds the Birgeneau Chair in Educational Disparities in the Graduate School of Education at the University of California, Berkeley. Her program of research focuses on issues of race, culture, and schooling. She also examines the relation between race and mathematic learning. She is the author of *Racialized Identities: Race and Achievement for African-American Youth*, published by Stanford University Press in 2011. She has also published over 30 articles in scholarly journals.

Carlos Cabana has taught middle and high school mathematics since 1990. He spent his first 20 years of teaching at Railside, where he also served as co-chair. He credits his Railside students and colleagues for his continued delight in working with students and his passion for helping them find their intellectual place in the world. After leaving Railside, he eventually found a new home at LIFE Academy, a small public high school in Oakland, California, where he is working to create a middle grades program building on his experience at Railside.

Barbara Shreve has spent 12 years teaching in high school math classrooms, including 10 years at Railside High School where she also served as department co-chair. Her experiences with students and colleagues at Railside deepened her passion for investigating how students talk and work together, and how teachers and students together build environments where every student has the opportunity to make sense of important mathematics content. She currently works as a math specialist in Oakland Unified School District, supporting teacher leaders and teams of teachers in their work with the Common Core State Standards.

Estelle Woodbury is a learner exploring what it takes for every student to have powerful experiences in school mathematics. She currently works for the Oakland Unified School District as a part of the Leadership, Curriculum, and Instruction mathematics team, which allows her the opportunity to do focused work in mathematics learning and teaching with principals, teachers, and students. As part of the Railside team, she realized the importance of creating a classroom community in which the learning was as strong as the contributions

255

of its members and how powerful the experience was in their development and decision making as citizens in the world.

Nicole Louie studies mathematics teaching and learning at the University of California, Berkeley. Her research focuses on secondary mathematics teachers' efforts to expand what it means to be "good at math," examining the challenges that this work poses for teachers and the resources that are necessary to support it.

Jo Boaler is a professor of mathematics education at Stanford University, the editor of the Research Commentary Section of *The Journal for Research in Mathematics Education* (JRME), author of the first MOOC on mathematics teaching and learning, and CEO of www.youcubed.org. Her book *Experiencing School Mathematics* won the Outstanding Book of the Year award for education in Britain. She is an elected fellow of the Royal Society of Arts (Great Britain), and a former president of the International Organization for Women and Mathematics Education (IOWME). She is the author of seven books and numerous research articles. Her latest books *What's Math Got to Do with It?* (2009) published by Penguin, USA, and *The Elephant in the Classroom* (2010) published by Souvenir Press, UK, both aim to increase public understanding of the importance of mathematics and the nature of effective teaching approaches in the U.S. and the UK.

Ruth Cossey is a professor at Mills College School of Education. She is the director of Teachers for Tomorrow's Schools teacher preparation program. Her research focuses on issues of mathematics, assessment, equity, and urban education. She is the co-author of *Teaching as Principled Practice: Managing Complexity for Social Justice* published in 2004 by Sage, and *Family Math* published in 1986 by the Lawrence Hall of Science at the University of California. She is an author of Math Reasoning Inventory, a web-based assessment tool published by Math Solutions, 2013 at mathreasoninginventory.com/home/.

Victoria Hand is an assistant professor of mathematics education at the University of Colorado at Boulder. She has theorized and examined empirically participation gaps, or differences in opportunities to participate productively in classroom mathematical activity for students from dominant versus nondominant ethnic, racial, and linguistic backgrounds.

Ilana Seidel Horn is associate professor of mathematics education at Vanderbilt University. She studies equitable secondary mathematics teaching, with a focus on urban schools as a learning environment for teachers. As a part of her study at Railside, she had the privilege of teaching alongside many of the contributors to this volume. In her book *Strength in Numbers: Collaborative Learning in Secondary Mathematics*, published by the National Council of Teachers of Mathematics, she wrote about much of what she learned from these colleagues.

Lisa M. Jilk is a researcher at the University of Washington and a consultant in a number of urban school districts. Her work focuses on reculturing high school mathematics departments and building teachers' collective capacity to implement and sustain Complex Instruction practices, so that all students have opportunities to learn rich mathematics and understand how they are smart. Prior to this work, Lisa was a high school math teacher in Minnesota and at Railside High.

Judith Warren Little is the Carol Liu Professor of Education Policy at the University of California, Berkeley. Her research focuses on school workplace cultures and relationships that affect teacher learning and career commitment, and on policies and practices of professional development. She has published widely in the areas of teachers' work, school reform, and teacher policy. She is an elected member of the National Academy of Education.

Rachel Lotan is the director of the Stanford Teacher Education Program and professor (Teaching) at the Graduate School of Education at Stanford University. Her teaching and research focuses on aspects of teaching and learning in academically and linguistically diverse classrooms, teacher education, sociology of the classroom, and the social organization of schools. In her previous position as co-director of the Program for Complex Instruction at Stanford University, she worked on the development, research, and worldwide dissemination of Complex Instruction, a pedagogical approach to creating equitable classrooms.

Karen O'Connell has been teaching at the middle and high school levels for almost 15 years. Her time at Railside as both teacher and department co-chair helped her realize just how much commitment, collaboration, and hard work is required to create a department community that believes every student can and will learn rigorous mathematics. Currently working as outreach faculty for University of Washington, Karen works intensely with a local math department to create a Railside-like math community.

Megan E. Staples is an associate professor of mathematics education in the Neag School of Education at the University of Connecticut. Her research focuses on student and teacher interactions in secondary mathematics classrooms with the aim of understanding how teachers organize student collaboration and support mathematical inquiry. Her primary teaching responsibilities are within Neag's secondary mathematics teacher preparation program.

Ruth Tsu is an independent consultant whose focus is on supporting teachers to learn the principles and strategies of Complex Instruction in order to improve the teaching and learning of mathematics for all students through equitable interaction in the classroom. She has presented numerous workshops and provided coaching to practicing teachers nationwide, in addition to teaching preservice teachers at the University of Washington, Tacoma. She was the chair of the mathematics department at Railside for several pivotal years, providing leadership for the department as they detracked their mathematics program and developed tools for teaching mathematics in heterogeneous classrooms.

Maria D. Velazquez is an alumna of Railside High School. She credits Railside math and the relentless support of her teachers, family, and mentors for her college competitiveness. In 2010, Maria got her bachelor's degree from the University of California, Berkeley, where she was a McNair Scholar and conducted research on equitable math learning. She aspires to become a researcher in education policy.

Index

Note: Page numbers followed by *f* or *t* indicate figures and tables respectively.